Summerville

Fr. Leo

St. Nathy's College
1810 – 2010

Reflections and Memories of Past Pupils

Compiled and Edited by
Fr. Leo Henry

Publishing History
First published in the United Kingdom in 2010

Published by
St Nathy's College

All rights reserved
Copyright © 2010 by St Nathy's

A CIP catalogue record for this title
is available from the British Library

ISBN: 978-0-9566002-0-2

Printed in the United Kingdom

Typeset and cover design by
Tom Brown
ellisedwardspublishing@hotmail.com

Printed and bound by
MPG Biddles Ltd
24 Rollesby Road
Hardwick Industrial Estate
King's Lynn, Norfolk
PE30 4LS

I dedicate this book to the memory of my brother P.J.,
Leaving Certificate Class of 1969,
who died on September 30th 1982;
and of Jim Brehony and his nephew Brian McNicholas,
who died tragically, travelling to St. Nathy's College,
on September 6th 1990.

Preface

My great granduncle, Fr. Edward Henry Connington D.D. (later known as Dean Connington), taught in St. Nathy's College before he was appointed its first priest President in 1878. I was a student at St. Nathy's College from 1970 to 1975 and I have been a member of the academic staff at St. Nathy's College across four decades, from 1986 to the present. Thus, on account of my long association with St. Nathy's College, I am delighted to make a contribution to its *centenary celebrations with this publication of memories and reflections from its past pupils.

No one publication of memories could comprehensively cover such a time-span as two hundred years. This is a modest, and hopefully worthwhile, contribution detailing personalised accounts of what school life was like at St. Nathy's College down through the decades. It is anticipated that these reflections will trigger positive memories in the minds of its readers and that it will honour St. Nathy's College and its educators, many of whom have gone before us to the Lord; may they rest in peace.

At the heart of any educational institution are its teachers. When students reminisce, they recall much – the buildings, the events, the smells, the sport, the spirituality, the discipline etc. However, there is one constant among them all and that one constant is the teachers. Students always remember their teachers and the relationships they formed and developed with them. It is true to say that the teacher is at the heart of the school; that the teacher is at the heart of information; that the teacher is at the heart of formation; and that the teacher is at the heart of transformation. The key to a school of quality is the relationship and the quality of that relationship between its pupils and its teachers. To the many hundreds of teachers, those recalled in this book, and the many, many unsung heroes and heroines, I, on behalf of their former pupils, laud them for their contribution to the quality of education provided down through the decades at St. Nathy's College.

I wish to sincerely thank all who contributed articles for this publication. The response I received was forthright, positive and courteous. I compliment all of you for your cooperation and your integrity. All who contributed are included. Some declined, while others were not ready just yet to publish their reflections. Ailing health prevented at least one past pupil from writing his memories, namely the retired Archbishop of Tuam, Dr. Joe Cassidy. Only Joe, in his own inimitable style, could have written his own memories. However, I must share that in one of our conversations, Joe reflected: "When I was a student at St. Nathy's, times were frugal. No one had much. Yet the humanity of the teaching staff was laudable. The priests humanised the place. They provided the students with an education that was academic, classical, spiritual and holistic. I genuinely was lonely the day I left the College."

Finally, I wish to thank all who encouraged and supported me with this initiative. I wish to express my deep appreciation to Michael Lafferty and his team at Lafferty Group for the sub-editing, lay-out and design of this publication.

Mo mhile buiochas libh go leir.

Fr. Leo Henry.
St. Nathy's College.

Foreword

' *Mol an óige agus tiocfaidh sí*' the seanfhocal says and it came to mind many times as I read through the fascinating collection of memories of school days that is 'St. Nathy's College, 1810-2010; Reflections and Memories of Past Pupils'. Time and again, the contributors testify to the power of the positive remark, the encouraging comment, and the sympathetic ear of the teachers they had the good fortune to meet. Clearly, the truly good teacher is the one who not only loves their subject and has the skills necessary to communicate it, but also – and primarily – they believe in each and every one of their students, and love them.

For so many of the writers in this book, it was a teacher or teachers who made the difference. If there is any teacher who doubts the value of their vocation, then they could do no better than take up these memories and read. At a time when too often only the failings of men and women, as well as priests both religious and lay, who taught in schools in the past are given public notice, it is refreshing to have the balance redressed, and the extraordinary dedication and compassion of the vast majority of the teachers in our past recognised and applauded. That alone makes this volume an entirely worthy contribution to the celebration of the bi-centenary of St. Nathy's College.

Yet for many other reasons too this is a very worthwhile publication. It is a chronicle of changing times in Ireland, in cultural, economic, social and religious circumstances, and above all, in education and schooling at second level. The earliest contribution comes from a student of St. Nathy's in the 1920s. The latest comes from a student who has just finished in the school. There are memories here from almost ninety years of youthful life and schooling in Ballaghaderreen.

The majority of these memories, inevitably, come from men who were boarders in the school. Boarding schools of the type that was St. Nathy's have now had their day. From the historical point of view, this book provides an invaluable record of what life was really like inside what were often seemingly sparse and rigid structures. One tastes the spirit of stricter and poorer conditions of life than we are now used to. But this book also records the indomitable spirit of youth that overcame the sparse conditions of the place and the era: there is much about fun and an awful lot about games and sport in this record. How vital games and sport were in the lives of young people at every stage of the period covered here! Plus ça change…

For these and many more reasons, I am delighted to welcome this publication. I salute all the past pupils who took the trouble to put pen to paper, or finger to keyboard as the case may be. *Nár laga Dia sibh.*

I thank Fr. Leo Henry who took on the task of finding contributors, cajoling them to write, editing and seeing the book through to publication. *B'fhiú an tairbhe an trioblóid, a Leo.*

Though the contributors, for the most part, are past pupils of St. Nathy's, it is good that there are essays here too from the other schools that eventually amalgamated with St. Nathy's in 1995, and whose history is now part of that of the modern St. Nathy's. These are primarily the Vocational School (founded in 1935), St. Joseph's Convent School (founded 1933), and the shorter lived but highly appreciated St. Jude's School of Commerce.

From the start, St. Nathy's has been the diocesan college of the Diocese of Achonry. For many, many years, when there was little state support for second-level schools or for teachers, priests of the diocese were often the sole educators there. In this book, there are many testimonies to the selfless and highly appreciated educational effectiveness of the contribution of these men. It is gratifying to see that the men and women, who are their successors in more recent times, are equally appreciated by their students. Catholic education, at present, is beginning to find its voice anew in Ireland, and it is grounded on the commitment and competence of men and women who experience their profession as a call, a vocation to be in the image of Jesus the Teacher. May the students of St. Nathy's now and in the future experience their teachers, as so many clearly did in the past, as deeply caring and highly competent in their calling, and may they have memories of their time in St. Nathy's for which they will always be grateful, and thankful to God.

Most Rev. Dr. Brendan Kelly,
Bishop of Achonry.

Message from the President
of St. Nathy's College

I extend a warm welcome to the reader of this very impressive collection of memories and recollections from past pupils of their times spent in St. Nathy's College.

When you browse through these articles, either as a past pupil, a present day member of the school community or as an individual with no immediate connection to St. Nathy's College, I trust that you will enjoy reading and learning about school life in times past and that you will also gain an insight into the long and distinguished history of this College.

I would like to thank all who contributed articles to this collection. I am indebted to them for sharing their experiences of school life with us, many relating to life as a student many decades ago.

I wish also to thank and compliment Fr. Leo Henry for his great commitment, dedication and hard work in undertaking the compilation and editing of this very diverse collection of material from our past pupils. His completed work now ensures that a very important part of our history will never be forgotten and will be preserved for all future generations.

Fr. Martin Convey,
President,
St. Nathy's College.

Contents

• 1 •
My Secondary School Days at St. Nathy's College
Thomas McGettrick (R.I.P.)

LC1923; Bishop of Ogoja, 1939-1973;
Bishop of Abakaliki, 1973-1983

We were told, as we came towards the end of our primary school, that some of us would have to leave the farm. The farms were so small they could not support more than one family, so many parents planned that some of their children would take on a trade, prepare to go to America, or get just away from the family home. My mother always insisted that the three of us, my younger sister, brother and I, would all have to try to get something for ourselves. Thus, on the second Tuesday of September 1919, my mother packed my bags and put them on the old sidecar and my father drove me the nine miles to Ballaghaderreen. I received a small scholarship, and my parents were delighted to get one of their children on the way to a profession.

After Catholic Emancipation, every diocese established a secondary school or a diocesan college from which it could prepare students to enter Maynooth, the National Seminary. So the Diocese of Achonry bought an old barracks, situated almost in the town of Ballaghaderreen, and fitted it up for a day school. Later, when new buildings were added in 1914, it became a boarding school and housed some 80 boarders. It had classroom space for at least 100 students, with a science hall and an oratory, where the Blessed Sacrament was reserved. This became the diocesan college of Achonry Diocese.

On that Tuesday in September 1919, I found myself in the dormitory in St. Nathy's beside a student called Jack Finnegan, who became my life-long friend, and later an engineer. Although he is now deceased, I hope he is engineering in Heaven. We felt lonely on that first night away from home, yet we were regaled to a pillow fight, with one side of the dormitory attacking the other. The fight continued unabated until the door opened and the Dean came in. Putting on the light, he warned us all that if this occurred again, we would all be sent home to our parents. We enjoyed the battle, which my side claimed to have won. That gave me a fresh start in college life and made me happy to share in the games of the other boys.

Strange to say for a diocesan college where boys were being prepared for the priesthood, we were not over burdened with religious exercises. We had mass in the morning and the rosary in the evening, as well as a beautiful oratory in the top storey where we could go to pray during the day if we wanted to or when the classes were not being held. The rosary at night before retiring was said by the prefect. We very seldom had benediction. Although we had religious knowledge in class, we did not offer it at the State examination. Naturally, no one worried about it. We were more worried about the subjects that we would be taking for the State exam. Usually there were about 25 students in a class, which included a few non-boarders; out of that number, eight or nine went on to study for the priesthood. In our class, there were 25 of us; four went to Maynooth, one went to Salamancar, and four others went to All Hallows and other missionary colleges. The other 16 went to lay vocations, one became an engineer, two became doctors, four worked in banks and the others picked up jobs throughout the country.

The one thing that exercised a great missionary influence on us was the Maynooth Mission to China. It was founded in 1916 and every year a priest from the Mission Society came from Dalgan Park to the school to appeal for vocations to the Chinese Missions. We all became interested in China and I remember that in my fourth year, I wrote a letter to my mother saying that I would like to join the Chinese Mission. I got an answer back the next day, and obviously she did not agree with my ideas at all. She reminded me that she and my father had sent me to school and that, if I wanted to be a priest, I should concentrate on the home mission, and not to go out foreign climes in case something dreadful might happen to me!

We settled to life in Ballaghaderreen, not knowing what would happen to us in the end, but always thinking of the green fields far away. We had classes every day except Sunday, with a half day on Wednesday. We hated Sunday and, although we liked the mass, we disliked the walk. Everybody had to go on a five- to six-mile walk on Sunday. We enjoyed the bracing cold air of the mountainside, and we enjoyed walking up Coulloheeran Hill, but when we came back, we got nothing to eat except two cuts of bread with jam on them, and maybe some butter. We had our evening tea at seven o'clock.

Thankfully, there was one great threat on a Sunday evening. The happiest hour of the day came when we were permitted to visit St. Mary's Parish Hall, which was beside the college. There we enjoyed a play, opera or a film.

On the staff of the College, there were six priests and two lay people. The President of the College during my first two years was Fr. Hugh O'Donnell; afterwards he became a parish priest at Straide, Co. Mayo. He was succeeded by Fr. Ambrose Blaine. There were five other priests and they all gave us a good education. Most of them were kind, although some of them occasionally chastised us, which we did not appreciate. Generally, the students were well behaved and got on positively with the staff.

Fr. Blaine taught us Latin and he was considered to be the best Latin teacher in the West of Ireland. Many of his students got first place in Ireland, and many got scholarships.

The subjects I had to take were Latin, English, mathematics, history, geography and Greek. In my first year, there was no science teacher and we had to wait a year before Fr. Tommy Curneen came from Maynooth. He had a science degree and began our science instruction.

The first year I passed in all subjects. In my second year I attempted honours, but I did not succeed; I failed mathematics. To be fair, I hated examinations, especially written examinations. I did not mind orals, but I could never write down all the things I knew. However, I passed middle and senior grade. In 1923, we had to go to Sligo to do the Matriculation. We were all very happy with the papers until we came to Greek. How disappointed we were when we were asked to translate a passage from a Greek book we had never seen! We all thought we would fail the examination. As we found out later, there was a mix up. The exam given to us was meant for the First Arts. I got my Matriculation Certificate and I was relieved.

The other priests were Fr. Eugene Foran, who taught English and Irish. He was a very good teacher and we always were successful in English. Fr. John Kirwan taught us Greek. As far as examinations were concerned, Greek was an easy subject! Fr. Peadar Vasey was the nicest of all the professors; he was most helpful and advised us on how to study. Science was taught by Mr. Collier, a layman. Another layman, whom we disrespectfully called 'Toby', taught us history and music. He was Mr. Cullen.

The four years went by rapidly; junior, middle and senior grades! Then we were launched into another world.

The monotony of College life and the tedious hours of study were often relieved by the pranks of some students. We were a good crowd of students, mostly farmers' sons who knew what work was; but some of us used to engage in sport, which the College did approve of.

There was a classmate of ours named Michael Durkin. He was an intelligent fellow and during his time in the College he took a feverish delight in doing strange acrobatics. He could climb a drainpipe up to the second floor of the building, enter a room through the window and find cakes that students had kept for feasts. He would take them down and divide them among the students, even to some who owned the cakes! He never kept things for himself. One of the things we all admired him for was his knowledge of Latin. He read the Latin Classics and from these he learnt how the stone throwers and catapult people, attached to Caesar's army, used their skills. He made a catapult with which he began to fire stones at the jackdaws that used to have their siesta on the chimney pots of the College. From a vantage point at the back of the College, he would fire shots, which could be very dangerous. Although he never aimed at people, he succeeded in killing the jackdaws and breaking some of the chimney pots. The President complained about the chimney pots and said that if he found any student throwing stones at them, he would expel the student. When our hero finished his studies at the College, he went to England and joined the British Army. He later went on to India, where he became a colonel in the Indian Army.

I took part in a little prank in my second last year before we went home on holidays in June. I decided to have a party in our dormitory of fifteen students. In order to have a party, we would have to get milk, lemonade, mineral drinks, sweet cake and biscuits. We had to prepare for this. To acquire the milk, four of us left the dormitory about 4am. It was quite bright on this summer's morning and we went out to the shed, where two of us milked a cow while the other two stood guard. We milked the cow and kept the milk in a trunk in the dormitory, and that night we had a little feast all to ourselves.

One evening before I ended my career at St. Nathy's, Fr. Blaine called me and asked if I wanted to go to Maynooth to become a priest. I said I had always wanted to be a priest, but wondered if my parents could keep me at Maynooth. "Would you like to go?" he asked. I replied: "I would, if I was recommended." "You may begin to prepare to go to Maynooth after the summer holidays," he then said. That was the way students were selected for the priesthood. The President of the College selected a few students, whom he thought showed signs of a religious vocation, and recommended them to the Bishop, who then sent them to the seminary. That put me on the road to Maynooth!

This article was written by me, using adapted extracts from Bishop McGettrick's autobiography, Memoirs. Kind permission to use these extracts was granted to me by the late Bishop's niece, Sr. Christine.

• 2 •

Looking Back

Jim McGarry (R.I.P.)

LC 1930; Solicitor

I went to St. Nathy's in 1925. Memory plays tricks and recollections may not always be true, but the following random notes are my recollection of those days in St. Nathy's. One of my clearest memories is of my first day there. My older brother had already been there a couple of years. I was twelve years old, and nothing will ever obliterate the memory of the hackney car setting off for Collooney, as Jack and I stood in the bleak and ugly street, watching it take my father home. Already I was painfully sick with a homesickness that never left me.

At nine o'clock that night, the chimes from the Cathedral banged out Home Sweet Home, while I covered my head under the bedclothes. In my first year, there were 68 boarders and less than 20 dayboys in the school. Nearly all came from the counties Roscommon, Mayo and Sligo. More I think from Mayo than either of the other two counties.

Until I arrived in St. Nathy's, I had led a nomadic life. I have no recollection of ever being in the house except for meals and to go to bed. Nor have I any recollection of ever doing homework for school. It was no wonder the schoolmaster said to my father, when he heard of my assault on the groves of academe, "If you take my advice, keep that fellow at home and save the money for him, because I could not knock anything into his head." That is how I arrived in St. Nathy's, with an unusually big head with not a bit of learning in it.

The change, from the carefree and timeless life I had led to a life ruled by the clock and regimented every minute of the day, bewildered me. Class was hell. Playtime was not much better, since it consisted of endless walking round the walk of the waterlogged playing field. Study was an intolerable bore. There were two ball alleys, but a first year never set foot on either of them. The football pitch was no Croke Park. Practice on it meant dodging the puddles or sometimes wading through a pool of water. Any other part of the grounds was out of bounds. Friendship with older boys was unhealthy. Why? Nobody told us.

Our timetable was:

Bell – 7.30am
Mass – 8.00am
Breakfast – 8.30am
Class – 10.00am
Lunch – 1.00pm
Class – 2.00pm
Dinner – 3.30pm
Study – 5.00pm
Tea – 7.00pm
Study – 8.00pm
Prayer – 9.00pm
Bed – 9.30pm

Study was supervised by two prefects: one at the top end of the study, the other at the bottom. In those days, we all changed from outdoor to tennis shoes before study (although we did not play tennis).

There was no communication between teachers and pupils; contact ended with class. Unbelievably, in a diocesan seminary, religion was not taught. In five years I never had one such class. We were sent to the Cathedral once or twice a term to go to confession. Apart from the annual retreat, during which talking was forbidden, religious training did not exist. How then, can one account for the number of boys who became priests? Was it a case of ignorance being bliss? It was the year I did the Inter Cert that the first pupil teachers were appointed on the results of the exam. About eight of my class became pupil teachers. They had extra subjects for the final two years – oral Irish from a local man, who was a native Irish speaker, singing and drawing. While they were at such classes, the other eight of us had no classes.

About my time, maths ceased to be a compulsory subject for the Leaving Cert. After the Inter, I abandoned the subject but had to endure the class. Consequently, without Irish or Maths, my future was very limited.

Every year, new boys were baptised under the tap outside the gate to the playing field. A name was given, which lasted not only your time, but that of any members of your family who came after you. Sometimes baptisms became unruly if the person to be baptised objected and had the strength to rebel. On the other hand, half the fun evaporated when there was no opposition. That is what the wise ones did.

There were no such things as trips outside the confines of the College. The only exception would be a rare visit by parents. Many boys did not even have these visits. The prefects went out every Wednesday and Saturday and brought in messages, mostly sweets to those with 6d to spare.

Parcels from home were an almost unknown luxury. There was no place with a lock on it to secure any personal belongings. On the odd occasion that a parcel of edibles arrived, it was a case of eating it all in one go or take the risk that no matter what hiding place was used, it would disappear. Most times the culprits would be known because there were a few students – called Feckers – who had developed pinching to a fine art.

Smoking was forbidden and was only indulged by a small minority of the more senior boys. The favourite place to smoke was an old corrugated iron "Jacks" to the rear of the back ball alley. Occasionally some were caught and chastised according to the method of the teacher who caught them.

Every week our laundry was sent to the Convent Laundry. The annual fee was £1 or £2. If one wanted to take the temperance pledge, one went to the Convent. I needed an excuse to get out of town one Sunday to meet someone and said I wanted to take the pledge. I got out, took the pledge but missed out on the tryst. I still have the pledge, except for wine with a meal.

During the summer term, there was an outbreak of devotion to the Thirty Days Prayer. This was particularly so with boys who had idled for the previous two terms. Our faith was pathetic and the devotion ended with the exams. During a Mission to Collooney one year, I told my mother that I thought I would be a priest. She replied, "Nonsense, better be a middling layman than a bad priest."

• 3 •

St. Nathy's College
1925-1930

Thomas P. McGettrick (R.I.P.)

LC 1930; Primary Teacher

I entered St. Nathy's College, the Diocesan Seminary for Achonry, at thirteen years of age in the autumn of 1925. The only memory that remains with me of that particular day is indeed a strange one. I do not remember leaving home or arriving at the College, nor do I recall events as they might be written into a diary during my five years there. But on that first day, I am standing looking up at a heavy iron object, suspended by strong pulley cables on the gable wall of the old building, and, in a shed nearby, there is a Ford car with a hood that could be raised and lowered. The contraption on the wall hung there for the duration of my stay, sometimes high sometimes low. It had some function to perform in supplying gas for the Bunsen burners in the science room. The car was the property of Fr. Curneen, who taught mathematics and science, and we were told it was the first and only one in the College at the time.

It is obvious, of course, that hunger, lessons, recreation, rest and lots of other matters began to demand that I should stop gazing heavenwards and get my eyes down to the proper level. If I had said, down to earth, it was in the football field they would be most of the time, deep in mud, which was an almost permanent feature of that arena. We spent all the winter in the College and very little of the summer.

When the first-year students arrived at the College, there was a communal baptising ceremony at the tap outside the gate leading to the football field. Each student was hauled there by two or three officiating ministers, and the more the subject intended for the water resisted this parody on God's first grace, the better the ministers liked it, so it was wise to submit feebly. The senior students who did this were not always the rough kind; it was a piece of usually harmless horseplay which was a tradition in the College.

The only instructions we actually got in hygiene or etiquette was to polish our shoes. Every morning after breakfast, there was a procession upstairs to the trunk room in the old college. The Matron carried out spot checks on the corridor into the classrooms and, if you were caught without the shine in the footwear, you were sent back.

Two developments, which today are necessary for formal domestic needs, had not at that time reached rural areas. There was no electricity and no water laid on to dwelling houses. Most of the students came from country districts, from the farming community. There was a high percentage of students whose fathers or mothers were teachers, or whose fathers were policemen – or rather ex-policemen as the Garda Siochana had then taken over under our own native government. As each diocese had its own college, St. Nathy's got very few students from outside the diocesan boundaries. Two students, I remember, were from Kerry and two were from America but had relations in the diocese. There were also a few whose diocesan affiliations were to Summerhill College, Sligo.

Boys in their teens had come into a world of new things – electric light, central heating, bathrooms, toilets (called jacks) and all aspects of community life. I recall how much students, especially the younger ones, suffered from chilblains throughout the winter. This was supposed to be because they used the radiators too frequently to warm their hands. There were a number of toilets in a unit off the recreation hall, which was the first part of the building one entered on the way in from the football field and the ball-alleys. These had to carry the burden of the day's activity until students went upstairs to bed. Little deformed Johnny Duffy carried out mopping operations all over the College. He was seldom seen without the mop in action. Sadly, there were those who thought that because of his lowly status in the scheme of things in the College, he was a suitable subject for their idea of fun. I saw him in tears.

There was a large jug called a ewer on a locker at the end of each bed, and it was here the morning ablutions were carried out – the water was cold. The baths in the bathrooms were never used.

The fee paid by students to the College was forty pounds a year. County Councils gave scholarships providing for free or subsidised entry for boys and girls to secondary schools. There was also the Broderick Scholarship, which was given out by the College itself to boys wanting to enter the College. Were it not for th cese scholarships, some parents would not have been able to afford to send their children to secondary education.

On entering the College, boys who had won scholarships or whose standard of primary education was observed to be high were put into classroom number two. The others were put into number one. The College thrived on examination results and this was earmarking the students in number two to bring future honours to the College. Some of them did and some of them did not. Yet, if my memory serves me, the boys in each room had to accept the same teaching. Remedial teaching and career guidance were unheard of in those distant times, and some who entered with weak primary foundations were left behind at the starting point. It would be accepted that throughout the four – or more often five – years students spent at St. Nathy's, the teaching was at times of a standard that neither the weak nor the strong derived full benefit from it; but it was those who were weak that lost out most. Irish and mathematics were subjects that confused many boys. Maybe you had to be born for Mathematics, like being able to sing. Fr. Curneen, who later became President of the College, took care with his teaching and was patient with the students. He also taught experimental science and made it an interesting subject.

Difficulties associated with the classroom in which Irish was taught had little to do with the language, or with the students' willingness or ability to accept the teaching provided. No matter what the subject was, it would only be natural for students awaiting the arrival of the teacher with the assurance that if written and oral preparation were well done, they could expect approval. This was not always the case with Irish. It was unpleasant for everybody else in the room when one of their classmates was severely and undeservedly punished. When a teacher singled out a student for frequent and perhaps unreasonable censure, he was said to have a 'set' on him. It was a pity that neither his ability as a teacher nor his priestly vocation caused him to make an effort to establish a better relationship in the case. This professor had the reputation of being a scholarly man; when he later gave up teaching and one met him, he was quite a likeable man. The world takes a lot of understanding.

The College is not remembered for its walls, windows, corridors, or surroundings. It lives with us still because of the students of our time and the teachers who taught there. Canon Blaine, the President during my time, was a fatherly figure who knew we needed discipline and who rarely went beyond the bounds of calling an errant student a humbug. The failings of those who worked under him were in most cases slight compared with their efforts on our behalf in the classroom. There are many boys that I never met or heard of again. They were successful men in their various professions – Dr. Igoe; Dr. Waldron; Garda Superintendent M. Crehan; teachers Joe Butler and Eamon Regan; my namesake, Jeff, to whom I will refer later, died a very short time after qualifying as a teacher; Solicitor Jim McGarry; Dr. P. Heraughty; District Justice O'Hara; P. Reid; and so on. Come to think of it, some good St. Nathy's did must be lurking somewhere in those last lines.

At the beginning of each year, the President appointed two prefects from the final-year class. Their duty was to oversee the conduct of the students in the study-hall, and to a lesser degree in the dormitories and the grounds of the College; they were always students whom the President regarded as of exemplary character. One sat in a high desk at the top of the study-hall and the other at the end. Students could not move from their desks, nor were they allowed to talk. Senior students did not adhere strictly to these restrictions. Rarely, if ever, did a priest appear in the study-hall.

This prevention of even limited freedom was extraordinary. Each day the students carried from the classrooms the various problems associated with the lessons of the day, yet a student could not, even with the best intentions, seek help from a student nearby. This discipline was too rigid and, even assuming that it was necessary, the prefect's way of enforcing it was cruel, often even savage. There was no way one could complain. In the dormitory, the prefect's duty was to see that the lights were put out at the correct time. No clock was needed, the cathedral chimes ringing out the quarter of an hour told the time when all operations began and ended throughout the day.

Handball and football were the only forms of recreation, if one were to exclude walking. Each Sunday there was a walk into the country. We left the College in marching order, but gradually extended into a broken line. Students liked to take a road along which there was a shop. On one occasion, some of the leaders reached a public house in Carrowcastle and took some intoxicating drink. This was an incident we talked about often. One of them laughed a lot on returning. If he had met any of the priests, he would have been detected. Teenage drinking was unheard of then.

Those who did not play games spent the time walking round the football field, or in wet weather up and down the recreation hall. This was monotonous exercise, but there was no other recreation available. Reading was allowed in the study-hall on Sunday night, but one never got the kind of book one would like to read. It was selected for you by Fr. Kirwin, who taught English and knew what was good for you.

It was difficult to get a place on one of the ball alleys unless you were a senior. It may sound funny now, but playing marbles – or 'taw' playing as it was called – was a common and enjoyable form of recreation with the junior students. This took place in an open iron-roofed shed near the ball alley. Maybe it points out the simplicity of the time and the need for something better to do, because no one plays 'taws' now.

When the teachers departed for their various rooms after classes were over, the students were for the most part left to make the most of the remainder of the day on their own. In general, there were acceptable relationships between the students. An occasional bout of fisticuffs might break out and a junior might be pushed about if he were not observing the proper respect for a senior, but these things were passed off. There were a small few who did not always act in accordance with those around them. On one occasion, I think it was during my first or second year there, a feud developed which almost split the students into two camps. I have tried to get to the root of this and was told that it had its beginnings five or six years earlier in a Mayo versus Sligo confrontation. How true this is I do not know, but I clearly recall that on one particular night it would have developed into serious gang warfare were it not for the timely intervention of the President – who had been told in time by one of the prefects. His arrival at the football field with his whip worked wonders in dispersing them; I have a vague idea that it was settled by single combat soon afterwards. It certainly was not a Mayo versus Sligo affair on this occasion.

The refectory was, of course, a very important place in our lives. Breakfast was tea and bread; I do not remember there being any variation from batch loaf. For variety, as some wag said, we got bread and tea in the evening, but with butter.

Each table seated eight and they were in two rows down each side of the room. Seniors sat at the head of each table and juniors – usually first-year students – sat at the end. The only type of etiquette enforced was that the seniors got first choice of the butter at breakfast and tea, and of the potatoes at dinner time. Each of these items came to the table on a dish, and by the time the dish arrived at the junior end of the table, it was often easy to eat all that was left on it. In this, as in other things where one might feel hard done by, one just put up with it. There was a code that was not transgressed about complaining to the authorities. There was always plenty of bread, cuts as we called it, and more was available at the serving table at the top of the refectory if needed. Dinner was a fairly substantial meal with little variety from day to day, cabbage for long periods in season, turnips for long periods, and so on. There was slight variation in the meat.

Friday in those times was a day of abstinence, and there was no proper meal to replace the meat dinner. Various concoctions were tried without success. Fish, which was good for the brain, was never served. In fact, other than the humble herring, fish was seldom seen on Irish tables at that time. There was one mess that we actually called 'concoction', the contents of which we never agreed on and most of us found it unpalatable, but one had to eat something. I remember there were rumblings about not going to the refectory as a kind of strike action against the food, but I do not recall that it was ever carried out. There was a cut of bread and cocoa at midday.

The prefects were allowed out town during recreation on Wednesdays and Saturdays, and students could purchase sweets, biscuits and other confectioneries if they had the money. Parcels from home – always containing a cake – arrived for some students, especially for St. Patrick's Day and November. One had to hide a parcel carefully in a locked locker or trunk as some students – known as prigs – were adept at finding them and appropriating them to their own use. To be a prig was not a character destroying thing, it meant you were clever that way.

During meals, but not always, the priest whose week it was for saying Mass walked up and down the refectory saying his Office. His business there was to keep us silent, when it would be a pleasant way to have a meal to be able to talk freely with those at the table. On one occasion, the professor of Greek noticed that I was laughing and called me a blackguard in the sternest tone of voice. He did not like laughing anyway; if he was seen smiling, it was talked about as an event.

If one felt ill and stayed in bed, Bess the Matron would take your temperature and, regardless of whether it recorded at or above the standard figure, you got no food for the day. If a student was ill enough to require medical attention, he would be removed to the infirmary in the old cottage. This seldom happened. On one occasion, there was a flu epidemic and many of the students were struck down with it.

There was Mass each morning and always prayers at night. Johnny Duffy, I think it was, rang a heavy hand bell which sounded all over the College to call us in the morning. There was no formal religious instruction and you left the College as uninformed officially about God's role for you in the scheme of things as when you entered it at thirteen. There was a retreat each year conducted by a priest of a religious order. It lasted for three days and during that time, all students went around in silence. God would speak to you during this silence. Perhaps it would be more fruitful if the priest spoke for Him. This was an opportunity for discussion groups to consider vocations, careers, life's problems as the students saw them, so many things, under the guidance of the priest and with response from him. The retreat was a worthwhile exercise and one felt better for having made it well.

Martin Coffey, from down the town and who had some professional experience as an actor, staged a play with the senior students each year. The night of the staging was a great occasion as there was a good deal of freedom for the players and a high tea after the performance. Students had to act female parts in these plays.

Soon after the students returned in autumn, an impromptu concert was put on in number two classroom. There was a stage in this room and it was here that the plays were staged. At the concert, the new arrivals had to do their party pieces. The seniors were the organisers, and were probably the same gentlemen that carried out the baptisms at the tap. If the selected artist was slow or entirely stubborn about taking his bow, he would likely be hoisted on the stage anyway. One timid youngster, who no doubt was telling the truth, said all he knew was a verse of the Tantum Ergo, so they told him it would do.

Occasionally we got down to entertainments in St. Mary's Hall, which was beside the College. There were great travelling play companies at that time; Dobell's was one of them. There were also excellent concerts with local talent organised by Fr. Roger McCarrick. He was the Diocesan religious examiner for many years and had the reputation of having picked many boys who became priests afterwards. We got to St. Mary's on the night that the Dempsey/Tunney fight was shown on the screen. It was a silent film. We cheered ourselves hoarse for Dempsey because at that time there was some ill-feeling towards the Kiltimagh students and Tunney had Kiltimagh connections. I think it had something to do with the feud to which I referred earlier. Tunney won that fight for the heavyweight championship of the world. Our cheering could not change the result.

Every student in the College got a nickname soon after arriving. The professors had their nicknames as well, and students and professors were usually best known by their nicknames. Some did not mind, some did. I remember thinking that Johnny Biscuits was a real name. I heard no other until I referred to him as such. I had every reason then to find out his real name. There was Click, whose real name was Brennan. He was named after the famous Co. Sligo footballer of that time. He had very sore knuckles which he often used to express the way he felt inside. If I could write all the names down and give the reason for them it would be great fun. There were Kruger, Bun, Dreoilin, Spot, Broder, Snib, Cuckoo, Spinx, Spart, Turkey Egg, Wuff, Spideog, Mouse, Bill Cody and dozens of others. I was Mutt and my namesake, who also came from the same national school as I did in the same year, was the Jeff to whom I have referred above. Dr. Stenson christened us in order to be able to distinguish one from the other in the classroom. I remember calling on him years after when he was parish priest in Collooney and he had not forgotten.

Inter-college competitions in football leading to All-Ireland finals began in my time, and they were great social occasions with the very best to eat. I played against St. Mary's, Galway, Summerhill, Sligo and Tuam. The O'Rourkes from Ballisodare were fine handballers. They played against the All-Ireland champions – I think it was a man called Perry and his partner – on the College alley and actually beat them.

Smoking was forbidden at St. Nathy's – there were some, perhaps a dozen or more, who did not obey this rule. There was plenty of opportunity in the shed that I have mentioned, or on the back-alley facing away from the College, to light up.

Servants on the staff I remember too: Joe McCann, staid and trustworthy, a loyal advisor of Canon Blaine's in attending to the farm attached to the College; Mick Quinn, carefree and good-humoured; Johnny Duffy and an old man we called Moko, who came to work each morning across a plank leading into the football field from the road along which he lived. This was the plank that certain students went out over at night on secret romantic missions. It took them onto a quiet road leading out from the town. Word reached the President of the goings-on and he waited in the dark at the intended rendezvous and kept the appointment instead of the girls. He caught two and one escaped. They were expelled from the College and the event set up a chain of enquiry and intercession that went on for some time. There were grounds for accepting that those who went out did so just to upset the fun for the real playboys. In the end, they were taken back to the College and finished their studies there. The students in general felt this was the best ending there could be to an unhappy event that caused the greatest disturbance in the College during my time there.

These are my memories. When I opened my story, I was standing at the gable wall of the old college, aged thirteen. A few years ago, I was in Ballaghaderreen and went through the wide, high gates again. That many-windowed view from the gates was the same as it was sixty years before. I went round to the right where there had been a wide way down by that gable to the football field and ball alleys. The way was all built up. I went over to the other side. On that side, the windows of the 'top big' and 'middle big' dormitories had looked out, on many a dark morning, at Ballaghaderreen fairs gathering in the field underneath. This side was now open the way the other side had been then. Down here I noticed, as Yeats said in a different context, all changed, changed utterly.

To the right, I saw the ball alleys with extra walls built for the way the modern game is played. As I moved a little nearer, I heard voices, the sounds of vigorous action and the smack of a ball, and I knew the senior students were in there. Two small boys were playing on the side alley. I have not told in my story that juniors rarely got on to the cement-floored alleys to play. The side alley was like playing against the gable of a house, with a rough street out from it, and I wondered if it was only the shape of St. Nathy's that had changed because I had to play there long ago too.

It would be wrong to think that I have lived my life in the diocese and I know that St. Nathy's has kept pace with developments to meet the needs of modern education, extra subjects, better teaching skills, more recreational facilities and more freedom. It must be a good thing still, as it was in our time, that among the students themselves there was an acceptable code to regulate their lives outside the areas where the teachers had control. The junior on the side alley will one day be a senior, and if he thinks he can do better than was done to him, the opportunity will be there for him. But I hope the system no longer applies to potatoes and butter.

Tempora mutantur et nos mutamur in illis.

Note: This article was written in 1987.

• 4 •

St. Nathy's in the 1920s
Patrick Heraughty (R.I.P.)
LC 1931; Medical Doctor

I arrived at St. Nathy's in the late afternoon of an early September day in 1926, to what I think may be a unique introduction to schooldays. I was taken to the matron's quarters and given tea with bacon and egg. It was the last time I had bacon and egg in St. Nathy's, but it was a lovely gesture and arose from the belief that I had come all the way from Innismurray Island on that day, when in fact I had come only from our alternative home in North Sligo. Apart from a month at Colaiste Connacht the previous July, it was my first time away from home. I did not know anyone – neither boys nor staff – and I think it says much for the spirit of St. Nathy's that I settled in quickly and easily, and still have friends that I made there.

Once installed, what does every young schoolboy think of first and remember always? Food, of course. No anxiety relating to food in St. Nathy's ever arose because it was wholly predictable and immutable. For breakfast and tea, we had bread – baker's and butter with tea which already had sugar and milk added – so any little foibles one might have about the additives were quickly dismissed. There was as much bread as one wished, but butter was rationed and the amount was small – a commendable pre-empt of the modern cardiologist' recommendations. We sat eight to a table, two Leaving Cert boys at either side at the top, two first year Leaving Cert boys next, two intermediate boys below and, at the foot of the table as was proper, two new boys. In these days, we still kept the classification used before the introduction of the Leaving/Intermediate epoch and called the Leaving Cert class Senior Grade, next Class Middle Grade and then Junior One and Junior Two, in that order. The head of the table rationed the butter by spreading it around the inner rim of the plate and dividing it into eight equal parts. Incidentally, and for good reason, our tableware was enamelled.

Our midday meal was again predictable. Apart form Fridays, we had roast beef or roast mutton with potatoes in their jackets. Helpings were generous –

second helpings of meat available and potatoes unlimited. The vegetable was, for all the first term, cabbage; for the second term, turnip. Friday lunch was a very generous helping of bread pudding with tea, bread and butter. We never had fish or eggs – the reason given being that some would not eat one, some would not eat the other and some neither. It must have been the most healthy diet ever designed as for four years, with numbers increasing from 90 to 105, there was only one case of serious illness and that was a case of tuberculosis meningitis – a disease that is not food related. The wholesomeness of the diet was, perhaps, the acceptable reasoning that resulted in the President, Vice-President and Matron taking holidays when 85 out of the 90 boarders were down with flu in the spring of 1927. The third-ranking member of the staff took the matter more seriously and the poor man spent his nights wandering from one dormitory to another, administering drinks of water but very obviously worried and helpless. He was unable to get medical help because of the epidemic and perhaps, in the case of flu, it would have availed him little in those days. We all survived unscathed.

Our next ranking interest in 1926 was the staff, five priests and the two laymen, later augmented by the addition of another layman. Our President was an upright, sterling type, but we suspected that his interest in the farm attached was, at worst, a good second to his interest in the school, which I hasten to add he never neglected. For reasons, which we always related to matters agricultural, classes might often be curtailed by 15 or 20 minutes. He was until the last term of school an eminently patient and reasonable teacher, but when last term came, he inevitably decided that we would all fail in his subject. The result was that we were taken away form general study to special classes where the benevolent teacher of the first two terms became the irate terror our last. We survived and I think that results-wise, no class ever let him down.

He had some strange but effective methods of helping slow learners. One of those was his 'hay foot' 'straw foot' method; the name deriving from the story of the army recruit who did not know his left from his right foot and who was brought into line by his sergeant major, who had him tie a rope of straw around one leg and a rope of hay around the other, and then instead of 'left' 'right', he called 'hay foot' straw foot'. The application was that if two possible solutions existed, and it obviously was not one, it should be the other.

On one occasion, he had helped a student to translate a sentence to 'Caesar, having crossed the hill, saw the hostem'. I must say he more than helped him all along to the 'hostem'. Hoping for a semi-miracle, he allowed the pupil to stare long and intently at 'hostem' before asking him what it was. He was encouraged by a radiantly intelligent beam on the pupils face as he triumphantly announced 'the imperfect subjunctive'. End of story.

He also took class in apologetics and perhaps because he found it difficult to communicate with us impartially with his profound knowledge of the subject, he was not very successful in holding our attention. On one occasion he spotted me in a vacant rather than pensive mood, and abruptly put the question 'Where is God?' to me. Not realising that he was asking me the second question in the Short Catechism, I did not realise for some time why everyone laughed when I replied 'in Heaven'.

The Vice-Principal was a literary genius who taught both English and Irish. His striking attitude was his ability to focus on one word and discuss all its shades of meaning in different positions in prose and in poetry. He was humorous and obviously brilliant. When in class he mudged that he had given us as much as we could digest, he would direct us to read, while he did so himself, either from his office book or from some other publication. Sadly, the time thus offered us was not always used to the best advantage – more often it was taken as bonus break.

Our teacher of science and mathematics was of the true academic school. Others did – and I am sure with justification – sometimes use corrective measures involving the use of hand or cane, but he never did. Perhaps it is a psychological reaction that when physical means are used, then one feels you have paid your debt, but in his particular case, one felt mean and ashamed if either by omission or commission you offended him, on his evidencing disappointment with one. We respected him and, immature though we were, appreciated him.

Our teacher of Greek and English, right the way through to the senior classes, was a strict disciplinarian and a painstaking teacher and student, but we always thought, a man with a well concealed sense of humour. He was never late for class and had his sessions so structured that he would stop as the clock struck with a perfectly timed conclusion. He corrected essays and term examinations with minute accuracy and always wrote helpful comments. Having made a favourable comment, in great detail, on the last essay I submitted before I sat for Leaving Cert, he added: 'But if your hand writing does not improve, I shall insist on your getting a Vere Foster headline copy,' – I was one of the class juniors of course, taken out of second study to write index cards for the books from his library left by Archdeacon O'Rourke to St. Nathy's. If anyone is having difficulty with some of those index cards, I promise, if requested, to try to decipher them and have them typed.

The priests took charge of the general functioning of the school in rotation, and this included supervision at meals. We were to keep silent in the refectory, but unless talk reached a crescendo, we were not ordered by any of the others to absolute obedience. In the care of our Greek and English teacher, however, silence for the duration of the meal was absolute. This could be very boring, especially if one had finished eating for some time before dismissal from the refectory. He wore a hat which was in shape, a trimmed down version of the tall hat. He left this crown downwards on one of the serving tables while he walked up and down the refectory. One evening, some bright spark got the idea of amusing himself by flicking small pieces of bread into the hat as the owner walked in the other direction. Several others took up the performance with the result that, when grace had been said, the hat was found to be filled with pieces of bread and a hurried exit from the refectory ensured that there would be no 'on the spot' investigation. When, after nothing further was heard about the affair for 24 hours, hopes were high that the incident was over. However, after grace had been said before tea on the following evening, there was a very definite announcement: "I hereby terminate the tea, leave the refectory."

This meant that, except for those who reacted quickly by grabbing some bread, no one had anything to eat until breakfast next morning. Our response was 'fair enough, you win and no hard feelings'. We appreciated him with mute admiration.

The fifth member of staff was a kind, friendly man who became ill shortly after I came to St. Nathy's, so I did not have the pleasure of being a pupil of his. He was replaced by a quiet but strong and efficient administrator who understood young people and acted on the principal of mutual trust. This reminds me of a rather funny incident during one of his weeks on duty. We were called at 7.30am, a very reasonable time, and were due in the oratory at 8.00am. Generally, the priests on duty visited the dormitories between 7.30am and 7.40am, but he generally did not do so. One morning he was about earlier than usual and called into our dormitory about six or seven minutes before 8.00am to find us all in bed – nevertheless, with our acquired efficiency we would still have been in the oratory at 8.00am. He was very disappointed and after standing in silence by the door for some moments, he finally expostulated: "You supine wretches" -a delightful term of phrase – and walked away. He had been a very fine athlete and devoted much time to helping the football team. Again, he was not one of my teachers, but I was happy to have been much better acquainted with him in later life.

The senior of our lay teachers was Toby, who taught history, geography and singing. Even then he was elderly and portly. He had, perhaps because of his advanced years, developed a respect for older boys, but apparently believed that an occasional light slap on the cheek was good for younger ones. I had a practical experience of this. He had a habit of half sitting on the edge of the front seat in class and I happened to sit in the same seat in my Intermediate year. We had him for class on Monday morning and again on Saturday. At this time, I found it necessary to shave once weekly and did so on Sunday. On Monday morning my smooth face was on occasions the target for his open palm. By Saturday, I was sufficient hirsute to earn his respect and could and, mea culpa, did give the most outrageous answers without punishment. I do not know if Toby was his real name, but it seemed most suitable. Years later, his very charming daughter was a patient of mine and introduced herself by saying "I am Toby's daughter." I was very touched.

As regards singing, he held that anyone could sing if only a technique was tried and the effort made. Surely, his experience with me must have changed his mind. He was very much loved.

The second lay teacher was a brilliant mathematician and scientist, but he was so far ahead of his students that he found it almost impossible to impart his comprehensive knowledge. He was friendly and witty, and I think he really pitied our affliction of limited intellects.

Three of our class decided to sit Honours Mathematics in Leaving Certificate, and were given special tuition by another member of the staff. They were unfortunate in that the paper was very difficult. When the boys came out from the examination, our teacher happened to be walking in the recreation ground with their special tutor. When the paper was produced, the special tutor found it so difficult that he admitted that he scarcely knew where to begin and so appealed to our friend, who took out a twenty cigarette packet containing two cigarettes, lit one of the cigarettes, put the other behind his ear, tore open the packet and in less than ten minutes had solved all six questions.

During our Leaving Certificate year, he announced one day that we were to have an inspector from the department next day, adding that as we obviously knew next to nothing about mathematics, he was not expecting much from us and implied that he was unconcerned about the inspection. The inspector arrived the next day and, as luck would have it, picked on the wit of the class, who was also one of the best students, and asked him: "What are you doing?" He was certainly astounded by the answer: "Sums." After a long enfostulation of the point that sums meant addition, he repeated the question and received the answer: "Mathematics", which evoked the further question: "Do you think I came into a Greek class?" When he eventually elicited that it was a problem in arithmetic, he asked that it be enunciated, wrote it on the blackboard and proceeded to demonstrate how the problem should be solved. He finished with a flourish by underlining his result, but was immediately brought to reality by the voice of the boy he had interrogated saying: "You got the answer wrong, Sir." He stared at the board realising that this was indeed so, dropped the chalk and without further comment walked out the door. Our teacher smiled, wiped the board clean and proceeded with the class. No one ever tittered, but there was a shared understanding that 'such is life'. There was a deep, if unexpressed, bond between him and us.

Our third lay teacher, who came in my last year, was not afflicted by having me as a pupil, but appeared to be a very fine person. What I heard of him after I had left St. Nathy's confirmed that this was so.

The new part of the College was, for its time, a very fine and solid building. It held our classrooms, dormitories, science hall, oratory, priests' bed and sitting room, and spacious tiled bathrooms in which, though laid on, the hot water never flowed. Anyhow, we were young and in the summer the cold water was less cold than in the winter.

Our morning ablutions were performed on a long, marble-covered stand, which ran the whole length of the centre of the dormitory. If one needed a mirror, one provided one's own.

The new building was joined to the older part of a tile-floored recreation hall. Mention of this reminds me of an incident when another boy and myself were consuming some tinned meat, purchased in disregard of the very proper rule against buying such, in an apartment of the recreation hall. We heard an adult footfall in the hall. While I stayed to conceal the container, my pal strolled out to reconnoitre. He returned almost immediately to announce: "It is only the Bishop." This was long before Vatican II.

In the older part of the building was the dining room, and above it the trunk room where we kept our obligatory school boy trunks, which were really unnecessary in St. Nathy's where all bed clothes, except sheets, were supplied. The trunk room was also where we polished our shoes – observation of which was conducted later by the matron as she stood at the entrance to the class area. Beyond the trunk room was the library, where we had worked on the cataloguing of Archdeacon O'Rourke's books.

Extra academic activities were Gaelic football and handball. I was only peripherally involved in these, not so much from lack of interest, but from the fact that when at the age of 12 years, I have been found to have a cardiac murmur. I was forbidden to take part in field games or in any physically stressful activity. On Sunday afternoons we had long walks, of two to three miles, in the vicinity generally; these were generally overseen by the prefects, sometimes accompanied by the priests on duty. Except during Lent, we were allowed to go to the pictures on alternate Sunday nights. These were the only occasions on which we might see the other half of the world and...

> 'When all the world was young lad
> And every tree was green
> And every goose a swan lad
> And every lass a queen.'

We were not interested in geese or swans, but all the lassies were queens.

The great annual diversion was the play produced at the end of the first term by the Leaving Cert boys. One of the advantages arising from this was that it was shown in the local concert hall, where the good Sisters knew the desired reward and thus the cast was treated to a high tea. A play designed to give parts to at least the whole class was chosen, and if a few extras were needed they were acquired from the next class. A la Polonius, I did enact Professor Tim – not too well, I fear.

Inevitably there were factions within the school, the main one being a Sligo versus Mayo division, but like all things Irish, this was characterised by the fact that boys from a town in central Mayo were members of the Sligo grouping, and boys from a town in Sligo were in the Mayo grouping. This particular faction was entirely absent from our class and I like to think that we were well thought of by staff and fellow pupils.

An incident that did touch us occurred on our last day in school. All others had gone home and, while we waited for our last examination, we paraded aimlessly in the recreation hall. One of the staff came into the hall, I am sure with the intention of saying goodbye to us, but having approached us he blurted out: "If any of you boys are ever around here, we will always be glad to see you," he turned around and walked away to, I think, conceal a mist on his glasses.

Could things have been better in St. Nathy's? I think that speech training was badly missed. We could all have done with it and many of us still could. Culture, both in the fine art aspect and in social manners, was not portrayed. There was no attempt at career guidance as regards higher education or business careers. If one expressed an interest in religious life, guidance and direction was available – as was proper since the school was founded for the primary purpose of educating young men towards the priesthood.

Despite any shortcomings, unless it were one's own fault, one left St. Nathy's with a reasonably good education and, very definitely, with a profound sense of loyalty and sincerity in all things. Happy days! – and when thyself with shining foot shall pass!

• 5 •

Recollections

Patrick Fleming

LC 1938. CEO Co. Cavan and Co. Dublin VEC

At 89 years of age, the very name St. Nathy's College brings back a flood of memories. With some 150-200 other boys, I sojourned there between 1933 and 1938. Many who were then my classmates and friends, are long in Heaven, where I hope to rejoin them at some future date. It was a happy school then and I am confident that trait has survived. Almost all the teachers were natives of the Diocese of Achonry, and this meant they had a very good understanding of each student's home environment. Those were some of the years of Ambrose Canon Blaine's presidency.

He taught us Latin with the aid of his famous 'skeleton', but that was just a small part of his every week's work. His teaching team seemed to be influenced by his example, rather than by instructions. The outcome of that was a smoothly running institution with us, the students, as chief beneficiaries. The following were also members of the teaching team during that particular period: Fathers Curneen, Folan, Colleran, Wims and Walsh, as well as Messrs Collier and O'Reilly. Two others I remember with affection because of their contribution to our well being are John Duffy, in the food department, and Miss Harris in the Infirmary.

Fr. James Colleran was our trainer for football and athletics. He was from Curry and one of seven brothers. In 1933, a boy called Michael Keegan scored 426 in Inter-Cert Greek, a consequence of which was that we got the whole day free. Billy Durcan of Swinford was the best all-round athlete of my time. He excelled in several sports and won the national trophy in handball for four years in succession.

Ours was a distressed community in the latter part of the nineteenth century and on into the 30s and 40s of the twentieth century. For me, access to St. Nathy's College meant the difference between a University degree and a shovel job with Mc Alpine around London. Why would I not be grateful to my parents and to my teachers? It was their help that made the difference.

The Trunk Room

In the thirties, one part of what had previously been a barracks now functioned as a dormitory. It was known to us as 'the trunk room'. Unlike the new college alongside, it lacked central heating, so it was the older and hardier students who slept there. To compensate for the lack of central heating, a coal fire was provided at one end.

Because of its relative remoteness, the trunk room was less closely supervised and, of course, we took advantage of this. A favoured practice when we assembled there after the Rosary was roasting fresh eggs in the fire's 'griasac' before getting into bed. Billy Durcan and Padraig Gallagher were thus engaged, when one of the other boys, returning from the distant toilets, shouted: "Mussy is coming up the stairs." Hurriedly, Gallagher pushed his egg into the hot coals. Durcan, reluctant to sacrifice his, grabbed the roasting hot egg and threw it into his open bed nearby, then got in and drew up the blankets as quickly as possible.

In all probability, Canon Blaine was primarily concerned about the risk associated with our open coal fire. He stood looking at it for a moment in silence. Then he turned to speak to us – probably to urge the need for care. Just as he was about to speak, an explosion occurred in the fire behind him. It was Gallagher's egg exploding. We knew, he did not, and maybe nobody ever told him. After rearranging the fender, he left the room without saying a word.

There was a short period of silence, while his footsteps could be heard going down the stairs. Then the silence was abruptly broken by a scream from Durcan, "I am destroyed by this roasting egg," (or words to that effect).

• 6 •

Reflection

Padraic Carney

LC 1945, Consultant Gynecologist

In September 1940, a twelve-year-old boy, accompanied by his parents, arrived on the steps of St. Nathy's College. On entry, they were directed to a small room off the main hall where they were welcomed by the Dean. Shortly thereafter, the parents departed leaving the boy alone to his own devices in a strange place. Away from home for the first time, he felt dejected and scared. As the days passed and as he mingled with other incoming students, he adapted to the new environment and accepted the fact that he was now a very small fish in a large pond.

By the fall of that year, World War ll was in full swing and although the country was not directly involved in hostilities, it was a time of food shortages, petrol rationings, and limited travel. Despite these problems, life as St. Nathy's, though spartan, was orderly and predictable. The daily routine started with Mass, followed by a simple breakfast. Classes occupied the mornings and afternoons with a break in between for the main meal of the day. A short free period was fitted in after classes, prior to the first study period. Following an evening repast, second study time lasted until it was time to retire to the dormitories for a much-needed sleep. Our free time, especially on weekends, was occupied by walking in groups around the grounds or by playing football.

From day one, I was drawn to the football pitch, although as a lowly first year, my activity was initially confined to chasing loose balls behind the goal posts.

With the passage of time, I settled in and took advantage of the learning and sporting activities that were offered. Friendships were formed, some of which have lasted to the present day. It was always a treat when the occasional parcel arrived from home, but the contents had to be consumed quickly or well hidden, otherwise they disappeared from one's locker. Once a week, the Matron opened her shop at the end of the exercise hall and we eagerly waited in line to make our purchases of candy bars and sweets.

The Christmas, Easter and summer holidays provided a welcome respite from our confined existence in an all-boys school. As a group, our teachers did a commendable job and posed no problem for the bright student, but for the less committed or poor performing, rather harsh verbal or physical treatment was not unusual.

In particular, I have pleasant memories of Fr. Foran, our English teacher, who made Shakespeare come alive in the classroom and instilled in many of us a love for the English language. The same can be said about Fr. Colleran, who made Geography both interesting and educational. Loving sports as I do, the arrival of Fr. Paddy Towey during my last two years made my days much brighter. His competitive spirit and coaching skills elevated our game to a new level. Emphasising the need for mastering basic skills and the commitment required to excel at the game, he enabled many of us to have success in later years at inter-county level. Last but not least was Fr. Joe Higgins, whose task it was to instil in us proper manners and clear articulation. His elocution and etiquette sessions assisted in no small way to our success in later years.

In 1945, my senior year at St. Nathy's arrived and the end of my high school days was fast approaching. I had the honour of being selected as the senior prefect, an office that required certain responsibilities and duties. The role allowed me to develop leadership skills and acquire judgment in handling difficult situations. This last year required hard study as we prepared for the Leaving Certificate and Matriculation Examinations. Having spent five of my nine teenage years at St. Nathy's, the twelve-year-old boy who came through the school gates in 1940 was now a seventeen-year-old adolescent eager to move on and pursue further challenges at university level. My St. Nathy's experience had provided me not only with a sound basic education, but had inculcated in me a thirst for knowledge, a keen interest in Gaelic football, good study habits, and the need for discipline and hard work if one is to succeed in future endeavours.

In July 2008, my family and I had the privilege of a guided tour of the present St. Nathy's by Fr. Martin Jennings and Fr. Leo Henry. What wonderful changes have taken place since my graduation? Now a co-education facility with state-of-the-art academic and sporting facilities, as well as an expansive and diverse curriculum, today's students are indeed fortunate to attend such a fine institution. Oh, to be young again and to be a student! But then the old St. Nathy's also had something special. Though not so grand, it did teach us survival skills and instilled in so many a burning desire to succeed.

• 7 •

Political Journalism
and the Back Alley

Ted Nealon

LC 1945; Journalist, Politician, Author

On a wet Wednesday in March, Aidan and Frank Durkin had a visit from their parents in Bohola. Nothing unusual about that. During my time in St. Nathy's, Wednesday was a half-day and there were always parents up for a visit. Mainly parents with cars, like teachers.

What made this visit unusual was what the Durkin parents brought with them. For, in addition to the porter cake and the G.A.A. newspaper cutting for Aidan and the chocolate for Frank, they had with them a bag full of election lapel badges!

I still remember the badge today in all its detail. It was about two inches in diameter with a background of the American flag in full colour and superimposed on this, in black and white, a head and shoulders picture of Bill O'Dwyer. Aidan Durkin had one for everyone in his class, including me, and Frank had one for everyone in his class. In addition, because my bed was next to Aidan's in the old dormitory between the bottom oratory and the top oratory, I also qualified for a full-colour poster that was more or less an enlarged version of the lapel badge with some extra wording.

After that we were all part of the election campaign. It did not matter that the election was for Major or faraway New York, or that it was between the Democrats and the Republicans of whose policies we were totally ignorant. After all, Bill O'Dwyer was an uncle of two of our schoolmates and a past pupil of St. Nathy's, and he was running for what, as far as we were concerned, was a job just below that of President of United States. What more did anyone want to know? Furthermore, most of the boarders then came from the emigration counties of Sligo or Mayo where they had more intimate knowledge of the streets of New York than those of Dublin. I myself had twenty-seven first cousins in New York compared to three in Ireland – and those three were the family of a returned Yank!

So we wore our badges and backed our man until we saw Bill O'Dwyer safely through the primaries and safely into City Hall with a sweeping victory.

Even without a favourite son like Bill O'Dwyer, we loved our politics in St. Nathy's. Not that the College did much to encourage our interest or improve our knowledge. The teaching of history stopped dead at the turn of the century, just when it was getting interesting. There were no civics classes. There were no newspapers allowed in the College and no radio. Even the most likely of the professors could not be cajoled into political debate or discussion. They even refused to pontificate on politics!

Despite this lack of source material and adequate briefing, we still loved to talk and to argue politics, and in this we were only reflecting what was happening at home around the firesides of Sligo and Mayo, at the crossroads and outside the church gates on a Sunday morning.

We were totally inhibited by our lack of knowledge of the social and economic issues. In that we were not much different from the Dail Deputies of the day. At that time, politics were very simple, you were for De Valera or you were against him. The nearest you got to seeing a live politician during our St. Nathy's days was the odd glimpse of James Dillon, and, truth to tell, we had more interest in the quality of the bread he baked for us in Monduffs than in the quality of his speeches!

The political arguments amongst the boarders were regular and vigorous. At election time in the great world outside, debate became more frequent and more furious. Amongst the more regular and dogmatic contributors was a John Healy from Charlestown. He was a year behind me but had already made his career choice. When he left St. Nathy's he was going to be a journalist, and he could not wait.

After St. Nathy's, John and myself went our separate ways, but seven years later we were together again in the newsroom of the Irish Press papers in Burgh Quay, then the best newspaper in the business. A further four years on and we were together again in the Irish Times offices in D'Olier Street, with John as the editor of the Sunday Review and myself as news editor.

This was a tabloid Sunday paper of the Irish Times with a circulation of 189,000. We set our target to push that circulation above 200,000. In seeking ways to do this, we went back to our experience in St. Nathy's and the interest that we knew existed in politics in the West and all over the country.

Here we felt might be the magical formula to increase circulation. At that time, the reporting of politics was incredibly staid. No comment, no colour, no satire and, of course, no fun. It was all treated with great reverence and simply amounted to reporting what Mr. De Valera said or Mr. Lemass said, or Mr. Dillon said or Mr. Costello said in one dull column after another. We decided that we would change all this. We would introduce a new kind of column to Irish papers. It would go behind the scenes; it would have comment; it would have satire; it would have gossip, but above all, it would have inside knowledge. Indeed we called it 'Inside Politics' by Backbencher.

This ran in the Sunday Review for three or four years and later was continued on by John Healy himself in the Irish Times for many, many years. It became the most famous political column in Irish Journalism. It was loved and it was feared. It was, in those Sunday Review days, extremely fair or, as one prominent politician put it: "equally offensive to all sides." It became a runaway success and transformed the style of political reporting in this country.

Those political discussions that we had in St. Nathy's, as we sheltered by the ball alley from the cold winds in from 'Bacagh', may not have done much in progressing political thought in the country, but I like to think that they may have led to a very significant change in the way politics was reported and presented to the people.

· 8 ·

Vocational Education in Ballaghaderreen

Oliver Hynes (R.I.P.)

Principal 1949-1959

In a recent study carried out for the Government, Consultants Area Development Management Ltd was asked to list Ireland's most disadvantaged and advantaged towns. In that study, Consultants placed a heavy emphasis on the availability of the various forms of post-primary education. It is of interest, therefore, to take a look at how Ballaghaderreen fared under this heading. Let us first take a brief look at the educational scene in general.

In the early years of the twentieth century, the only form of post-primary education available was the academic education provided by the Church authorities. Under this heading, Ballaghaderreen was well served by St. Nathy's Diocesan College for boys and the Convent Secondary School of the Sisters of Charity for girls. However, these schools were intended mainly to provide for boys and girls entering the religious life. Those who did not have a religious vocation or those for whom academic education was unsuitable had no alternative form of education available. Training or the study of practical subjects was frowned on as non-educational. Chalk and talk was the order of the day, with very little effort to encourage students to think and learn for themselves.

Then came the 1930 Vocational Educational Act. It was to bring the most momentous and dramatic change to Ireland's education system for more than a century. For the first time, the Church was not to be the only provider of post-primary education. The State was now prepared to provide secondary level education of a new and exciting kind.

Throughout the 1930s, 1940s and 1950s, new schools were erected across the country. One of the earliest ones was Ballaghaderreen Vocational School, which opened its doors for the first time on the 1st of September 1939. The buildings and equipment were of a very high standard and were staffed by highly and specially trained teachers.

But Ballaghaderreen School, like the others, was not to have an easy run for many years. The Church-run schools now had competition for the first time. To make life more difficult for Ballaghaderreen School, its opening coincided with the outbreak of the Second World War. Travelling any distance to schools became difficult or indeed impossible. Bicycles and tyres, foe example, were luxuries that could only be obtained on the black-market at exorbitant prices.

The first headmaster of the new Ballaghaderreen School was M. J. Tiernan, a specially trained local Ballaghaderreen man. He captained that first team consisting of Irish teacher Peadar O' Nuadhain; domestic science teacher Miss A. Reidy (later to become Mrs. Lack Coen of the local Coen's Hotel); Dr. James Ruane (later Professor and Head of the Agricultural Science Faculty, UCD). That team provided day courses for boys and girls in their teens in Irish, English, mathematics, domestic science, woodwork and building construction, agricultural and rural science.

But the day school was only part of the new picture. An extensive range of night classes in a vast variety of subjects was provided for adults in the local school itself, as well as in rural halls and national schools, old renovated buildings, farmhouses, kitchens and specially erected prefabricated buildings throughout the length and breath of the parish. Life-long learning had begun. Places like Lisacul, Cloontia, Derrinacartha, Frenchpark and Kilmovee had classes and training brought to their doorsteps. Long after schools were in darkness, the Ballaghaderreen Vocational School and its classes in the far-flung surrounding areas were still open and lights in every room late into the night was a familiar and heart-warming sight.

As well as the day and night classes, educational bus tours for students to a variety of centres were organised throughout the year. The annual bus tour to the RDS Spring Show in Dublin was a main attraction. Games such as football and camogie also had an important slot on the educational timetable.

For the record, M. J. Tiernan was followed as headmaster by Peadar O' Nuadhain. He was the headmaster during the early post-war years and did a remarkable job in keeping a scheme of day and night classes going during those difficult years.

Oliver Hynes, who later became chief education officer for County Monaghan and County Galway, succeeded Peadar O' Nuadhain as headmaster.

Another well-known member of the early teaching staff was Mrs. B. O'Reilly (nee Kitsy Chapman), who succeeded Mrs. Coen as domestic science teacher. Two other local and nationally acclaimed teachers in the school were Maureen Glynn and Mary Ann Callaghan, teacher of commerce.

Pat Hunt took over at the helm when Oliver Hynes left in 1959, and the last headmaster of the school before its closing as a post-primary day school in 1995 was Alex McDonnell.

The Ballaghaderreen Vocational School served well for almost sixty years. Make no mistake about it, Ballaghaderreen – and indeed Ireland – would be a poorer place today but for the Vocational Educational Act of 1930. Before that, only the brighter students who won scholarships or the well-off could afford a post-primary education. All that changed with the coming of the new Act.

It was the young men and women who passed through these schools, aided by a dedicated and enthusiastic teaching force, who laid the successful foundation for both the agricultural and industrial development that was to follow. Farmers, clubs, Macra Na Feirme and the National Farmers Association were founded and fostered by the teachers of vocational schools and were manned by their former students. Those organisations did more for agricultural development and for the instilling of self-respect and confidence into rural Ireland than did many previous years of teaching and exhortation. The success of industry depended almost entirely on the ability of the technical school to provided education and training. It is imperative that Ballaghaderreen should never forget the structures, and the men and women in them, who served it so well.

We must keep the past for pride.

This article was written for Voices. Margaret Garvey and Gary Hynes gave me their permission to include this article in our publication.

• 9 •

Memories of St. Nathy's College

Thomas Flynn

LC 1949; Bishop of Achonry 1976-2007

When the autumn of life gathers around us, greying what is left of a once heavy head of hair, enforcing discipline on a gainly gait and reducing physical strength, we look for compensation of another kind. Memories fill many a gap and enhance our experiences. The great problem or, perhaps, advantage of memories is that they can be very selective. So, when I look back at my student days in St. Nathy's, it is often the pleasant experiences that come to mind or the humorous aspects of the distressful days.

Above all, I remember many of my fellow students. Some of them are already with the Lord, while others have distinguished themselves as priests, doctors, scientists or teachers, not only in Ireland, but right across the globe. I remember as a first year getting our first 'class exam' in October. We got one question in geography: 'Write all you know about Java'. We did not do so well on that outing so we got a replay a week later!

There was another 'first year' experience which I cannot forget. I was a 'day boy' and at lunchtime one day, we got word that a German plane had landed just outside the town. The war was still on and this was too much of an attraction to be missed, so a group of us set off walking to find it. It emerged that it was neither German nor near the town. It was British and about five miles away. We reached our destination but it was too late to get back to St. Nathy's for class. We had hoped that we would not be missed but we were.

I still remember one bit of advice we got for writing English. We were told that adjectives were very important and that we should spend some time in selecting them: 'throw them up in the air and look at them before you choose the one you need'.

In those days, day boys were second-class citizens, or that is what we perceived ourselves to be. All activities revolved around boarding life. Boarders were in the majority and we were tolerated. I was never a good businessman, but some of my fellow day-boys plied a lucrative trade on chocolate and toffee bars. These traded well at a time when food was very scarce, and the dean's main occupation was touring the local towns for loaves and bread. These were the war and post-war years when anything edible was valuable. There was a lot of hardship in those days and yet there was great security. Very few people had locks on their doors and most houses kept the door on the latch day and night.

In spite of hardship, or perhaps it was because of them, there was a great idealism among the students. There were twenty six students in my class for Leaving Certificate and seven of us went on to study for the priesthood. That was not particularly good in those days; the following year, thirteen out of a class of twenty eight followed the same road to priesthood. I am forever grateful to St. Nathy's College for the insight it gave me into priestly life and the encouragement it provided among the way. I would be happy if I, for my part, could impart a similar vision of the dignity and value of each and every person, and try to walk along the road of life with people, particularly in their hour of need.

In those days, we did not have the choice of subjects that is on offer today. We were limited, too, in our choice of games. We had Gaelic football and handball, with little else. There was only one football field where the basketball courts and the new blocks of classrooms are located in the present. This was shared by juniors and seniors. The sharing was not quite equal, with the seniors taking the larger share. The handball alleys were also shared in an equally unequal fashion, yet we produced some of the best handballers in Ireland and won a number of Connacht titles in football.

We performed our concerts and plays on stage and these were in Irish or English. There was also drama adapted for the occasion. I remember the day we brought a goat into the class and hid him behind a bookcase. He emerged from his hiding place in the middle of class, but an old experienced teacher spoke to him in a kid-like manner, while beckoning a student to take him out. The incident was over in a matter of minutes. However, the goat was retrieved for the following class and behaved as he had done previously. The teacher on this occasion was not as skilled in 'kid' behaviour. He did not see the joke and, with threatening menaces, he organised a 'posse' to remove the offending creature. To make sure the animal was removed from the building, he accompanied the 'posse' to the side door. However, before he could reach the classroom again, the goat was passed in through the window and reinstated in its hiding place behind the bookcase. We were all on our best behaviour prepared for the inevitable. We had not long to wait until a pair of horns appeared at the end of the bookcase and the outraged teacher conceded defeat. Peig Sayers had vanished from that day's class.

When you are old, you look back to the past for memories because the future is moving quickly into the past and is getting shorter and shorter. But when you are young, there is very little past and a vast future, which seems to be limitless. The future will have most to offer when it fuses the energy and enthusiasm of youth with the experience of age. St. Nathy's College has a memory going back for two hundred and yet its students have never aged; they are still the teenagers they were two centuries ago.

The 'points' system, as we know it today, is relatively new. This does not mean there was no pressure from exams in the olden times. In those days, before the advent of 'free' education, the real pressure was for scholarships and there were very few of these. Roscommon County Council offered two university scholarships for the county! Without one of these, university education was closed to the majority of students. Expectations were not as high as they are today; some would say they were more realistic. At any rate, we survived and I have no doubt that newer generations will rise to greater heights and help fashion a world where we can all feel at home in the love of God and find a ready and supporting hand in one another.

Beir bua agus beannacht.

• 10 •

Reminiscence
Noel Dorr

LC 1951; MRIA; Secretary General Dept. of Foreign Affairs;
Ambassador to London and United Nations New York

It was cold, very cold, that winter of 1946/47. As memorable for us who lived through it as children as Oiche Na Gaoithe Moire – the night of the 'Big Wind' – must have been for our great, great grandparents.

It was my first year in St. Nathy's, the diocesan college, where all our teachers except one – Billy O'Reilly who taught us maths – were priests of the diocese. I had arrived there as a boarder in September 1946, thanks to a scholarship. I was twelve, going on thirteen, the oldest in my family, and I was away from home for the first time. All of twenty-five miles. But with transport and roads as they were at the time, a year after the war, it might as well have been five hundred.

I do not remember exactly when the snow started that winter, after Christmas I think, but once it started it went on and on and on. Towns were cut off from each other by huge snowdrifts for weeks until roads were gradually opened by men with shovels. No contact with home. No phones of course, we would hardly have known how to use one, and in any case the lines were down. No letters or food parcels or visitors. Wartime rationing still in force, and to cap it all, bread, our staple food, ran short because of a strike.

Altogether not the best introduction for a small boy in short trousers to five years of boarding school life.

In later years, things were less harsh, though still well short of the cosy toast and muffins in a sixth-former's study after cricket that we read about in English public school stories of the time. In our case, it was football played with a heavy, soggy ball in wet and muddy fields on dark November days. This was followed by cold showers to wash off the mud. There was always a rush from class to get a place on a handball alley, which could then be taken over by a senior boy if he exercised his accepted right to 'bully' you off the alley. If this happened, all that was left to do was interminable rounds of 'the walk', a paved footpath around the four sides of the football field.

A strange lingo or 'cant' evolved, which seemed to have its epicentre in Charlestown, though I have heard since it connected to Tuam – a 'sham' was a man, a 'bloan' a woman, for example.

We had sausages with breakfast twice a year, on the 1st of November and St. Patrick's Day. For the rest of the year, only occasional food parcels from home would break the monotony of a limited post-war diet.

St. Nathy's, like other diocesan colleges around the country at the time, must have constantly had to maintain a precarious balance between the facilities it could provide and the level of fees it could charge if it was to keep education affordable for the boys of families in the region. So some mothers, anxious to supplement the diet which the College provided for their darling sons, would send bulky parcels from time to time that contained butter, jam, home-made soda bread, cakes and even eggs to be taken raw in the morning. We stored the good things in the locked 'do-boxes', as we called them, under our bed and shared them later with the others at our four-person table in the refectory. In my case, the parcels were hand delivered on Saturdays by the Morrin's Dry Cleaning van from Foxford as it made its rounds of neighbouring towns; my uncle drove it.

Sweets and chocolates could be bought on occasion from the 'shop', which opened for a short time one day a week by the matron. Then there were the bars of chocolate smuggled in by dayboys from the town and sold to boarders at a substantial mark-up. Sometimes the purchaser, a budding entrepreneur, sold on the chocolate, square by square at a handsome profit.

Other memories return as I write. The ghost of Jacob Henthron walked at night late in October, we were told, on the stairs in the very oldest part of the College. Not a name we would have invented for ourselves. Who or what was he? Was he buried in the old graveyard nearby? Why was his spirit restless? There was also the 'solemn silence', which we were supposed to maintain, but did not, from 'lights out' in the dormitories until after morning mass in the Oratory. A disciplinary measure, no doubt, but one that we were given to believe was tinged with religious significance. We did not understand why at the time, but I can see now that this was a vestige of the previous century, when diocesans colleges founded with a particular aim of ensuring a supply of priests for the diocese were classed in Church thinking as 'minor seminaries'. Every year, even in my time, a number of those who sat the Leaving Certificate still took the direct path from St. Nathy's to Maynooth and back again, seven years later, to the diocese.

I remember too the strange kind of ritualised aggression, which an anthropologist would surely find of interest, that was late-night 'polishing' raids, in which an intrepid few from one dormitory would leave sleepers in another dormitory across the long corridor abashed to find their faces blackened with boot polish when they awoke in the morning.

In recalling a now-distant past, should one be kind or honest? A little of both perhaps. Nicknames were prevalent and could be cruel. Reading books, apart from set texts, was hardly known, indeed, hardly possible since there was no library. The general atmosphere of our closed world, confined to the college buildings and three muddy fields, did not encourage difference or cultural aspirations, it was perhaps closer to 'Lord of the Flies' than to 'Our Boys'. Punishment – with the hand or various implements – could be severe for some; it was frequent and widespread, but just a normal part of life.

However, that was a different time – let us not speak of these things now in an anniversary year. Better to recall some of the good or droll things instead. How pleased our class – 4A if I remember correctly – was at its own ingenuity in devising a trick to head off the beatings freely meted out by the priest who taught us Irish for failures at poetry memorisation. We wrote the text of the Irish poem assigned for that day in chalk on the blackboard using the letters of the Greek alphabet – we had to study Greek at that time too. Those of us called on to recite the poem from memory would read it from the blackboard behind our teacher, who, if he glanced at it at all as he entered the room, assumed that what was written there had been left over from a previous Greek class.

The hue and cry – unsuccessful of course – and the search for clues, I mean for crumbs, when some brave souls from our dormitory broke into the kitchens late at night and stole the Christmas cake prepared for the Bishop. For good measure, they also took a jar of the suety filling for the mince pies that they thought was jam and which, concealed in a jug, they surreptitiously spooned out on to their bread and ate at table later.

Then there was the day when, to our surprise, for the first and only time, we were marched out to attend the circus which had pitched its big top on the fair green across the wall from the College. The priests, our teachers, were to supervise us, but were apparently forbidden by canon law to enter the tent, and so were obliged to remain outside. It did not make for good order on our part inside. A riotous and anarchic night followed as from our darkened second floor dormitory windows, we watched the older, bolder boys climb over the wall for a late night assignation – by their own account at least-with some of the girls from the circus.

Best of all, towards the end of my five years, were the Shakespearean plays produced by Fr. Sean Tiernan, with the help of Fr. Tom Lynch. They took us into a different world. In another life, Fr. Tiernan would have achieved fame in the theatre world as a director. As it was, he was barred by Church discipline at the time from attending the professional theatre. So, on summer holidays in London, he got permission from kindly theatre managements to stand in the wings and watch plays from there, while keeping to the letter, at least, of the canon law code. I can say that I had a part in the very first play he directed in St. Nathy's – an English comedy called It Pays To Advertise. It was preformed only internally in the College. I still remember how mortified I was when my parents came over to Ballaghaderreen to see it. They were the only outsiders in the audience that night.

In the following years, Fr. Tiernan became more ambitious and sanguine about what we could do. Were we good? Well, whatever the truth may have been, he made us believe we were. So he directed us in As You Like It and, the next year, in The Merchant Of Venice. (I had left when he produced 'Hamlet' a year later). Dare I mention now the distinguished future Archbishop who played Rosalind the year I played Orlando, and who played Portia the next year when I played Shylock? Or name those, including some retired parish priests, who played other parts? Better not – perhaps it would embarrass them. But memories returned recently when I found the text of As You Like It among some old papers. I also recalled that final scene a year later in The Merchant of Venice when Shylock, baulked by Portia's legal acumen, dropped his knife. That one night, it stuck quivering in the stage floor: it had never done so in rehearsal.

Fr. Tiernan and Fr. Lynch – and so many more – are gone now, gone into the world of light. What they did with us, and for us, helped form and shape our lives.

In illo temore. All of that was long ago and in another country. Memories are all that remain; but all memories – bad and good – recede and fade, and as they do their contours grow softer. It was a different time.

• 11 •

Remembering '48

John Doherty

LC 1952; retired Parish Priest of Gurteen

Like all past students of St. Nathy's, I have many memories, most of them happy, but some unhappy. However, the one I have chosen to record has nothing to do with class, study or the hazards of boarding, but is a sporting one, the All Ireland final of 1948, and the impression it made on my then young mind.

For one who rarely took an active part in sport, I grew up with a great love of sport and of Gaelic football in particular. It was not something I got from my family background, but rather from attending the boy's primary school in Charlestown. Going to school in Charlestown in the forties meant that you had to be caught up in the excitement and thrills of sport.

Boxing was huge in those days. Boys, especially from the town, vied with each other in collecting pictures of boxers, yet boxing was only a remote second to Gaelic football. When it came to Mayo football, our heroes were without doubt the team that won the 1936 All Ireland. Their names were spoken with awe. However, it was a memory handed down to us, as we were too young to remember the game itself.

The forties were lean enough years for Mayo with many disappointments, but always the hope of better things to come. Then it all happened in 1948. There was the titanic struggle with Galway before winning the Connacht title. This was followed by overwhelming no less than Kerry in the semi-final. Suddenly, the seemingly unthinkable had happened, Mayo were in an All Ireland Senior Football Final.

By the time the great day arrived, I was back in St. Nathy's beginning my second year as a boarder. Given the restrictions associated with a boarding school and the lack of contact with the outside world, the build-up to the game in the College and the hype and excitement that went with it was really memorable. On the morning of the game, I was awoken at a very early hour. For a brief moment, I did not know what was going on, but I still sensed something special was in the air, not unlike going home for Christmas. The dormitory I was sleeping in overlooked the fair green. I was aroused from sleep by the murmuring voices of three boys who were sitting at an open window. There, braving wind and rain, they were watching the cars speed by eastwards on the road beyond the fair green, with a murmur of excitement each time they recognised – or thought they recognised – a car from Charlestown, Swinford or Foxford.

On Sunday mornings, the President always said Mass for the students. After Mass that morning, as he and the more pious of the students remained on in the Oratory, their prayers were rudely interrupted as the body of students hastily left the Oratory, blessed themselves with Holy Water and shouted 'Up Mayo'. Later, we got a stern rebuke from the President, Canon Thomas Curneen.

For the game, we had one radio that was located in the classroom known as the stage hall. As far as getting a position near the radio, it was not a case of 'first come, first served'. A strict pecking order was observed with the seniors occupying the 'Hogan Stand' seats beside the radio. I and my likes were relegated to the fringes of the crowd. Though Croke Park could be noisier, there was really little, from a Mayo point of view, to cheer about in the first half as Mayo failed to score, largely because they played against an almost a gale force wind.

However, the second half was something else. There was continuous wild cheering as Mayo clawed their way back. The cheering reached a crescendo when Mayo, near the end of the game, drew level. Where I was situated, I heard absolutely nothing but the news that was relayed from one to another back to the end of the crowd. At last the shout rang out: 'It's a draw, it's a draw', meaning the sides were level. Then there was silence. Cavan took the lead with a point. Almost immediately, the cheering rose again as Mayo drove forward and were awarded a close-in free to level the game. Again, with the cheering crowd, I heard nothing. Then there was an ominous silence drifting outwards from those nearest the radio. The game was over but I was not sure and neither was I sure of the result. Though I feared the worst, I had vainly hoped it might be otherwise. As the crowd drifted away in silence, I remember asking someone what had happened. He just looked at me, said nothing and walked on!

During the next few days, we heard much about the controversial ending to the game as the referee blew full time before the official time was up. Then there was the bizarre scenario of the close-in free. Apparently a Cavan forward, Mick Higgins, ironically of Mayo origin, was standing too close to the ball. Despite protests from free taker, Padraig Carney, the referee did not intervene. So, Mick Higgins blocked down Carney's free and that was it! Carney, who was a past pupil of St. Nathy's, was one of the outstanding Mayo players that day, although he was then just twenty years of age and indeed, went on to be one of the all time greats of Gaelic football.

Years later, Carney must have captured the mood of the players that day when he described how, at the end of the game, he sat down in Croke Park and wept and wondered if there was any justice in the world. However, he also related how this seemingly unfair defeat only made him more determined than ever to succeed, and succeed they did in 1950 and 1951.

By 1951, I was an 'important' senior student and, for that game, I took my place on the 'Hogan Stand' close to the voice of Michael O Hehir! As far as we were concerned, it was a somewhat subdued affair compared to '48'; no wild shouting or cheering. Mayo were, after all, defending their All Ireland crown that year and did so in some style. After the game, there was no flag waving or indeed great excitement, we were just so proud and pleased to be, at least for another year, the best in the land.

Over the years there were many sporting memories to share, but none as vivid in my mind as that of the last Sunday in September of '48' as I, in company with over a hundred fellow students of St. Nathy's, shared the thrills, excitement and sadness of a famous All Ireland final.

• 12 •

Squeeze the Scrauve Cove!

Vivian Sheridan

LC 1952; Journalist

In 1947, St. Nathy's could boast one of the finest student refectories of any college of its size in Ireland. In those days, tables for four with white table cloths were only found in restaurants – and upmarket ones at that. Sadly, however, there the similarities stopped. The food was on the spartan side: the tea – pre-milked and sugared – smacked faintly of Sunlight soap, and the sliced beef at lunchtime sometimes featured interesting rainbow effects! Nevertheless, one had to remember that across post-war Europe, people were faring far worse and I never heard of anyone actually being poisoned! Besides, we were frequently assured that things were not much better in the priests' dining room behind the ivy covered Old Wing – a former British military barracks. Although this we took with a pinch of salt.

After dutifully delivering up our grey wartime ration books to the matron (nicknamed The Bess) on arrival, we gradually came to develop a taste for, and actually thrive on, the St. Nathy's fare! However, the yearning for home cooking was such that a burgeoning trade in parcels from home developed – something along the lines of Red Cross parcels in wartime POW camps. The goodies thus solicited from caring parents across three counties represented a welcome addition to St. Nathy's fodder and were very much looked forward to. Some contained hardboiled eggs, others home-made jam, soda bread or cooked ham. Barmbracks made a seasonal appearance around November. One loving Swinford mother had the inspiration to regularly ship a box full of fried Donnelly's sausages, which the generous recipient was good enough to share with his friends!

Not every student was supplied on a regular basis: some had to be content with rather eccentric offerings (like a well-remembered stone of cooking apples from Killasser). Nevertheless, there was some competition to share a table with those who had regular access to goodies. Exotic items such as apple tarts and potato cake could raise or lower a chap's standing in the community, while stinginess could lead to unfortunate events behind the back alley or on the football field.

The authorities exhibited a tacit acceptance of this trade and even provided lockers near the kitchen area for storage. However, a certain quantity inevitably found its way into the dormitories and was stored in an exclusive St. Nathy's invention called a Do-Box. This was a container of some sort that could be locked. Despite the 'solemn silence' edict in force in the dormitories, these would be furtively opened after lights out and the contents demolished between the sheets.

One memorable feature of the refectory was the lamentable state of the teapots. These battered and misshapen utensils were regularly subject to a mauling if they refused to yield up the last drops of liquid. To eager grunts of 'Squeeze the scrauve cove', they were thumped, pounded and pressured until it was apparent that nothing else was forthcoming. For anyone still thirsty, there were raids made on neighbouring tables to ensure that no teapot escaped unscathed.

The term 'squeeze the scrauve cove' was our first introduction to St. Nathy's slang. This strange dialect, it is said, had its origins in the Charlestown area. The 'scrauve' was the slang for a teapot. 'Each to his own bakes' meant 'every man for himself'. A 'Blone' was St. Nathy's speak for a woman. 'Cop the sham' meant 'spot the stranger'. A 'whitten cove' was a priest or religious person. A 'gammy glimmer' meant cross eyes. 'Lukes cove' meant 'look out' – a term much used by back alley smokers! 'A kick in the jeer' meant a rise in the behind!

No doubt this picturesque lingo has now disappeared and its origins will surely mystify modern students as much as they mystified us.

The annual November visit of the phantom Job Henthorne (called Penthorne's Night) was an occasion to be reckoned with – especially for the quaking first-year students. Unfortunately for them, the apparition seemed to have a special affinity with the New Wing dormitory which is where they were billeted. Other dormitories like the Top Big or Middle Big or even the Top Small, which directly overlooked the old military cemetery, seemed to be off the old soldier's ghostly beat.

No doubt Henthorne and his contemporaries breathed a sigh of relief when Nathy's ceased to be a residential secondary school, for I doubt that any nineteenth century phantom would be able to cope with a generation of twenty-first century student sceptics who would size him up, face him down, and end up making his afterlife a living hell!

The Teeth That Once Thro' St. Nathy's Halls

If O'Shea had not opened his big mouth, the weeks of exam preparation might have been a period of total tranquillity, even boredom. The school was empty except for the Leaving and Intermediate Cert students. It was a time of revision, reflection and welcome relaxation. Discipline was lax, food was marginally better and walks outside the College perimeter frequent. There was even a memorable and thoroughly enjoyable picnic excursion by special train to Lough Gara. Less memorable were the walks to local beauty spots – such as they existed – in the immediate vicinity of the town of Ballaghaderreen; less memorable, that is, until O'Shea opened his big mouth.

O'Shea, you must understand, had false teeth. One of these walks took us to the banks of the Lung River not far from the town. It was a lovely June evening as we loitered on the banks of the river, watching, and occasionally throwing stones, at a bunch of highly indignant swans. The Lung is not a noble stream by any means, but it is cool, wet and (when it is not raining) quite picturesque. O'Shea and a couple of his pals decided they would like a swim. The problem was that the Dean, who had accompanied us, had made it abundantly clear that swimming was out of the question. So a plan was devised: the Dean was distracted and the three swimmers disappeared around a bend in the river. Safely out of sight, they disported themselves in silent plunging and muffled merriment.

In surfacing from one of these manoeuvres, however, O'Shea opened his mouth either for a mouthful of air or from sheer delight. In any case, the result was the same – the false teeth fell out and sank to the muddy bottom of the river. A state of emergency was immediately declared and all three swimmers dived repeatedly in a desperate effort to recover the missing molars. All to no avail. The call up whistle was sounded, the peloton assembled, and O'Shea was forced to march back toothless to the College.

It was inevitable that his loss would be noted by the authorities and embarrassing questions asked. O'Shea, a noted talker and raconteur, could not be guaranteed to keep his mouth shut for long. Besides, there was the tricky question of sustenance – not all Nathy's fare was suited to toothless students. It was clear to everyone that the recovery of O'Shea's teeth had become something of a priority. Expert swimmers were called for and two volunteers – Adrian Moore and Donal Dorr – came forward. With the connivance of the remainder of the student body, they pluckily took off jogging for the Lung River each evening after supper.

As exam time approached, they continued their illicit evening canter – their nightly return eagerly awaited – but the Lung did not willingly give up its booty. Night after night they returned, downcast and empty handed. After about three or four nights, however, they unexpectedly arrived back early – and triumphantly! Word spread quickly and night prayers in the oratory were exceptionally noisy, with O'Shea the centre of attention as he flashed yellow tinted smiles in all directions!

Against all the odds, Moore had succeeded in disinterring the missing teeth from the bog-brown waters – and recalcitrant grip – of the languid Lung!

Another First for St. Nathy's. Another local legend born!

• 13 •

Annual Retreats in St. Nathy's

Farrell Cawley

LC 1954; retired Parish Priest of Kilmovee

Annual retreats in St. Nathy's College were taken very seriously. They lasted for three days, involved solemn silence, and the only means of communication was usually by way of a note on the back of the missionary magazines that we were given to us as reading material. During our 1953 retreat, the priest said the following prayer so often that I remember it quite well, and I have recited it often as a prayer, a prayer that has meant a lot to me ever since. It goes as follows:

Dear Lord, in the Game (Contest, Battle) of life,
I ask for a field that is fair,
A chance that is equal to all in the strife,
and courage to do and to dare.

And, if I should win, let it be by the code,
Of all that is honest and true,
And, if I should lose, let me stand by the road
And cheer as the winners goes by.
Amen.

• 14 •

The Saint Jude's
School of Commerce

Mary Gallagher Coyle &
Margaret Gallagher Mulrennan

In premises between the Square and Barrack Street, I first encountered the marvellous Miss Bea Regan and her superb St. Jude's School of Commerce. I had attended a half-course at night while still keeping my job in Duff's ladies department under the watchful eye of Mrs. Kielty.

Later I was to do the complete course before embarking for New York to seek my fortune in the 1950s. In Miss Regan's class, desks were laid out with Underwood and Royal typewriters, their keys covered so that we could learn by touch rather than sight. There were approximately 12 pupils then and we paid modest fees. Bookkeeping, typing and Pitman's Shorthand were our curriculum. Pupils came from Castlerea, Carracastle, Frenchpark and other outlying areas. Some cycled to Ballaghaderreen, while others stayed in lodgings. The famous Mary Towey, who lived where the AIB Bank is now, provided some accommodation. She was a lady of great kindness and wit.

As Miss Regan's Academy expanded, St. Brigid's Hall was used. Trusted girls were sent upstairs to do their work unsupervised. We wrote with pencils and biros, learning trial balance, accounts, profit and loss, and so on. Shorthand was difficult at first, alphabet and sounds, symbols and light. I found it hard but it was all preparation for employment in a big city. We looked at advertisements for jobs in newspapers and all chorused "how much", mentally subtracting rent and travel, etc.

On completion of the course, we received a recognised School of Commerce of St. Jude Certificate. This certification was recognised for all Civil Service Departments, Aer Lingus, E.S.B, Irish Lights, the County Councils and banking, as well as a qualification for England and America. There had also been another school of commerce earlier in Main Street run by another Miss Regan, aunt of Paddy, Joe and Jack Regan, whose premises are still on Main Street.

Mary Gallagher Coyle

Like my sister Mary, I also attended St. Jude's Secretarial School run by the marvellous Miss Bea Regan. It was approximately 1958 and it was still on Barrack Street. As it expanded, it moved to St. Brigids's Hall. In my group were Larry Noone (R.I.P.), Carmel Hickey (R.I.P.), Breege Kelly and Emmanuelle Walsh of Charlestown. I loved the little Underwood typewriter and made fast progress. As well as bookkeeping, shorthand and typing, Miss Regan made sure all her charges knew the Christmas Novena 'Hail and Blessed'. I imagine in today's world – stifled with political correctness – how such an innocent requirement would draw criticism.

Margaret Gallagher Mulrennan

• 15 •

Going Home for Christmas

Gregory Hannon

LC 1955; Parish Priest of Ballymote

I had my first experience of going home for Christmas at the age of thirteen when I was a boarder at St. Nathy's College. Even though homecoming was very much part of our yearly routine, it took on a special significance at Christmas; it was our first break since September and was a happy release after three months spent within the rather austere walls of St. Nathy's.

The build up started once Advent came, and it was heralded by a very spirited singing of the Adeste Fideles, which concluded night prayer in the College Oratory.

Eventually the long awaited day arrived. There had been little sleep the previous night; despite frequent patrols by the authorities, the singing and the craic had continued into the small hours.

Then, long before the morning bell rang, we were out of bed and putting on our Sunday best – including the trousers that had been placed under the mattress a week before to give it a knife edge crease. A flashy tie, of course, was essential and we had great fun experimenting with the new-fangled Windsor knot. Great attention was also lavished on the hairdo; most of us went for the sleek oily look that was moulded from jars of Brylcreem; though some also sported the more daring crew-cut.

It was then on to the last hurdles of the morning; a final exam and the annual report. We all gathered in the study-hall to hear the President report at length on all aspects of school life. While he, no doubt, made a great impression on the Bishop, our thoughts and hearts were elsewhere; already the cars were pulling in; already Gurteen beckoned.

No sooner had the Bishop finished speaking and giving us good advice for the holidays – lots of praying and little or no dancing – than the dam burst and there was an almighty dash for the front door and the waiting cars. Hurrah! We were free at last; we were going home for Christmas!

Soon I was back in the warm glow of the family circle and enjoying my first tasty meal in months. What matter if the house seemed to have shrunk in size or if, for the moment, the local news and gossip seemed a little strange! It was now Christmas time in Gurteen and once more I was part of that happy scene.

• 16 •

Rough Boys with Healthy Minds

Pat Lynch

LC 1956; Parish Priest of Tubbercurry

Looking back at it, after more than half a century, it is the most remarkable thing. One hundred and eighty or so young men knelt and prayed together in the College oratory, and did so with deep respect. This was all the more extraordinary as the Oratory at that time consisted of two large classrooms that had had the dividing partition removed. There was no dim religious light – just four large windows, beautified, certainly, by four reveals made of pitch pine. The sky, a tree or two and the tops of the one or two headstones in the adjoining cemetery served as stain-glass. For all that, the room was sacred and respected. I have no memory of it being disrespected, despite the fact that it was very crowded.

Thinking of it all now, I am reminded of a recent remark by an old man who came to admire a church that had just been refurbished: "Now that the place of worship is beautiful, what about the worshippers!" Worship of the sacred is from within, a disposition of the soul.

On every morning of the week, Mass was celebrated; and depending on the vocal accomplishments of the priest, very often it was a Missa Cantata – chanted in plain song by both the priest and the students. A student at the harmonium provided the accompaniment. One must ask if the ancient medieval chant provided something that we have lost – a music with a long and tested tradition that lulled one into prayer and to a sense of mystery and the sacred. Think of the fact that many students stayed behind after Mass, for several minutes, to give thanks, and there you will find evidence of inner disposition.

There were holy hours on Sunday evenings, given, very often, by the President, and delivered with a touch of devotion that was palpable. We prayed and sang and bowed our heads as the Monstrance was raised in blessing – the scent of incense adding to the sense of the numinous. But there was another exercise, which for many reasons would be unthinkable now. During Lent and Advent, we rose a half hour earlier for meditation. Many of the priests, after they had led Morning Prayer, helped us through that half hour with reflections, suggestions and short periods of quiet. All of it was formative and led to spontaneous devotions on the part of the students. I remember the 'jostle' to make the Stations of the Cross on Lenten evenings. No, there was no jostling; the centre aisle (and the only aisle) was narrow and the students were many. Lent had acquired a meaning and so had Advent. I remember being amazed by a student from Foxford who told me of his practice of saying 4,000 Hail Marys during Advent as preparation for the feast of the Nativity; and I remember being even more amazed when I found that many other students were given to the same practice. It amounted to saying three rosaries each day. How could the Mystery of the Incarnation not mean something inspiring to those who prepared so well for it? And out of all this – not forgetting the greater influence of home – vocations blossomed.

Deliberately I have kept to moral, psychological and religious formation. There will be others who will expound on the other aspects of life in that closed, restrictive and, in many ways, artificial environment. My objective is to state that it was not without its merits. Many people over the years have said that it was a great preparation for life, even if, in a negative way, they added that if one survived there, one was capable of surviving any set of circumstances. I do not know about that, but I do know that it produced many fine men. Without their knowing it, the students themselves had a profound influence on each other. Of course, there was vulgar, boisterous and rough behaviour; one hundred and eighty boys housed at close quarters could hardly behave otherwise. Nevertheless, with profound gratitude, I must claim that despite the normal 'rough and tumble' that teenage boys bring with them in large quantities, I never once came upon anything objectionable while I was a student there, or in the fourteen years when I taught there afterwards.

Some of the very influential things that came my way as a student in the 1950s have remained with me ever since. An example might help. One young boy – we shared a seat for two years – was the very life of the place. Yet on one occasion I noticed that he was very 'down'. In those days, we were very timid of sharing feelings. I had to ask, in the end, if anything was the matter. Yes, he had fought with someone two days before and could not pray; he could not say the Our Father because he could not get past 'forgive us our trespasses, as we forgive…' It was a telling moment when, a day later, he told me he had gone to his adversary and asked forgiveness. His joy had returned. For all of the 'rough and tumble', there was something very healthy in the student body, for I never really came upon anything vicious or deliberately hurtful. Rows (in small quantities) yes, retaliation I was not aware of. Nor was I aware of any spitefulness against any individual on the part of the teaching staff.

Have I painted with a rosy hue? I hope not. Imperfection and human frailty are always to be had. It is true that some of the staff – they were small in number – had missed out on the art of teaching; they had little understanding of people less gifted intellectually than themselves, and they certainly did not value that basic principle of teaching practice: praise the young and they will flourish. Yes, I remember on several occasions being beaten on the hands with a cane. I never resented it and I do not believe that it did me any harm. Despite the caning, which was very much part of the teaching practice of the time, I can still say that I never witnessed brutality.

St. Nathy, Patron of Achonry Diocese

1898, new home of St. Nathy's College

Edmonstown Park House

1916 – new extension completed

Entrance to St. Nathy's College with 1916 building

St. Nathy's College with preparatory work for 1984 extension

View of 1950's buildings from first-year dormitory

Quadrangle and garrison

External view of new gymnasium, with new playing courts

New 60x30 handball court with glass backwall

Internal view of new gymnasium

Students in construction studies classroom

College Refectory

Connection between 1984 and 1995 extensions

Stairwell, Oratory end of main corridor

Main corridor, 1916 building

Students at prayer in new College Oratory

Altar and stained glass sanctuary window of
the College Oratory

Redecorated College Oratory with new
stained glass windows

Personally, when I was ill in my final year and I needed help, I was the recipient of great kindness from several of the teaching staff.

What was much more evident than corporal punishment in the St. Nathy's of the 1950s was the outstanding quality of the teaching. A thorough grounding in the Classics – Latin and Greek for the modern student – as well as in mathematics, English and Irish, should not be dismissed. Any student who went forward to third-level education was well prepared. Of those who sought employment in other areas, whether at home or abroad, none should have been disadvantaged.

The experience of St. Nathy's, as I knew it, was a great preparation for life. Morally it was sound, intellectually it was advanced, and psychologically – for almost everyone – it was both strengthening and formative. For the present writer, the experience was happy, holy, hard going and very often humorous. For all of that I am very thankful.

• 17 •

All Ireland Champions 1957

Eamon O'Hara, Captain

LC 1957; Episcopal Vicar, Nottingham Diocese

On the 8th of September 1952, I left the security of my small, close-knit family of a widowed mother and a younger brother to go to St. Nathy's. Living in a rural area, one had to go to boarding school to experience the pain of separation from family and the excitement of a new and different life. I was fortunate to know boys from my primary school, Castle Rock, and from my parish of Tourlestrane, who were already in Nathy's.

A few years prior to this, I saw the St. Nathy's team play the Connaught final in 1949. My uncle – Fr. James Edward O'Hara – was the coach of that successful team and I knew some of the team members: Eamonn Walsh, Ned Durkin, Willie Sheeran and Jimmy O'Grady. From that day onwards, and being interested in football, I had aspirations of one day playing for St. Nathy's.

On Sundays and Wednesdays we played football on the two fields near the College, which were ankle deep in mud in the winter and rock solid in the summer. Very little happened the first term and it was a struggle trying to cope with Latin and Greek.

We got our only cooked breakfast on the 1st November. After that, all that was left to look forward to was the Christmas holiday. Going home for the first time was a great experience, but the return after Christmas was one of the worst. The weather was cold and wet, and the home sickness was even worse than it had been in September.

Both the senior and junior football teams played inter-college matches, but they were not very successful. We looked forward to these matches and were very disappointed when we lost. Our second year was even less eventful than the first, the only difference being that my little brother had joined me and we had to share the same bed. Things got a bit more serious in third year; we had the Inter Cert exam at the end but, more significantly, I was hoping to make the junior team. Everything went well until I broke my collar bone.

With the dawn of the fourth year, an air of confidence, maturity and hope was beginning to emerge. I was made captain of the junior team. Many of the boys in our class were friendly with the fifth years. We started off with a hard game against Summerhill, Sligo, which ended in a draw. Soon after that, we beat St. Muredachs Ballina. After Christmas, we had the replay against Summerhill at Sligo. It was disappointing because we were beaten by three points. A few days after the match, Fr. Johnnie Walsh, who was the rector at the time, called me over to him and told me he was considering expelling me from the College because I let down its good name by being booked by the referee. To make matters even worse, he would not allow me to play in the combined Connaught Colleges side for which I was picked. He was, to say the least, a little impulsive and of course nothing happened. I did play for the Connaught side, but we were beaten by Leinster. That completed my football exploits for that year.

The college football year of 1956 to 1957 was going to be very different! I was made captain of the senior football team on our return in September. We started our campaign by playing St. Mary's in Galway, and even though we conceded the only goal of the whole campaign, we beat them easily 3-7 to 1-6. There was then a big change in the College coaching staff. Fr. Padraig McGovern, who was our coach, was appointed to a parish and Fr. Tom Lynch took over at the helm. Two totally different characters, but both very committed and very professional in their own way. Next we beat St. Muredachs 1-8 to 0-6; and then Summerhill Sligo by 2-10 to 0-6. People outside were beginning to take a great interest in our team, none more so than Johnnie McGoldrick, who was a real football fanatic. He wanted the panel of players to be super fit and pleaded with Fr. Johnnie Walsh and Fr. Tom Lynch that our diet should be supplemented, so we were issued with raw eggs and multi-vitamin tablets. The raw eggs were broken into a glass and a drop of milk was added. I personally found this difficult to consume but, as captain, I had to show a good example.

In the Connaught final, we played St. Jarlath's from Tuam, who had dominated football in Connaught for most of our time. It was a game we had to win. The tension was razor-sharp before the match. From the throw in, we got off to a great start and soon built up an early lead, making it a commanding lead by half-time. In the second half, Jarlath's came at us strong and began to whittle away at our lead. We never relented and somehow managed to hold on and win by a point, having failed to score at all in the second half. We then had to play the Division Two winners, who were CBS Roscommon. This was a bit of an anti-climax and we thought we had only to turn up, but we got a rude awakening. We played with a strong wind to our back in the first half and only led by 0-3 to 0-1 at half time. After a heated team-talk at halftime, we got our act together and won comfortably by 2-10 to 0-1.

We were now in the All Ireland semi-final and were drawn against the Munster champions Colaiste Iosagain, Ballyvourney, with the game to be played in Killarney. They had played a couple of drawn games with St. Brendan's Killarney in the Munster final. We had no idea what they were like but presumed that they would be very difficult opponents, especially because of the reputation of Kerry football at the time. It was a week of high tension in the College and on

Saturday the 12th of March, four or five cars were booked to take us to Killarney. We had lunch in Limerick and later that evening arrived at our hotel in Killarney. After our evening meal, Danny Scannell, who worked in the forestry, took three of us out on a sight seeing tour. Danny had worked in Sligo the previous year and helped Tourlestrane win their first senior Sligo championship.

Sunday morning was taken up with the celebration of mass, followed by breakfast and a look at the Sunday papers. We had a light lunch before the game. Peter McDermott was the referee. Colaiste Iosagain got off to a great start, scoring the first point. However, they did not score again until near the end of the game and we ran out easy winners by 3-7 to 0-4. There was great relief and much joy! We returned to the hotel to have dinner, where we were joined by some of the Kerry football dignitaries, including Dr. O'Sullivan, the chairman of the Kerry Co. Board.

One outstanding memory of this game for me was the fact that the teaching staff of St. Jarlath's, whom we beat in the Connaught final, brought down the Jarlath's team to Killarney that day to support us. On Sunday evening in the hotel, when most were in high spirits, Danny Scannell – whom I mentioned earlier – asked Fr. Walsh if I could be granted permission to play for my parish team in the inter county club championship against Tuam Stars. I think there was reluctance in granting permission but he did, and Fr. Walsh came to me on the morning of the match and warned me not to get injured.

The next two weeks went by very quickly with the excitement increasing with each passing day. No one wanted to sleep on the night of Friday the 12th April. The team were off to Dublin the next day and the rest were breaking up for the Easter break. At about midday on Saturday the 13th of April 1957, our team set off for Dublin to compete in the All Ireland College's Senior Football Final against St. Colman's College, Newry. Our first stop was Croke Park to sample the stadium and the playing surface. We then proceeded to the Grand Hotel in Malahide. Later that evening, Liam O' Hora, a past pupil of the College and the then national film censor, arranged for the players to see a movie in one of the cinemas in O' Connell Street.

On Sunday morning, our routine was the same as for the previous match. Our team was in confident mood, largely because of our easy passage in the semi-final. Years afterwards, I learned St. Colman's were just as confident because they had also won their semi-final by twelve points. The game was early in the afternoon because it was the curtain-raiser to the Tyrone versus Galway National League semi-final. We got off to a good start, scoring the first point and at the interval we led three points to two. In the second half, we played much better and we went on to win convincingly by 1-7 to 0-4. The game was described in the Irish Independent the next day as dull. The referee did not help matters, he whistled for every little infringement – very different to Peter McDermott in the semi-final. The nature of the game did not matter; what did matter was the result. I climbed the steps of the Hogan Stand to receive the cup, much to the delight of the team, our mentors and our supporters. It was interesting to note that the first person to congratulate me was Bishop Fergus of Achonry diocese. We then watched the Galway and Tyrone match from the stand. After getting back to the hotel, we had a celebratory meal and were joined by a number of past pupils from the Dublin area. Later that evening, seven or eight of us went to a dance in Bray, where we met up with a number of the Galway players.

Next day, after some shopping in the city centre, we headed west and arrived in Ballaghaderreen about 9.00pm, where we were greeted by a huge bonfire in the town square and hundreds of people.

As I conclude my memory of this great success, I have deliberately not mentioned any of the squad by name. This is because each squad member gave their all and each in his own way contributed to our success.

An interesting aside, more than forty years later I was executor of a priest's will. This priest came from Banbridge in County Down. He had attended St. Colman's and often talked about the players there. The priest had cancer and, as he was coming closer to death, I asked him in a most sensitive way questions like where he would like to be buried and if he knew of an undertaker in Banbridge. He told me he was very friendly with Tommy Keenan, which meant nothing to me at the time. After the priest's death, I contacted Tommy to make the necessary arrangements. In the conversation I told him I played college football against lads from that area. He asked: "In what competition?" I replied: "The All Ireland College's final of 1957." His reply was, "I played in that. In fact, I was the captain of the St. Colman's team." I smiled and added, "We have spoken to each other before; I was captain of the St. Nathy's team." I travelled over for the funeral and met Tommy, the McCartin brothers and many others including some of the priests that were on the staff of St. Colman's.

• 18 •

A Stroll Down Memory Lane

Padraig Maye

LC 1959; Secondary Teacher

Friday the 12th of April 1957 was another one of these nice and pleasant days. An end of term exam was scheduled for the morning and afterwards most of the students were going home for Easter holidays, while others had to remain behind, still recovering from the raw eggs and vitamins taken at 11.00am.

A perceptual buzz was evident in the corridors. The barber had been up the evening before during first study, laundry had come early that morning, and rumour had it that we were going to see a picture that night, which meant getting to stay up till 11pm.

Of course, this was not your normal weekend at St. Nathy's. Something out of the ordinary was astir. The next day, we left for Dublin at 2pm, thrilled with the extra pound in our pocket – compliments of the Past Pupil's Union. On reaching the city, our first stop was Croke Park. For many of us, it was a place we heard about on radio. Therefore, with a certain amount of awe and anticipation, we rushed up the stands and down on to the pitch. One of the company was heard to remark: "Not a bad looking field." My recollection of the visit was the deceptive distance of the fifty-yard line – it seemed so close to the goalmouth. I think the towering stands created an optical illusion; however, I was rudely awakened next day.

At 6pm, we finally arrived at the Grand Hotel in Malahide, and some past pupils and friends were there to greet us. After checking in, four to a room, we were off to O'Connell Street with bated breath. I wonder what happened in 1966 to those names we carved on the pillar. Later, it was off to another film – two pictures in three nights for free – will wonders ever cease? This time, Liam O' Hora, the film censor and past pupil of St. Nathy's, treated us. With a feeling of relief and exhaustion, we got to bed at midnight, too tired even to worry the dean, Fr. James Gavigan.

Before we knew it, the 14th of April 1957 dawned – it was to be a historic day in St. Nathy's footballing history. Yes, today St. Nathy's were in the All Ireland College's Senior A Final. Who would have believed it way back in September of 1956? Over the years, St. Nathy's had just won two Connacht Senior titles, in 1928 and 1949, even though they lost many finals by the most slender of margins. Perhaps the school year of 1956 to 1957 would be just another one of those dismal years. Nevertheless, this new season was extra special. The Hogan Cup competition had recently being revived after a lapse of eleven years. St. Patrick's College, Armagh, had been the custodians of the cup since 1946. This year the winning college in Connacht would represent the province.

Our first outing on October 14th was against St. Mary's, Galway, which we won by a score of 3-7 to 1-6. Ironically, this was the highest score recorded against St. Nathy's that year and the only goal conceded by the defence – mind you, it was a penalty. The next day, an outbreak of mumps swept the College. By November 18th, everybody was back to full health for our game against St. Muredach's, Ballina. Again, we were victorious with a score of 1-8 to 0-6. As yet, we were causing no great excitement in football circles. Then again, we never got to read the local papers. It was three months until our next game on February 17th.

In the meantime, six of us played junior football. Our opposition in senior was Summerhill. This was a vital game for us as Summerhill had run St. Jarlath's very close earlier. For the first quarter, the outcome seemed uncertain, but then St. Nathy's hit a purple patch and went to win eventually by 2-10 to 0-6.

Still our bogey team St. Jarlath's remained. This time, we were playing them at home in the Abbey – or the "Cabbage Garden" as it was humorously called. That day, March 10th, was a very windy day and we happened to play with the advantage in first half, but at the end of fifteen minutes, the score was deadlocked at two points all. Then St. Nathy's began to get the upper-hand and led by 1-5 to 0-3 at half time. For the GAA pundits, this lead was nothing to be confident about and to tell the truth, this was the case. St. Jarlath's began to tenaciously claw back the lead. Point by point, the margin of difference drew closer and closer. Fr. Tom Lynch's discarded cigarettes began to pile up along the sideline, and were possibly picked up by some thoughtful student. By the proverbial skin of their teeth, St. Nathy's held on, despite getting no score at all during the second half. It was with a great sense of relief that the final whistle blew and St. Nathy's had finally won their third Connacht title.

Afterwards, the De La Salle Boys band escorted us into town and up to the College. That night, we got to see the picture 'Sitting Pretty' – sounds exciting – and the prefects got us a free day on Monday. Just over a week later, we met Roscommon CBS, the Division B Champions, in Castlerea in a match that would decide who would represent the province. This was a very one-sided affair, with our team winning by the easiest score of 2-10 to 0-1. Clearly our secret weapon – the raw eggs and vitamins – was paying off, yet everybody believed our successes was down to good old fashioned training and strategy. In the background, Fr. Padraig McGovern's leagues and regimen had developed and seasoned us.

Roll on Killarney. March 31st was one more step towards the Hogan Cup. We were meeting Colaiste Iosagain from Ballyvourney, the Munster Champions, in the All Ireland Semi-Final. Again those 'Hefty Western Boys', as we were called, had an easy victory. Our system was to play the more robust players down the middle, with those who did not thrive on Maggie's food on the wings. The game was decided by half time when already we had a big lead. Even the referee asked us to take things easy. St. Nathy's eventually won by 3-7 to 0-4. My greatest memories of this trip were the luxury drive south in Tommy Denby's taxi, the journey out to the Killarney lakes, and the opposition as they spoke in Irish.

Now it was Palm Sunday and Canon Walsh said Mass for us early. A few 'butterflies' were beginning to surface. Earlier, we had slipped out to get some Sunday papers, a little secretly as old habits never die. One headline read: "St. Nathy's Favourites for All Ireland." It went on to say that: "St. Nathy's team is probably the best to ever represent the College. The team is well-balanced in football skill, weight and height, and with such match winning assets at their disposal, it is unlikely that the Ballaghaderreen College boys will return empty handed from the metropolis" – it must be a past pupil who wrote it! We had our customary 'spiff' from Fr. Tom. His comment on the paper was: "I expect Nathy's to win, but our backs need to be on their toes if they are to hold the Newry attack." Of course, without saying, the offence was taken for granted.

At 2.45pm, our game began. It was the curtain-raiser to the League Semi-Final between Tyrone and Galway. The occasion was a little nerve-wrecking, so the standard of play was not up to expectations. Nevertheless, St. Nathy's emerged as the new Hogan Cup holders by a score of 1-7 to 0-4. We had done it! Imagine a small school from Ballaghaderreen emerging as best football team in Ireland. What did we care if the papers commented: "Too many petty infringements and a fair amount of deliberate fouling at the rate of almost one a minute." We had won and nobody could take that away from us.

After the game we had a celebration meal back at our hotel. The cup was filled with champagne for the more adult followers and we got our lemonade. Needless to say, the thought of alcoholic drink was far from our minds. What we were interested in was the dance at the Grand that night and the late self-service 'take away' from the hotel kitchen.

Before we realised it, it was time to get up. We had an early start to the city centre and then another fine meal at the Clarence. After a brief stop-over in Mullingar, we arrived back in Ballaghaderreen at 9pm. Many of our supporters were at the Square and numerous bonfires were alight throughout the town. A band escorted us from the Square up to the College, where we were all introduced. Some of us lucky ones got to go home that night.

Now, as St. Nathy's College celebrates its historic bicentenary, we try once more to relive and commemorate that eventful day. I hope this article helps to refresh the minds of those involved. I intentionally avoided mentioning any member of the team so far because everybody in his own unique way contributed to that glorious year and nobody has to be singled out. The following made up the panel: J.T. Cribben, M. Hanrahan, G. McManus, M.

Joyce, C. McGuire, T. McGuire, E. Stenson – R.I.P., M. Ruane – R.I.P., E. O'Hara – captain, S. McMahon, J Madden, T. Kilcoyne, J. O'Grady, J. Boland, P. Maye, M. Kilcoyne, T. O'Connor, J. Maloney, A. McGrath, M.J. Tansey – R.I.P., D. Caulfield, J. Maloney, J.F. Kelly and A. Murtagh.

• 19 •

Mistaken Identity

Seamus Caulfield

LC 1958; Professor of Archeology at U.C.D.
and founder of Ceidhe Fields

Not knowing a single person when I went to St. Nathy's, I inevitably ended up at the 'orphan's table', the long table at the end of the refectory where unclaimed first years spent their first year. Because I had spent the first week or two as temporary guest at one of the tables up the refectory until someone's younger brother arrived, I ended up in the last seat immediately inside the door. This guaranteed me a certain level of popularity because of my strategic location, which gave me virtual control of the two first-year side alleys. The front alley was for the seniors, the back alley was for the second and third years (and unofficially for smokers and fights), and the concreted area outside the west side of the two alleys was marked out as two single-walled alleys for the first years. First on the alley commanded two places, next on got the third place and the owner of the 'elephant' (the official competition handball from Elvery's) first hopped on the alley got the fourth place. Placed as I was in prime location inside the door, I had a five- to ten-yard head start on the stampede for the alleys everyday, and particularly when we had a free day. Most days I would make it first to the side alleys, straddling the white dividing line with a foot in either alley or hopping two bars carried for pals on the two alleys; in all controlling six of the eight places available.

In the race for the alleys, if carrying a ball for a friend, it was very important to carry it in the right hand. If the left hand was not free, the acceleration down the front corridor had to be braked in order to take the left turn at the bottom of the stairs. If the left hand was kept free, it was possible to actually accelerate into the turn and, by swinging on the newel post at the foot of the stairs, to produce a slingshot effect that propelled one at greater speed into the next leg of the race. By the time we got to the second term, I had mastered the slingshot manoeuvre to perfection.

Then one free day after breakfast, armed with an elephant in my right hand and another in my pocket, I was at full tilt, my left ready to swing around the newel post, when Father X, bedecked with berretta and reading his Divine Office, stepped off the end of the stairs just as I reached the same spot. Fifty years later, the image is still frozen in my mind's eye: Father X sliding on his behind, propelled by my momentum down the rest of the corridor, his berretta and breviary sliding beside him. As I rushed to his assistance and to apologise, Joe O'Grady, following behind, was already helping him to his feet and handing him his berretta and breviary. The last I saw of the incident was Father X swinging a punch at Joe. I realised that I was the beneficiary of a clear case of mistaken identity and I continued my race to the alleys. Joe has just recently told me that yes, the swing made perfect contact with his jaw, and how Father X, with dignity and honour satisfied, continued up the corridor, resuming reading the Divine Office as if the thirty-second interlude had never happened.

I cannot recall if I even held a place on the alley for Joe!

Staff

Youngsters in Ireland today and those who went through St. Nathy's in the 1950s – that means anyone under sixty – have two silly misconceptions about the 1950s. Firstly, they seem to think that life was lived in a grey dismal world, and secondly that it was dominated by pious, po-faced, respect-demanding clergy.

On the first point, I need only point out that just because the record of the 1950s survives in black and white images does not mean that we did not live life in full colour, as teenagers in every decade have done.

On the second point, because all our teachers – except Billy Reilly – were priests, we lived with priests literally around the clock, and I have to say that my memories of them are fond ones, even of those priests we feared in the first and second year because of the excessive use of the cane on occasion. What I remember most is a sense of fairness and their welcome for a good argument in class, in particular Fathers Cawleyeen, Reveen, Tolly, Lynch and surprisingly Flam. This, coupled with a certain lack of reverence for things held piously sacred at the time, left me with a feeling from an early stage that we were among men first and priests second.

Like Reveen's less-than-resounding endorsement of Knock Shrine: "As good a place as any to say your prayers." Yet, Knock is where I head to, if any 'toir' comes to me, and I would say this is because of Reveen's attitude, not in spite of it.

Or the black humour of Flam that marked the death of any unfortunate parish priest in the diocese. Flam – feeling as incarcerated as the rest of us and hoping to get released to parish duty, but by our time too old to be sent to a curacy – was believed to have more than a passing interest in any vacancy which occurred. Which was why, on our hearing of the death of a parish priest in the diocese, Flam would get a prolonged standing ovation in every class with shouts of: "You will get it this time, Father," and in every class, the same response from Flam, "Maybe. And you know, that namesake of mine is the bane of my life. If it was not for him, I would have had a parish long ago," suggesting that there could be a downside to the discovery of the wonder cure penicillin a decade earlier.

Or Flam, recounting the parable of the 'Good Samaritan' and explaining why the priest, coming upon the man lying on the roadway, passed by: "Sure, was not the man robbed already."

Then there was a great debate between Tolly and Reveen, a debate which started in the priest's refectory but which had spilled into the classrooms, where we were expected to be the jury as to the merits or demerits of the hit tune of the time 'Sixteen Tons'. Tolly saw the song as a deeply spiritual example of what was later to be highlighted as liberation theology, a cry from the heart of the enslaved. Reveen was having no part in it; his theatrical sensitivities were offended by "over sentimentalised melodramatic bull".

Ta said uilig ar sli na firne le fada. Ar Dheis De go raibh a n-anamacha uasal.

• 20 •

The Value of a Classical Education

Thomas Mitchell

LC 1958; MRIA; First Catholic Provost Trinity College Dublin

I came to St. Nathy's at the beginning of my teenage years with a great sense of excitement and anticipation. I came from a rural background and had never been away from home. It was a great adventure to go to boarding school, to meet other students from a great variety of backgrounds, to live a totally different way of life, and to face new academic opportunities and challenges.

This reality, as so often is the case, did not exactly match the expectation. There were aspects of life that proved less than appealing. It was, in many respects, restricted and regimented; some of the security and many of the comforts of home were missing; it demanded a certain toughness and independence, qualities that, in my case, needed some time to be acquired.

However, the positive side far outweighed the minor hardships and upsets. Friendships flourished amid the shared experiences of the classrooms, on the walks during recreation periods, on the ball alleys and playing fields, or during clandestine discussions after lights out in the dormitories. There was a great sense of fun and a rare excitement attached to all extracurricular diversions, and for me there was the discovery of the unique pleasure of learning, of acquiring greater knowledge and understanding of man and his world. I found in St. Nathy's an ethos that stressed the value of education, that respected and valued things of the mind and intellectual achievement in whatever direction. It encouraged intellectual effort and provided an excellent environment for study. The teaching and general concerns for the academic well-being of students were exemplary.

For me, the greatest impact of my educational experiences at St. Nathy's was the discovery of the richness and pervasive influence of the world of ancient Greece and Rome on our western culture. The Classics were splendidly taught and had an honoured place in the curriculum, their educational value and centrality taken for granted. I was fascinated by the languages, by their use of forms, by their structural preciseness, and especially by the primal importance of Latin as the begetter of romance languages, as the language of the church, and as the intellectual language of all of Europe for more than a thousand years.

The languages were a gateway to the interdisciplinary study of an absorbing civilisation that shaped every major aspect of our western culture. The literature, the history, the political ideas, the philosophical concept, the art and architecture, all of these areas of classical antiquity revealed new aspects of the capacity of the human intellect and imagination, and the great continuity in the evolution of European civilisation.

I was captivated and before I left St. Nathy's, I knew I wanted to pursue the studies of Classics at university. I left very well equipped to do so, with a sound base of knowledge, good study habits, and above all, a curiosity and enthusiasm for learning that had been strengthened by an environment that carefully fostered the idea that intellectual growth and pursuits, as well as knowledge and understanding, were of fundamental importance to a full, happy and successful life. I owe a great deal to St. Nathy's and am delighted that it continues to flourish as a major centre of education.

• 21 •

St. Nathy's Bicentenary

Seamus Cunningham

LC 1960; Bishop of Hexham and Newcastle

Close on to 50 years is a good spell of time – but two centuries is something to write home about. That is the thought that inspired me to put pen to paper and express my congratulations to St. Nathy's for its amazing ability to survive so long in a world that is changing so fast and is using up its resources so quickly.

My formative teenage years were spent at St. Nathy's College in the 1950s, a time when resources were always a challenge for the staff and students. It was still a time of recovery after the Second World War. For the record, I was a student at St. Nathy's between 1956 and 1960.

I have not been back to St. Nathy's for five decades. When I was there, it was a boarding school where pupils went home only for Christmas, Easter and the gloriously long summer holidays. Why is it that I remember the school terms, the work and the regime more clearly than the holidays? I suppose it is just a curious aspect of human nature.

We were up at 6.30am every morning, as I recall, and it was lights out by 10.00pm for all students – no matter what age you were. Everything was timed by the bell. All this was done under the eagle eye of the College's President, Canon Walsh. I do not instantly remember his first name. Perhaps it is true that those were the days when the clergy did not appear to have first names!

Alongside the Canon were two members of staff I remember very well – for their kindness and for their example as much as for their teaching. Fr. Cawley taught me English and Fr. Flynn was our Latin tutor. I have fond memories of them both. So too of Mr. Billy O'Reilly, who taught us maths. He stands out in the memory as the only layman in a fraternity of priest teachers.

Half a century on when the announcement was being made about the thirteenth Bishop of Hexham & Newcastle, the historians in our midst here uncovered a curious coincidence – and not just in the name of a previous Bishop of our diocese in the north-east of England. He was also named James Cunningham, but that was not the only twist of fate, for he too had attended St. Nathy's as a day pupil. He was sent by his parents from his home in Manchester to stay with relations in Ballaghaderreen and to attend St. Nathy's College. He attended the College for a few months. James Cunningham was Bishop of Newcastle & Hexham from 1958 to 1974.

In the matter of formation, a vivid memory comes back of annual visits from a procession of vocation directors from England, Scotland and Wales – but also from countries much further afield including Australia, New Zealand and the United States of America. As I recall, a statistic of the time was proudly given that half of each Leaving Certificate class would go on to continue their studies at the seminary.

Suffice to say that by the time I left for St. John's College Waterford in 1960, the foundation for my vocation was already laid. For that, I shall be forever truly grateful to St. Nathy's – for the prayer life of the College, the retreats and the dedication of the staff.

• 22 •

The Sisters of Charity

Margaret Garvey (nee Murphy)

Member of the Board of Management St. Nathy's College

The devastation caused by the Great Famine and its aftermath of hunger, poverty and fever was still in evidence in the Ballaghaderreen area in the 1870s. Dr. Francis McCormack, Bishop of Achonry, laid the foundation stone of the Convent of Our Lady of the Sacred Heart, Ballaghaderreen, at Friar's Hill on Corpus Christi in 1874. He was a life-long defender of the oppressed, his own family having been evicted when he was a boy. His motto was 'Facere et Docere' – 'Do and Preach'!

Preparations were made for the Sisters of Charity (founded by Mary Aikenhead) to establish a community. Mother Mary Arsenius, formerly Agnes Morrough Bernard, was asked to take charge of the new mission. She was in Mountjoy St. Convent at that time. Her health was not good and she worried about her forthcoming work. She met Fr. Charles of Mount Argus at St. Vincent's Hospital, which was run by the sisters. He was a constant visitor to the sick and the dying there, comforting them and giving them the Last Rites. She asked for his blessing: "I am to go as Superior to a new foundation in Ballaghaderreen and feel neither in body nor soul fit for it." He put his hands on her head and in his Dutch accent said: "Ballaghaderreen, Co. Mayo. Yes, you will go there and will be strong in body and soul and do a great deal for God's glory in the West of Ireland." This is the Passionist Priest who is now St. Charles of Mount Argus. On the 24th of April 1877, the little group of nuns arrived at the Ballaghaderreen Railway Station to be welcomed by throngs of local people, with Bishop McCormack, students, clerics and teachers from St. Nathy's College.

The work of the Sisters included tending to the sick and poor, providing food and clothing, religious education and establishing a new school. Young people became literate and cookery, laundry, knitting, needlework and weaving was taught in an effort to provide skills for those who had to emigrate and to provide those who remained in the area with a means of living. Thus, the seeds of second-level education were sown. Later, Mother Arsenius set up a community in Foxford, where she established the well-known woollen mills.

The Ballaghaderreen Sisters continued to serve in the locality with the help of local benefactors. Here I should mention that a member of the congregation, Sister Aloysius Higgins, held a life-interest in a share of the Glencorrib Estates, Galway, which was endowed on her by her brother – Colonel Gore Ousley Higgins – and was to be used for the maintenance of the community and their work. (*Father Denis Gildea's, Life of: 'Mother Mary Arsenius'*)

By 1933, a secondary school had already been established. There was a small fee for those who could afford it. In July 1944, the secondary school was amalgamated with the primary school to become 'Secondary Top'. This was Sr. Mary Martin's idea and was accepted as being more in keeping with the Sisters of Charity charism of 'Service to the Poor'. This was three decades before the introduction of 'free education' by the Government!

When I attended St. Joseph's Secondary School, Sr. Mary Martin was Principal. Our school motto was 'Caritas Christi urget nos,' - 'Love of Christ spurs us on.'

The uniform was a gym slip made from the navy wool/serge that was woven at Foxford and sewn by local dressmakers, with a white blouse and red cardigan, red woven belt and beret. There was earnestness and order in the school, with corridors quiet and polished, bounded at each end by statues, votive lamps and the flowers of the season brought by the students. Classrooms had desks for two with hinged lids and a space to store books. These books were looked after well in order to be passed on to younger family members. Many would have written inside – 'remember me, when this you see, remember me forever, remember the good old days we spent in school together'. In the classroom the big cast-iron radiators were fuelled by turf. Donations towards heating or simply turf by the load were given by the students' families.

The core subjects were taught, as well as physiology and anatomy as many girls favoured nursing as a career. The Sisters introduced us to art and to Gregorian chant. The year was divided seasonally and liturgically. Irish language and culture were encouraged.

We had a three part choir and we each took part annually in Feiseanna and concerts in St. Mary's Hall. The Diocesan Festival of Gregorian chant was held in early summer at the cathedral, with every secondary school in the diocese taking part. The great doors of the cathedral would be thrown open and hundreds of young voices could be heard singing the Gloria, the Credo, the Magnificat and the beautiful Motets after Communion. It was important to know church history and doctrine, to study Sheen's Apologetics, Catholic social teaching and the Encyclicals. Sr. Martin encouraged us to be familiar with the main points of 'Rerum Novarum', the important and influential work of Pope Leo XIII (1891) on the conditions of the working classes, also documents relating to marriage and education in modern society in the light of Christian teaching. We had copies of the Gospels and the Acts of the Apostles for reading. At least we could defend our beliefs and, if later we rejected this treasure of the church, we would at least know what it was we were rejecting!

For some it was an era of absentee emigrant fathers, long cycle rides to school in all weathers, and damp clothing during winter. We used the cookery room for our lunch and a drink of cocoa. Strolling players came to the school and made Shakespeare come to life. Dennis Franks, the Polish actor, came a few times with his 'Shakespeare without Tears' presentation.

Before the summer exams we had a retreat – a memorable time. There was Mass at 7.30am, no formal classes, study and silence (difficult for some), and a chance to walk in the convent grounds when the rhododendrons were blooming in pinks and purple.

We walked a tightrope between taboo and nature. Taboo almost always won – not because we were more virtuous, but because the climate of the time reinforced a stricter code of behaviour. Media and agony aunts had not yet driven a wedge between parents and children. Real romance flourished like sheebeens during prohibition in America. We were schooled in an era of delayed self gratification – political correctness was never our tyranny.

The 40s, 50s and 60s are presented as dull and oppressive, lacking in rights and equality, but this is a distorted picture. Obligation, not rights, was the byword then. Choice was limited. Need and austerity stimulated creativity. We were secure in our family and community. The drugs we used were iodine for cuts, vick for congestion and olive oil and castor oil for almost everything else.

We never formally graduated. We left quietly with our books, no roses or chocolates. Some of us never even saw our classmates again. The United States, England and Australia were the destinations of many. A few girls entered the religious life. We were in awe of the serious business of taking vows and wearing a veil, and maybe calmly ministering to the sick and needy in far flung regions.

Sr. Martin kept in touch with past pupils for years. She spent the last years of her life in her native Dublin, her eyesight failing. As a girl, she had met many of the men and women who made history in the early part of the twentieth century – Pearse, Eoin McNeill and members of Cumann na mBan and the early Gaelic League. Thomas McDonagh was her lecturer at University College Dublin when she studied for her masters degree in English. She and the Sisters of Charity we knew, together with the lay teachers at St. Joseph's Secondary School, were dedicated, self-sacrificing women who were ahead of their time in the spirit of true education. Their names read like a litany – Mary Martin, Joseph, Teresa, Bernadette, Rosario, Sarto, Brigid and Gonzaga. Some of them now lie in Kilcolman Cemetry and elsewhere under simple crosses, 'Memory o'er their tomb no trophies raise'.

Mar fhocal scoir, ba mhaith liom suaimhneas a ghui orthu siud uilig a ta ina lui i gCill Cholmain agus aiteanna eile.

The Sisters of Charity who made their way from the railway station on that April day in 1877 were a powerhouse of optimism, faith and hope for the local community. They left Ballaghaderreen in 1971.

The Sisters of Mercy continued their work in education in Ballaghaderreen until the secondary schools were amalgamated in 1995.

• 23 •

My Memories of St. Nathy's

Noel Conroy

LC 1963; Garda Commissioner

In the late 1950s, I first entered the gates of St. Nathy's College. At that time, Ireland was a very different place to what it is today. The decision to send me to St. Nathy's was made by my late parents. They decided to do so as there was no secondary school for boys in our local town of Belmulet. The Mercy Convent was there for girls' education. My brother Paddy had been sent to St. Nathy's before me; I guess it was because Mrs Maguire, our local primary school teacher, sent her boys there that my parents decided what was good for them was also good for us.

I was transported to St. Nathy's by car for my first visit. After that, I took the bus from my local village of Eachleim to Ballina; there changed onto the Dublin bus; travelled to Ballaghaderreen; alighted at the Square and headed with my suitcase up to the gates of St. Nathy's. It was a journey that I made many times, so many that it is engraved in my memory.

One of the most striking first images of St. Nathy's for me was that the priests wore the full length soutane. We seldom saw them in their black suits. Priests wearing black suits was what I was accustomed to, as this was the attire in which my local clergy presented themselves. Fr. Francie Cawley, who taught us English, had a very kind personality and he brought out the best in us boys. I remember him fondly. Another gentle soul was Fr. Michael Giblin, who was our Irish teacher.

Fr. Gordon gave us our grinding in Latin and Fr. Tom Lynch trained us in Gaelic football. He had a passion for success with our football teams. Indeed, he had coached the senior football team to All Ireland success the year before I arrived. St. Nathy's at the time held the reputation for having one of the best football teams in Connaught and over the years, it produced some great inter-county players. St. Nathy's was strict in the 1950s and 1960s, and Fr. James Gavigan was the Dean of Discipline. He kept us all on the straight and narrow, and silly excuses were seen through. However, I must admit that he was an extremely fair and understanding person.

Our school day began with Mass followed by breakfast. From there we went into our classrooms. The first term ran from early September till Christmas, with no mid-term break and definitely no weekends at home! Once you entered the gates on the first day of term, you did not leave until Christmas holidays. My brother and I were so far away from home that there were no visits for us from our family. The local boys from Tubbercurry and Aclare had the pleasure of visits from their parents on the odd Sunday.

Films were shown on rare occasions and plays, as Gaeilge, were produced by Fr. Giblin. One I remember was 'Cor in Aghaidh an Cam'. We had half days on Wednesdays and Saturdays, but these afternoons were taken up with sport. Handball was one of the sports that quite a lot of the students played, as well as the very popular Gaelic football.

One of the great joys of our school life was the expectation and the reception of parcels from home. These were mostly full of sweets, cakes and biscuits. We all had little groups of friends with whom we would share our parcels. When our parcels were gone, the local day pupils helped us out. We gave them the few bob and they bought us in the goodies. The day boys were a very significant lifeline for us. One dayboy I remember well was Brian Mullen. His father had a shop down the road from the college on Chapel Lane. One of my most pleasurable memories is of the rum and butter sweets that he brought up to us. It was forbidden to bring these in but, to my knowledge, Brian was never caught. He seemed to have a happy knack of escaping suspicion.

When I became ill with appendicitis, Canon Walsh, then the President of the College, took me to Roscommon County Hospital. Mr James Dillon T.D. came to see me there. He obviously was sent in by the priests from St. Nathy's. He was very popular figure in the hospital on the day. I later became aware that the bread we consumed in the College came from one of his businesses, known then as Monica Duff's.

The regime of St. Nathy's prepared me well for the Garda Training College. When I joined, the first job in the morning was to dress our beds. This was followed by Mass, which was only compulsory on Sundays. Again, we had a certain allocation of time for study every day, but we were free at the weekends. Curfew during the week was at 11pm. Many students from St. Nathy's joined An Garda Siochana. Among them was my colleague Cormac Gordon, who was detective chief superintendent in charge of the drugs squad until recently. He was a distant relation of the late Fr. Gordon.

In conclusion, I would like to say that I am very grateful to my teachers from St. Nathy's. Those priests dedicated their lives to educating us young people to giving us the best start in life they could. As Garda Commissioner, I had the privilege of meeting the heads of police from other countries, and found that they had also been educated by Irish priests and brothers, and that they too spoke highly of the commitment of their teachers.

For all who have gone before us to the Lord, may they rest in peace in Heaven. For those of us still around, as we celebrate the bicentenary of St.

Nathy's, may we have good health to enjoy and make full use of the remainder of our time in this life. I wish St. Nathy's continued success.

• 24 •

"Carry On"
William Burke

LC 1965; President and CEO of Country Bank, New York;
Grand Marshall of the St. Patrick's Day Parade, New York, 1988

On the 6th of September 1960, my father drove me to St. Nathy's College in Ballaghaderreen. As I sat in the car, lonesome and speechless, my father said: "It's up to you now; I won't be looking over your shoulder." My mother had passed away so he was the chief cook and bottle washer.

I lugged my case in and at the door was a grim faced priest who directed me to the dormitory. The dormitory consisted of about 30 beds, which were allocated on a first-come-first-served basis. I hung around making small talk, and then we were invited to go downstairs to the refectory for our tea.

The next morning the bell rang at 7.30am. It was off to Mass and then breakfast. At this time, the prefects had all been chosen and were assigned to organise the tables in the refectory. It was four to a table, with the tables being assigned on a seniority basis. For the boys who were not assigned or picked to go to a table, there was a big table at the bottom for about 20 boys. Guess what table I wound up at… the big table. I was somewhat embarrassed at not having been selected for a four-man table.

After breakfast, the first-year students were ushered into a classroom. A stern priest, Fr. Doherty, announced that we would have to take an entrance examination. The first-year students would be divided into an 'A' class for the better students and a 'B' class for the struggling students. Guess what class I wound up in… the 'B' group!

The 'B' group was ushered down to a small classroom by the recreation hall, away from the main body and next door to the handyman's sleeping quarters. The classes started and were run by a group of fine, dedicated priests – although I did not think so at the time! These included Fathers Fleming, Lynch, Gordon, Flynn, Cawley and Tiernan, as well as the one and only Mr. Billy Reilly.

The first day that Mr. Billy Reilly came into our classroom, he looked up to heaven and said: "This is impossible," and for the next five years he just said; "Carry on."

Life in that first term was difficult. The food was poor and we were not allowed to wear top coats. There were no newspapers, radio, television or telephones, and the Dean took a hard look at all the incoming mail. Our first break came in late September when Fr. Lynch brought down a radio to a classroom and we listened to Michael O'Hehir's broadcast of the All-Ireland football final between Down and Derry.

The second break came on Halloween when we were served brack and cup cakes for tea; even the Dean was smiling and in a good mood. It may not seem like much now, but then it was fantastic.

We slowly moved into December and started counting the days to go before going home. Every evening during the break, we would listen to Ben Gallagher from Kilmatigue sing Christmas carols – 'I'm dreaming of a white Christmas' and 'Rudolph the Red Nosed Reindeer'. He would bring tears to a stone and we all shed a few ourselves.

Starting on the 15th of December, the barber from downtown would come up each evening to cut our hair. We all wanted to look our best going home. It was a shilling for a haircut and there was nothing fancy about it. The barber only had a scissors and a hand-held trimmer; and he had been known to nip an ear now and then!

On the night before the Christmas holidays, everyone in the dormitory had to sing, tell a story or recite poetry, so it was well into the morning before we got to sleep. The prefect in our dormitory was Padraig Keane from Curry. He was a great individual; he was friendly and gave us plenty of advice and confidence that carried us through our first term.

The next morning was the start of the holidays. We forgot the breakfast and the whole body of students were ushered into the main classrooms. The partitions were pulled back and we were introduced to the Bishop of Achonry, who was ready to give us his annual speech. Unfortunately, the speech was given in Irish and lasted for more than an hour. I did not understand a word he was saying and wished he would rap it up so I could head back to Tubbercurry.

I developed great relationships with my fellow students – Paddy Kilcoyne, Hugh Gallagher, Seamus Mullooly and Luke Snee from Tubbercurry; John Joe and Colm Casey from Charlestown; Al McDonnell from Crossmolina; Willie Curran from Irishtown; and the boys from Kilmactigue – Anthony Haran, Ben Gallagher, Paddy Gallagher, Jimmy Rooper and Bernie Lehiney.

As I mentioned, the priests were dedicated to providing the best education. The following are some friendly quotes that were directed at me during my stay, and even today I think they were humorous and I accepted them as hilarious.

Fr. Gordon: "This all seems Greek to you?"

Fr. Duffy: "One of these days, we will get beyond Mensa."

Fr. Flynn: "I presume Irish is not going to be your second language."

Fr. Fleming: "You would make a perfect picture for a postcard."

Fr. Walsh: "Everyone deserves a second chance."

Fr. Tiernan: "You are never going to be a scientist."

However, Mr. Billy Reilly got it right. One day, Mr. Reilly was studying at the window; reportedly he was exceptionally good at maths and had written a book. Anyway, he stopped reading, stepped to the blackboard and, with his chalk, proceeded to print a blackboard full of numbers.

He then swung around, pointed at me and said: "Can you solve this equation?" I had not paying attention so I just blurted out some numbers. He looked at me for about two minutes and finally said: "You are correct, you are an absolute genius and you are going places."

He looked up at heaven and said: "Carry on."

• 25 •

Mens Sane in Corpore Sano

Dermot Earley

LC 1965; Lieutenant General, Chief of Staff, Irish Defence Forces

When my late father, God rest him, told me one evening in 1957 that the local secondary school had won the Hogan Cup, I made up my mind that this was the school that I wished to attend after I had finished my primary education. I was not aware as a nine-year-old that St. Nathy's was in a different Diocese to us, even though we were living just eight miles away. The possibility of secondry-level education anywhere else was totally dismissed when in 1959 St. Nathy's contested the Hogan Cup Final again. Despite loosing to St. Joseph's Fairview, led by the late Des Foley of Dublin, God rest him too, I was heading for St. Nathy's. Dad was secretly in full agreement, although Mam was not so sure. "It is not all about football," she advised me one evening, but Dad interjected with words like balance, in development, holistic education and then he uttered a Latin phrase, which he later interpreted for me: "*Mens sana in corpore sano.*" In later life, I was to use that phrase often in encouraging young people to take exercise and to get involved in playing a game, any game. And so in September 1960, I began my life at St. Nathy's. As I look back now at those five years, I can recall enjoyable days (mostly), great teachers, having an identity, learning about life inside and outside of the classroom, and above all, compliance with my mum's wishes and participating in all sports.

Playing football was the release from any difficulties one might have in class or study, and the games we played on the top field or on any of the other pitches were great contests, great fun, and were the topic of discussion 'till the next game was played'. Three teachers were most helpful and encouraging to me in every aspect of college life, namely Fr. Tom Lynch and Fr. Con Gordon, may they rest in peace, and Fr. Jimmy Colleran. Fr. Tom was involved in '57 and '59 when St. Nathy's were at a peak in College Football. Fr. Con was our juvenile trainer and coached us in the skills and team play. We won the Connaught Colleges Juvenile Championships in 1963 – my first medal ever! Fr.

Jimmy arrived at the College as a teacher, as we did as students, in September 1960 and introduced basketball to the school. This was a new game and he taught us the skills of how to play. I thought it was a most wonderful game; second only to football.

Fr. Tom Lynch and I became lifelong friends. Under his guidance, we won the Connaught Championships in 1965; although St. Nathy's did not win a senior title in my time. The College has had great success in basketball over the years and it is wonderful to see and read of the endeavours of the pupils and their successes on and off the field.

But it was not all sport. Our teachers helped, motivated and encouraged (different ways – early 60s), and what we were taught in the classroom was complemented by advice outside the formal programme. In particular, I remember the introduction of debates by the then Fr. Tom Flynn, recently retired Bishop of Achonry. I enjoyed the new challenge and the requirement to develop one's ideas and thoughts quickly, sometimes with hilarious results (in relation to myself only).

St. Nathy's was both good to me and good for me. In 1957, my thoughts were only about sport. But life, as we all know, is much more than just that. I am grateful for what I was taught by committed and dedicated teachers and for what I gained from my fellow pupils. It is a pleasure to meet a St. Nathy's colleague at anytime.

Fr. James Gavigan was the Dean for the duration of my time there. He too has gone to his eternal reward, God rest his soul. He was strong and strict, but had a sense of humour. It was from him that I received one of his best pieces of advice ever. It was my first year and there had been a bit of bother. In sorting out the problem, he spoke to each class, talking of behaviour and respect. After a pause, as if to make an impact, he said: "If you want to know what a person is really like, give them a bit of authority." I have never forgotten that statement and I have used it many times in dealing with people both at work and at play.

In 1960, only two of the sixth class of our primary school went on to second level, myself and one other. Most of the remainder went to England or the US in their early teens. Some fought in Vietnam and some helped build parts of the US and the UK. Thankfully, the vast majority of those now leaving primary school go on to third-level education.

Sport was a simple strand for me in going to St. Nathy's, but I have received rewards of enjoyment from sport and satisfaction from the classroom that cannot be measured. For all of that, I am extremely grateful. In attempting to sum up my experience of life in St. Nathy's, I could not put it better than what was said by a consultant at my daughter's graduation as a nurse a number of years ago. He encouraged the new nurses to use their skills in a caring way because he said you must be a good person and have respect for all with whom you will come in contact. He added: "Your attitude is more important that your ability, your motives are more important than your method, your courage is more important that your cleverness, and have your heart in the right place."

Whatever can be said about us students, the attitudes and the motives of the College staff were sound. In 1965, as we walked away from St. Nathy's to further our education or get employment, confidence and courage were not wanting, and our hearts were set in the right place.

• 26 •

Some Memories of St. Nathy's in the 1960s

Nollaig Ó Muraíle

LC 1967; MRIA; Roinn Na Gaeilge, Ollscoil na hÉireann, Gaillimh

I entered St. Nathy's College (or simply 'Nathy's' as we usually referred to it) for the first time in September 1962; I was to spend almost five years there until I did 'the leaving' in 1967. Most of the first half of this period coincided with the very strict presidency of Fr. Tom Fleming (universally known by his nickname 'Flam'. Following his sudden death in March 1965, Fr. Fleming's successor, Fr. Charlie Doherty (known, for some reason, as 'George'), brought in a less severe regime – although it would still seem extremely restrictive by present-day standards.

Looking back over those years, after more than four decades, many memories come flooding back; many pleasant, some rather less so. One recalls classmates – as well as lads from contiguous classes – several of whom have remained good friends over the years, while others are encountered rarely, if at all. Some, sadly, have passed away – from my year I recall Joe Byrne, Dominic Lydon, Tom Brennan, Michael Keaveney, Tom McMunn, Pat Lynch and John Mitchell. Requiescant in peace.

One undeniable and unpleasant aspect of college life at this time involved the use of mean-minded bullying tactics by members of the senior classes against the younger boys. As I recall, this was a fairly serious issue when we were in first and second years, but then largely faded away. I wonder if those who were two or three classes behind my own were treated in similar fashion by some of my own classmates. My impression is that things did improve in this respect, but this may be merely wishful thinking.

Life in a boarding school was, of necessity, strictly regimented and could often be quite tedious. The Dean – Fr. James Gavigan in our first three years, followed by Fr. Andy Johnston – kept us on a tight leash. Some of the restrictions imposed struck me at the time as rather irksome, and some as downright ridiculous. There was the rule of not straying 'out of bounds', which meant that anyone who, without official permission, stepped outside the front door of the College, or who ventured outside the perimeter marked out by the path known as 'the walk' – even to the extent of crossing the drain that ran alongside the northern end of the tennis court – had committed an offence for which the punishment could be expulsion. Of course, in hindsight, there were plenty of good reasons – to do with insurance as well general discipline – why students should not have been able to wander at will wherever they liked, but this was never explained to us. We just did not go out of bounds because that was 'the rule'. One strange result of the rule, however, was that although I spent nearly five years in Ballaghaderreen, I never got to know the town, never having set foot in a single shop there in all that time. It is only in the intervening years that I have gained some slight familiarity with 'Ballagh' – once the principal town of east Mayo and now part of 'Mayo irredenta', the chunk of my native county 'lost' to Roscommon for reasons of local taxation in 1898. As compensation, we got Ardnaree from Sligo and Finny from Galway.

Some of us St. Nathy's students did not go in for sports much – in my own case, being always rather nearsighted, I think I would have been more of a hindrance than a help on any sports field, so my sporting activities were confined to playing a small amount of handball (badly) on the back-alley. Apart from that, those of us in the non-sporting category were confined to walking interminably round and round 'the walk'. I remember one classmate, Tommie Heneghan – now a parish priest in Brixton – inquiring plaintively how our situation differed from that of the inmates of Mountjoy Jail. Even 'going round 'the walk' was strictly regulated – one had to go clockwise! One sunny afternoon, Michael Carroll and myself (and perhaps one other), out of sheer boredom, decided to vary the routine and go round anti-clockwise – only to be confronted at the end of our short perambulation by the Dean, who, in the course of a severe dressing-down, inquired if we smart alecs considered ourselves 'the intelligentsia' (a term I was hearing for the first time).

Even more boring than those interminable circuits of 'the walk' were the long, tedious periods spent standing on wet days in the 'recreation hall' – not the large modern building which was probably Fr. Fleming's most enduring legacy, but the long, narrow hall with the red-tiled floor that runs along the side of the quadrangle opposite and parallel to the refectory. Another perch, from which we were routinely banished by the Dean, was the low wall in front of the 'jacks'.

Only in our final year were we allowed to spend some time in the classroom if it was raining – no doubt because we were (or were supposed to be) studying for the Leaving Cert. Among the few things that helped relieve the boredom were the films that were shown in the College on Sunday nights, perhaps once a month or so. Sometimes, on a wet half-day (Wednesday or Saturday), we were permitted to go – under the supervision of the prefects – to the cinema just outside the College gates for a special showing of a film. I recall those films (both internal and external) with a certain amount of nostalgia; many seem to have been either Westerns ('Cowboys and Indians' as we called them in the days before political correctness) or war-films (mainly about World War II), but there were also comedies and Alfred Hitchcock thrillers.

On filmless Sunday nights – and on other, very rare occasions – the 'library' was opened; that is, one was allowed to borrow and read for about two hours, during second study, a book from the usually locked glass bookcases that stood in one or two of the class halls. I have very little memory of the books – except, for some reason, Jules Vernes's Twenty Thousand Leagues Under the Sea and Dorothy Macardle's The Irish Republic – but the two-hours maximum limit on reading a book and the fact that there was no certainty one would get the same book when the library was re-opened a week or a fortnight later were most frustrating.

Other restrictive rules included the active discouragement of visitors and the complete prohibition of 'food-parcels' – the latter on the grounds (in hindsight, far from unreasonable) of preventing inequity between students whose parents could easily afford such luxuries and those whose parents could not. I remember in second year a neighbour from home, who had recently acquired a car, bringing my parents on their only visit to St. Nathy's during my five years there. The neighbour was the principal of the girls' school in Knock, and her son – my best friend in national school – had gone to college in Ballyfin, Co. Laois. She was incredulous when I told her I could not accept the sweets, biscuits and fruit that she and my mother had brought along; such items were included under the heading of 'food-parcels' and accordingly banned. I was persuaded to take just a few of the smaller items they had brought. On my way back to the classroom after the visit, I was met by the President, Fr. Fleming, who did not search me – as he was wont to do with anyone who had been in contact with the 'outside world' – but instead expressed his satisfaction that I was not carrying one of the dreaded 'food-parcels'. I did have several bars of chocolate and a couple of packets of sweets stuffed into my pockets, but I managed to evade scrutiny. I do not recall if I felt guilty at the President's unmerited words of commendation!

To my mind, the most nonsensical ban was that on newspapers – of all kinds, both national and local. I have always had a great interest in current affairs, but this was suffocated during my time in Ballaghaderreen. Yet, some of our teachers would comment freely on current events – most notably Fr. Tom Lynch, who could sometimes be diverted from a history or English lesson to give his views (usually quite trenchant and eloquently expressed) on some burning topic of the day. The result of the ban on all media meant that some of the great events of the period 1962 to 1967 almost passed us by. We heard of the Cuban missile crisis of autumn 1962 via rumours from the dayboys, until we persuaded our youngest teacher, Fr. Louis Dunleavy, to bring in a transistor radio so we could hear at least one news-bulletin. I recall that Fr. Louis – a fine strapping man (and consequently nicknamed 'Tiny') – was nervous that the President might hear the radio, so he kept the volume down so low that scarcely anyone could make sense of the bulletin.

The other earth-shattering event of the early 1960s was of course the assassination of John F. Kennedy on 22 November 1963. I can still remember the sense of palpable shock felt by the class when our prefect, Micheál Noone, announced at the beginning of evening study that President Kennedy had been shot and wounded that afternoon in Dallas, Texas. As we were going into the dormitory that night, the Dean told us that the president had, in fact, died. We went to bed with heavy hearts, wondering if this presaged a terrifying war between America and Russia. Over the following days, we learned of the swearing-in of the new president, Lyndon Johnson, and the killing of Lee Harvey Oswald by Jack Ruby, but we did not get to see or hear the president's funeral, although I did 'overhear' a small part of the ceremony from a small, 'illegal' transistor radio that one of the senior students had smuggled in – he and a small group gathered behind the toilets to listen to the commentary, through a great deal of static, until they dispersed on hearing that the Dean was approaching. I never saw the TV-footage of either the Cuban missile crisis or Kennedy's assassination and funeral until the twentieth, or even twenty-fifth, anniversary of those events.

In our second-to-last year, we did get a television set in the College, but it was mostly kept locked away in a cabinet in the 6A classroom, to be opened for the science programmes for schools broadcast under the title Telefís Scoile. The only other exception was on St. Patrick's Day, when we were allowed to watch the Railway Cup Football and hurling finals. On one Patrick's Day, we received the special privilege of being able to watch a ballad session with the internationally known Irish stars of the day, the Clancy Brothers and Tommy Makem. The same concession would not have been extended to the pop groups and showbands being lauded and 'promoted' by the young Louis Walsh, who was in a class about three years behind mine. Mention of music reminds me of one song that for me especially epitomises the popular culture of the time – Tom Jones singing 'The Green, Green Grass of Home'. I vividly recall hearing – just barely – those distinctive notes wafting across the 'Middle Big' dormitory long after lights out from one or other of the illegal transistors buried deep under piles of bedclothes to keep them safe from the sharp ears of the Dean (there were no earphones in those days!). Incidentally, the Dean was, for reasons that were even then utterly unknown, nicknamed 'Sike' or, according to some, 'Psyche' (perhaps because of his uncanny, even psychic, ability to spot trouble or mischief a mile off?).

A good deal of what I have had to say thus far has concentrated on the more negative aspects of life in the College – perhaps because they loom fairly large in memories of the place. Another topic about which we complained incessantly was the quality of the food, which often left a good deal to be desired – having had roast-beef for dinner five or six days a week for nearly five years put me off that particular item of food for nearly thirty years. There were, however, many positive aspects to our time in St. Nathy's, things for which I will always be grateful. Most importantly, there was a team of very dedicated, hardworking and conscientious teachers. I think I learned many worthwhile things from all of them.

Most of us, I think, were scared of Billy O'Reilly, who taught us maths and who, for a long period, was the only lay-teacher in the College. His threats could indeed be fearsome – especially to those of us who were not mathematical geniuses, yet we discovered over time that his bark was much worse than his bite. He seemed to be hardest on his own son, Derek, who was in our class.

In our first couple of years we learned the basics of Greek grammar from Fr. Mike Keegan. I recall him as being kind and funny – telling us, for example, to keep staring at the text and eventually some of it might sink in! He was succeeded after a couple of years by Fr. Tom Flynn – later bishop – who instilled in me a great love and fascination for the Classics, as well as a particular interest in the history of ancient Greece. In fact, I still have the typed notes he gave us on that topic. I also remember an absorbing slide show he gave us after returning from a holiday in Greece.

Our Latin teacher for the whole five years was Fr. Michael Duffy, a kind and humorous man whom ill-health cut off all too early. I owe to him a good grounding in Latin; I enjoyed Caesar and, to a lesser extent, Cicero, but for some reason I never warmed to Virgil. However, I found Roman history really fascinating and was very proud of the detailed notes I had compiled on the subject – although they mysteriously disappeared on the very eve of the Leaving. (That puzzle was eventually solved by Damien Tansey, more than twenty years later, but that is a story for another day!) A particular memory of Fr. Duffy is of him bringing in books on all kinds of strange and wonderful topics from which he would read extracts at free classes immediately before the holidays.

We had Fr. Tom Flynn's older brother, Fr. Bob, for Inter-Cert Irish and also, for a time, for science. He could be very humorous and, while sometimes given to uttering dire threats, behind it all he was a very kind man. Fr. Louis Dunleavy, who taught us Irish and history in first year, was the epitome of the 'gentle giant' and we were sorry when he left to minister in Florida. I think it was he who advised us, at an early stage of our sojourn in St. Nathy's, to keep a diary – although some others (including Michael Carroll) started at the same time, I seem to have persisted longest. Moreover, while the works of the others seem to have been lost over time, I still have three notebooks that cover the period between October 1962 and March 1963, and, following a break that probably represents a lost notebook, from December 1963 to October 1964. Most of the contents, it should be emphasised, are mind-numbingly boring and banal – lists of classes, schoolboy gossip and, literally, what we had for breakfast! But just occasionally, there are details that may be of some slight interest almost half a century later.

Inserted between the pages of one of the notebooks, I found a copy of a peace treaty between Michael Carroll and myself, in Michael's handwriting and formally witnessed by Pat Lynch and John Mitchell (both now sadly deceased). Accompanying it are two notes that help to explain the genesis of hostilities – the firing of some ink-blobs from a fountain-pen by Michael having apparently damaged a copy of mine. The first of the notes, dated '26/4/1963', begs forgiveness and adds 'I will give you any compensation, within reason, for your copy', and is signed 'Yours sorrowfully, Michael'. The second reads: 'Don't you think we should sign a ceasefire agreement and be friends? By the way, please give me your compass (my biro won't fit in mine).' Incidentally, the resulting 'treaty' has the following, slightly ominous, codicil: 'If any of the undersigned calls the other thick, bang goes the Treaty.' One can see how Michael ended up as solicitor for CIÉ!

For the Leaving Cert Irish course, we had the formidable Fr. Michael Giblin. He was a brilliant teacher with a marvellous command of the native tongue and a fund of entertaining stories. He could also be quite fearsome, being utterly intolerant of anyone not giving him his undivided attention. Although a gifted teacher, he told me in later years that he loathed teaching and hated every moment he was confined in St. Nathy's, he just wanted to work in a parish. Nevertheless, he prepared our class meticulously for the Leaving Cert; in fact, he had completed the set course by Easter of fourth year and spent the remainder of that year giving us a crash course in Celtic studies. He brought into class facsimiles of medieval Irish manuscripts including the Book of Leinster and the Book of Ballymote, read extracts from Cormac Ó Cadhlaigh's encyclopaedic book An Fhiannuidheacht, and talked about people who were active in the language movement (many of whom he knew personally). In my case, at least, he truly laid the foundations of the university course I was to pursue in Maynooth a couple of years later. Then, in fifth year, he returned to the Leaving Cert course, which he thoroughly revised with us. I do not think I have ever been as well prepared for an exam as I was for my Leaving-Cert Irish.

We were fortunate in our history teachers. For the Inter Cert we had the dynamic Fr. Jimmy Colleran, having had Fr. Dunleavy in first year, and for Leaving Cert we had the brilliant Fr. Tom Lynch. Fr. Colleran always came to class with meticulously prepared notes, but he often had difficulty controlling the class – he made the mistake of treating us all as adults and, sadly, the response he received was all too often more than a little juvenile. Rather naively, he indicated early on that he disapproved of corporal punishment, and this was more than taken advantage of. Fr. Lynch, on the other hand, declared regularly and with vehemence his disapproval of the campaign – then gathering momentum – to abolish corporal punishment in Irish schools. Such a development, he suggested, would mean the end of civilisation as we knew it. Yet I can never recall him having to resort to such a means of chastisement himself! Perhaps his experience of training the football team gave him an edge in controlling unruly teenagers. One funny or sarcastic remark from him could usually put the most robust challenger in his place.

Fr. Lynch's classes, both in history and Leaving-Cert English, were always wonderfully stimulating. He was so strongly opinionated that there was no room for neutrality in his classes, and he relished someone putting forward a contradictory viewpoint as an opportunity for a debate. He was also a brilliant raconteur and would readily bring a whole variety of topics into a class – sport (obviously), current affairs, politics (both national and international), as well as the subject in hand. Our English teacher at Inter-Cert level was Fr. Cornelius Gordon, whom I recall as quietly witty and encouraging.

Our most memorable science teacher was undoubtedly the inimitable and fiery Fr. Seán Tiernan. A tiny bundle of energy, one of his nicknames was, rather aptly, 'The Bullet' – he could be charming and very entertaining, but when he lost his temper, the class had better watch out! He had very strong views on a range of issues – I remember him being totally dismissive of the idea, just then coming to the fore, that smoking might damage one's health. He claimed that by the same logic, one could prove that wearing trousers was potentially harmful! But he was also quite visionary – he forecast, around 1965, the feasibility of a hydrogen-fuelled car. My abiding memory of him, however, is of how his whole demeanour changed when he would come into the class hall and announce, without any forewarning, that there was to be a house exam there and then. The charm vanished utterly and the exam took on a grim, even doom-laden aspect, like a visit from the Lord High Executioner himself. Ever since, when giving an exam to my own students, I make sure to make it as informal and unthreatening as possible. In our final year, we had Fr. Michael Joyce as science-teacher, who was not far removed in age from ourselves, and I began to enjoy the subject to an extent not done before.

In our first year, French was introduced as a subject and our first teacher was Mrs. Connolly, a kind and gentle woman who, I am sorry to say, was treated rather like Daniel in the lions' den. I felt really sorry for her as she tried to control the class and impart the rudiments of French grammar. Despite what seemed like a continuous rowdy disruption during that year, I seem to have learned a fair bit of basic French. Mrs. Connolly was succeeded by James Flanagan, who was only the third lay-teacher of whom we had experience. He made it clear in one of his very first classes that he would not stand for any nonsense, and it really worked! I enjoyed learning the language and regretted having to give it up after Inter Cert – I think I had to choose between French and history. In spite of the lapse of time, I found about a dozen years ago that I still retained sufficient of the language to make my way round Paris without too much difficulty.

Christian Doctrine was a subject taught by several different teachers, including Frs. Giblin and Gavigan, and later by Frs. Tom Flynn, Andy Johnston and Greg Hannon. The latter three, in particular, made great efforts to distil and explain the documents that were emerging from the Second Vatican Council, which had begun the very autumn we started in St. Nathy's and continued on until after we had completed the Inter Cert. Fr. Hannon, especially, was always ready for a lively debate on any topic that happened to crop up.

A memorable figure in our first year was the wonderful Fr. Francie Cawley, who was Vice-President before leaving to work on the missions in Latin America. He was a remarkably lively, funny and unstuffy man, small and wiry and almost always wearing a biretta on his bald head. With his twinkling eyes and ready smile, he seemed totally at odds with the prevailing regime. In class, I remember him most for promoting Ronald Knox's translation of the New Testament; while outside of class I recall his usually unsuccessful efforts to keep a semblance of order in the refectory when the President and Dean happened to be away.

In addition to meeting the staff in class, I had a chance to meet some of them in a different setting when in 1966 I was invited to join the 'editorial staff' of a college magazine, The Torch, which Frs. Tom Flynn and Jimmy Colleran had established in February 1965. The cover was designed by our classmate Tim Lynch. We used to have 'editorial meetings' in a room in the old college building at the back to the square, and I can still recall the pungent smell of the ink and the wax stencils in the Gestetner machine on which multiple typed copies of the magazine were printed, and not always very legibly. The final issue with which I was involved was one of that we were especially proud. Dated 16 May 1967, it featured pieces by students who had recently left St. Nathy's to do a variety of higher education courses or join various professions, as follows:

Arts degree, UCD (John Doherty);
Agricultural science, UCG (John Walsh);
Accountancy, Institute of Chartered Accountants of Ireland (Barry Butler);
The missionary priesthood, St. Patrick's College, Kiltegan (Luke Fitzmaurice);
Teacher-training, St. Patrick's College, Drumcondra (Micheál Ó Fearadhaigh & Michael Farry);
Law (an anonymous solicitor);
Medicine, UCD (Xavier Flanagan);
Banking, National Bank of Ireland, Clifden (George Butler);
Cadetship in the Irish army, Military College, The Curragh (Dermot Earley);
The diocesan priesthood, St. Patrick's College, Maynooth (Pádraic Brennan);
Engineering, UCG (Alban Carney).

I found each of those eleven accounts of life in so many different places utterly fascinating, and even today they are full of interest. One may note, incidentally, that among that group of students, one name stands out – that of Dermot Earley. In our time in St. Nathy's, he was our football hero, the man who saved the day in more than one encounter with our rivals from neighbouring diocesan colleges, Muredach's, Summerhill or Jarlath's. He is now Lieutenant-General Earley, chief of staff of Óglaigh na hÉireann, the Irish defence forces – and he is also deemed one of the greatest footballers never to have won an All-Ireland medal. Another interesting detail in that issue of The Torch was a series of photographs of all thirty-eight members of that year's Leaving-Cert class (my own). Taken by Fr. Hannon, each was accompanied by the student's autograph.

There are many other aspects of life in St. Nathy's on which I might write in some detail had I the time and space to do so. I have not mentioned, for example, the desperate, survival-of-the-fittest-type scramble to get to the College shop, open for just a short period each week, to try to secure the last bar of chocolate in the place. Or the equally desperate and often ludicrous efforts to stock up on all types of sweets and biscuits on our occasional trips to inter-college football matches in Charlestown as if we were about to endure a veritable chocolate famine – which I suppose we were!

Other aspects of college life I had almost forgotten until I began writing these reminiscences included getting a haircut from the barber in the locker room, or going in to see the nuns – especially the wonderful Sister Liguori who was not much older than ourselves – when feeling unwell, and hoping to be sent up to the dormitory for a couple of days' 'rest'; but how those days dragged when one was not really sick! On one occasion, almost half the College took to bed with various stages of flu, either real, imagined or pretended.

Then there were certain unpardonable crimes, such as running in the corridor, talking (even whispering) at study or after 'lights out', or not wearing 'house shoes' – heaven help you if the Dean caught you wearing your own shoes indoors! I recall just how treacherous those house shoes with their smooth leather soles could be on the marble stairs coming down from the first-year dormitory.

Other memories are of the weekly scramble for the laundry bags outside the 'ref', the ordeal of washing (and later shaving) with cold water, the occasional scares about Henthorn's ghost, and the counting of days until the next holidays – 'Up going home in 53 days' time!', as was written in a prayer book by a homesick fellow-inmate. And always the subject of food! The golden syrup for spreading on a thin slice of bread after class in the afternoon was deemed far preferable to the sometimes foul-tasting soup (known as 'juice') which was often served at afternoon lunch. More positively, there was the fry one sometimes got as a reward for serving Mass, the stew (which could vary from good to awful), or other very rare treats such as the quite delicious, but severely rationed, shepherd's pie (I do not think I have ever since tasted its equal), the mushy peas, the wonderful (and almost equally rare) fresh 'brown bread', dispensed in the 'ref' by the prefects who, were it not for the presence of the Dean, stood in real danger of being mobbed in a mini 'bread-riot'. By way of complete contrast, can one ever forget Fr. Tiernan mischievously preparing us for our meals by creating nauseating 'rotten-egg' smells in the science hall just before dinnertime?

I should perhaps explain that most of this account is based on my experiences as a boarder in St. Nathy's. We should recall that a small but significant portion of the student body consisted of day-boys, who attended College for class and organised sports, and some for supervised study. The day-boys were in many ways much more 'free' than the boarders; nevertheless, they experienced a number of significant restrictions, being perennially suspected of being engaged in smuggling contraband, notably sweets, biscuits and cigarettes, or posting letters for the boarders. That suspicion was far from groundless, with some of the day-boys having become extremely proficient and ingenious smugglers. Some showed themselves to have genuine entrepreneurial flair!

I hope that the foregoing fairly random collection of reminiscences, however brief, will give some idea of the College as it was between forty and fifty years ago. The place has changed utterly since then, developing and expanding most impressively – although I am happy to see that most of the core-buildings are still wholly recognisable to those of us who looked up in awe at the impressive front of the College with its Latin inscription, '*Collegium Sancti Nath[a]ei*', on that day in early September 1962. Just to show how memory can play tricks on one, I was under the impression – until corrected by Fr. Leo Henry – that the inscription was of the College motto, '*Robur Nathaei*' ('Nathy/Nath Í's oak' and, by extension of meaning, 'Nathy's strength'). This, however, occurred elsewhere in the College and was of course displayed on the pocket of the College blazer. This latter item of attire, incidentally, was a luxury to which many of us aspired, but which I, for one, could never afford.

It may seem strange to recall that no schoolgirl was ever permitted to darken the door of the College in those days – the nearest approach of those exotic creatures was on the 'festival day' each year when students from the diocese's convent schools came to Mass in the cathedral. Now girls and boys play an equal role in the new St. Nathy's and that has to be a healthy development. Since coming to NUI Galway five years ago, I have been privileged to teach graduates of St. Nathy's, both male and female, at undergraduate and postgraduate level, and it has made me very proud indeed of my alma mater – now with two centuries of honourable history behind her. *Go maire sí dhá chéad eile go héasca agus faoi ghradam!*

Appendix: Diary-entry on Cuban Missile Crisis, 1962

The surviving diaries (mentioned above) are in three notebooks which run as follows:

11 October [1962] (Thursday) – 7 December [1962] (Friday)
8 December [1962] (Saturday) – 5 March [1963] (Tuesday)
20 December [1963] (Friday) – 5 October [1964] (Monday)

The following is a fairly typical entry, albeit relating to a time of great drama in world affairs, but note how it is sandwiched between more immediate and mundane concerns. It should be borne in mind that when this was penned, my classmates and I were still in first year, having been less than two months in the College. Had we been in a higher class, we would surely have pressed the staff for more information on the dramatic events unfolding in the outside world. Here the staff were no doubt deliberately trying to prevent an outbreak of panic, while unsure themselves of what was likely to be the outcome to the perilous standoff between the Great Powers.

Oct. 23 (Tuesday) [1962]: Peck in fairly good humour. Tiny gave us first verse of 'Cill Aodáin' to learn for next day. When we went into 1A for Cath. Doct, everyone was asking us if we had heard that a World War had started over Cuba, but Fr. Colleran would not tell us anything about it. We had Fr. Dunleavy again for history and he told us all about President Kennedy's speech and the blockade of Cuba. After dinner, Tiny was teaching us Irish grammar. Hoff told us we have a fairly good chance of getting to Charlestown for the St. Nathy's v St. Muredach's of Ballina match on Sunday. I hope we go. I bought a sixpenny forecast from Ted Kennedy the other day for it. Billy was in great humour at first, but he got into a rotten mood near the end of the class and ended up by telling us that we will have two Maths exams. Juice for lunch. Wrote home at first study in answer to the letter I got at dinner... The Grade was on study tonight.

Explanatory note:

Nicknames for staff-members have been retained here. They are as follows: 'Peck': Fr. Michael Duffy; 'Tiny': Fr. Louis Dunleavy; 'Hoff': Fr. Tom Lynch; 'The Grade': Fr. Michael Giblin. The etymologies of most of those nicknames (except 'Tiny') are lost in the mists of time – even forty years ago, people were unsure where many of them had originated. Interestingly, Fr. Colleran is here referred to by his own name – his nickname was 'Jummy', which he inherited from his uncle, a former member of the College staff and later a canon. 'Billy' refers to Mr. Billy O'Reilly.

Incidentally, the Ted Kennedy mentioned was not the brother of the US President, but rather an enterprising fellow-student, rather older than me and my classmates!

Before concluding this article, I wish to offer my sincere thanks to Fr. Leo Henry, St. Nathy's, and to my old classmate Fr. Martin Jennings, PP, Curry, for various valuable suggestions and corrections. *Nár laga Dia iad*!

• 27 •

James Dillon and the Prize Essay

Michael Lafferty

LC 1967; Chairman of Lafferty Group

Times were very tough in the little village of Kilvaloon, just outside Ballaghaderreen, back in 1962. I was part of a big family that eventually came to number eleven children. There was no choice but to sleep four or six to a bed. We all helped out on the small farm by doing jobs like milking the cows, butter-making, feeding the cattle, spreading manure and haymaking, as well as helping my mother in the kitchen. In spite of all the poverty, I was regularly told that there was a great future ahead. This encouragement came as much from neighbours as it did from within the family. It gave me a great deal of confidence and determination.

In the summer of 1962, I did something very unusual at the time and went for a holiday in London to stay with my Aunt Nora and her husband, Tom. I had a wonderful time. In my euphoria on coming home, I called up James Dillon, the famous politician, from the phone box in the Square and arranged to see him. The great man gave me several hours of his time and talked at length about people and things I hardly understood. Dr. Noel Browne and Keir Hardy are two big political names he mentioned time and time again.

The big news that awaited me on my return from London was that my parents, with help from relatives in Ireland, England and South Africa, had somehow found the money to send me as a day-boy to St. Nathy's College. I was over the moon with delight, seeing college as the start of a process that would eventually help me along the path to an exciting future career.

Proud as I was to be a pupil at St. Nathy's, I could not avoid getting the impression that day-boys were somehow second-class citizens in the College in the 1960s. Sports activities seemed to be the exclusive preserve of boarders, but it was not a big issue for me. I was grateful just to be a pupil. Much more important was academic achievement – and this was brought home to me when I was demoted from Class 1 to 1A.

Without exception, the teachers were good and very hard-working – often going far beyond the curriculum at the time to organise regular debates and teach us about classical music. I was not very good at debating, but I always pushed myself forward in the belief that one day the experience would come in useful. It did, and I now find myself giving around one hundred speeches a year around the world!

I worked very hard during those first three years and did well enough in my Inter Cert exams to be promoted into the top class the following year. I was secretly pleased to have caught up with the townies, as we called the more affluent pupils from Ballaghaderreen. My parents and relatives were delighted and decided that I should become a boarder.

I was pleased about this, but totally unprepared for the spartan diet that came with boarding in St. Nathy's. Before long, I learned a lot about the taste of stale bread and sliced cold beef, and began to realise how lucky I had been at home with my mother's simple cooking. I will never forget the refectory, where Fr. Johnson, the Dean, circled the room at meals. Like most others, I had a jar of banned jam between my legs at breakfast and usually managed to apply some of it to the underside of a slice of bread before the Fr. Johnson came back into view. The horrors of an accident, when jam fell on one's trousers to leave a sticky mess, are still with me. So too are the cold showers and the experience of shaving with cold water.

The only respite from the College food came on Sundays, when parents were allowed to visit. My mother was wonderful, bringing in lovely sandwiches and lots of tasty slices of ham. I tried to make the ham last, but soon came to realise that it went rancid after a few days. On one occasion, a few friends and I were so hungry we decided on a gamble – we would clean the Oratory in the hope that the Sisters would be appreciative enough to give us a big meal in return. The gamble worked and the four of us had a regular job every two weeks until we left the College.

As my time at St. Nathy's drew to a close in 1967, there was much talk about the annual prize essay, which always seemed to have been won by a very academic senior – typically a pupil who was also a good Irish speaker – year after year. Although nobody mentioned me as a possible candidate, I decided to have a go. The specified topic for the essay was 'The Itinerant Problem in Ireland' and, desperate for inspiration, I decided to seek outside help. Could it be that there might be some recent government research that might help me, I wondered? So it was that I wrote to my old contact James Dillon in Dail Eireann.

However, the lazy summer weeks and months passed by and there was no reply from him. Then, to my great delight, with just a few days to go to the deadline for submitting the essay, a large brown envelope arrived in the post with a compliment slip from the great parliamentary orator. It was an unpublished official study of the very topic for the essay! I quoted liberally from it in my composition – and may have given the impression that I had done far more research than I actually had.

This is how Michael Lafferty came to win the 1967 St. Nathy's Prize Essay competition.

• 28 •

College Life as a Student
in St. Nathy's

Anthony McNamara

LC 1969; Chief Superintendent Mayo Division

1964. It seems like a different age, an indeed was a different age. An era long before the ubiquitous mobile phone, iPod or PlayStation, but no less exciting and adventurous for all that. My first time away from home, away from my family, away from the rugged beauty of Achill Island, was to attend the famed St. Nathy's College as a boarding student. It all sounded so exciting in that summer of 1964, as Kevin English and I fished in his uncle's curragh and planned our new lives and future which lay ahead of us. We had heard all of the stories of the teachers, mostly priests – some tough but mostly gentle – as well as of the dormitories, refectory, oratory, football fields and not least the handball alleys. Yes, St. Nathy's produced the finest handballers in Ireland; everybody knew that.

Alas! The stories never quite prepared us for the imposing and foreboding edifice that was St. Nathy's College, as our minibus drove through the gates on that dusky September evening in 1964. As first years, we were directed to the top-floor dormitory in the 'new wing'. It seemed like the largest room I had ever seen in my life and, with its high ceiling and well-worn timber floor, I wondered what the 'old wing' was like. I will never forget that first night; my first night away from home, in a strange bed, huge windows with no curtains or blinds, but most of all I remember the clock. Yes, that old clock on the Cathedral, which chimed religiously every fifteen minutes without fail and would continue to do so for the following five years I spent in St. Nathy's; but long before then it had entered into my subconscious. I had not been in bed by 10.00pm since I passed the age of ten years; but, on that first night in the College, I was and heard every bell chime until that clock struck 4am, I am sure.

Another sound that was to become as customary and tedious as the Cathedral clock was the morning bell at 7.30am, calling all to rise and pray. The daily morning mass in the Oratory at 8.00am was to be another custom that I had to get used to in my College days. Those early days were filled with excitement because so much was new. New classrooms; new subjects I knew nothing of such as French, Latin and science; new classmates from places I had never heard of like Cloonacool, Coolaney, Kilmovee and Keelogues; and the sporting facilities for Gaelic football, not to mention the famed handball. Dermot Earley, a fifth year who is now chief of Staff in the Army, was a colossus in our young eyes to be admired and emulated; what an example for any young boy in his formative years. Study and night times in those days was filled with loneliness and thoughts of home. What would my father be doing at this time; home from a hard day's work, his overalls splattered with cement, a days growth of stubble, after his tea and asleep on the chair beside the fire.

I did not know it then, but those were formative days in my life, a time that would shape my character and teach me lifelong lessons on equality, sharing, fairness, truth and honesty, and looking out for one another. As those early days rolled into weeks, and the weeks into months, those traits and the new college life surrounded us like an ocean wave. Now the thoughts turned to monthly exams, but even more so to the college teams. How would the 'Seniors' do against Summerhill in the first round of the Connaught Colleges Football Championship? Somebody called it: 'Cath Cnoc a tSamhraidh'. Then there was the Juniors, or was it the Minors and the Juveniles; that is where we came in to the reckoning. Imagine the chance to play for St. Nathy's and wear the famed green jersey. It was all so exciting!

Although I left St. Nathy's in June of 1969, and while sadly I have never been back to this day, in a funny way St. Nathy's has never left me. I pass the College on a weekly basis on my way to and from Dublin where my work brings me. I gaze at the windows at the top floor of the 'new wing' and many thoughts come flooding back to me just as if it were yesteryear. So many thoughts, all of them good. I can say that with all of the honesty instilled into me in St. Nathy's more than forty-five years ago. I remember the teachers – both clerical and lay – too numerous to mention individually and so dedicated to our education and development. I will remember that sense of equality and fairness instilled in us; how we were treated equally, regardless of our background. How you could only spend two shillings (what were they!) in the twice-weekly shop in the College.

In the days before free education, it was only right to remember Fr. Doherty, or 'George' as he was known to us as students; he was the President of the College during my five years there. It is a fact, although hard to believe in the inflationary times of today, that the annual fees for a boarder never increased over that period. It was due in no small measure to the prudence and diligence of Fr. Doherty that the fees remained at the sum of £80 per annum, payable quarterly. Although my late father never met Fr. Doherty, he was grateful for his careful husbandry at St. Nathy's and always had the big red £20 note ready for me each September, Halloween, Christmas and Easter. Money was not easily come by in Achill or elsewhere back then, but that was another lesson I learned in St. Nathy's subconsciously.

It's funny how life turns out sometimes. In my fifth year at St. Nathy's, and with no clear or even cloudy idea about a future career, four of us asked the Dean, Fr. Andy Johnston, for permission to go down to the Garda Station in

Ballaghaderreen to make an application to join the Garda Siochana; really, all we wanted was to get a few free classes away from Leaving Certificate preparation as most in the group had no interest of a career in the Gardai. In fact, two did not even make the height qualification! That chance visit to the Garda Station led me to a wonderful and fulfilling career of thirty-nine years in An Garda Siochana, which still continues (for another while anyway, God willing).

Here again is another funny story relating back to St. Nathy's. The first weeks in the then Training Centre (now the Garda College) in Templemore, were considered to be pretty tough for the twenty-seven recruits of the class of October 1969. So tough in fact that one hardy Kerryman had enough after a week and went home. But for a young eighteen-year-old from Achill Island, who had just completed five years in Nathy's, this was a holiday camp by comparison. I loved every minute of it.

Yes, as I look back on a successful career in An Garda Siochana, I have a lot to be grateful for. I think of my father a lot and I also think of my days in St. Nathy's, where, as well as receiving a good education, we were also provided with so much more that I cannot put into words.

I regret with my impetuosity of youth, I did not thank the President or my teachers at the time, although many are now gone to God to enjoy the well deserved fruits of their labours; I belatedly and gratefully thank them now. To those who still serve and follow in their illustrious footsteps, I say – may God bless you and keep up the good work.

'Robur Nathaei'

• 29 •

An Open Letter

Hughie Quinn

LC 1969; Scientist and Entrepreneur

It was a lovely Wednesday afternoon – a half-day at St. Nathy's – in mid-September during my first year as a teenager and I was trying to get a game of handball on the first year's handball alley – the one just at the end of the 'walk' – when suddenly I heard someone call my name and yell: "Tog out." I looked around to see who it was that was barking at me. He was a burly lad with huge thighs. I thought, well, this cannot be all that bad seeing that the one ordering me around looked like he could play football – the love of my young life – and since it was abundantly clear that there would be no handball game for me on this day, I accepted the call and set off for the dormitory to get my 'stuff'.

Sleeping in the New Wing

I arrived at St. Nathy's in the fall of 1964 when I was in my thirteenth year. I can still recall the fear that overcame me the minute I entered the building and saw the enormity of the high ceilings just inside the entrance hall of the 1914 building extension. Moreover, the length of that high corridor, with the designs on the floor running parallel to the walls, had the same effect on me as the white line on the road during my not-so-familiar car ride coming in from Charlestown to Ballaghaderreen.

I do not remember much else about the activities of that first evening except going to bed in the 'new wing', which was above what I would come to know later as the refectory and which had the stairs with the terrazzo finish. I had received a package of chocolate biscuits from my mother before leaving home (a novelty in those days, at least for me) and, when the lights went out, I tackled them, more out of fear of my intimidating surroundings than any great affinity for chocolate, which I never liked. I finished the biscuits and went to sleep. Suddenly, I was awake and, while attempting blind man's bluff in the dark not knowing which way I was pointed, I threw up the entire contents of my stomach partly on my own bed and partly between that of my neighbour and mine. I will never forget the balance of that night. I lay awake not knowing which way the toilet was if I should need to go again, and how I would clean up the mess I had created before I was 'caught' in the morning. I must have drifted to sleep eventually, because I have a clear recollection, even to this day, of being awakened by the sound of that infernal bell – the one strategically placed outside the door adjacent to the courtyard, directly opposite the old army barracks with the ivy-covered walls – only to find that the mess I had envisaged in the dark was twice as bad as I had imagined when viewed in the bright light of those dangling fluorescent bulbs hanging from the rafters. My prefect was from Bunninaden, a tall gangly fellow with red hair. He told me where to find a bucket and mop and, as quickly as I could, I cleaned up the mess while, at the same time, hoping that no one would remember who I was. Such was my first experience sleeping away from home.

Nomenclature

The boy with the huge thighs was from Sligo. That was a good thing for me, because Even though I knew that I was in the town of Ballaghaderreen, which is all of twenty miles, give or take, from where I come from in Sligo, I might as well have been in Timbuktu. I remember getting a lift to Charlestown once in our neighbour's dilapidated Volkswagen (not everyone owned a car back then) to see Mickey Kearns playing for Sligo in 1962. That was the game against Roscommon in which Paddy Christy, my own clubman, missed the penalty and the man from Bunninaden mis-kicked the fifty, only to present the great Gerry O' Malley with a gift, which he summarily converted into a match-ending goal.

Once outside of Charlestown, however, my calibration was turned off and, accordingly, one place was just as foreign to me as another. I was grateful then to find out that not only was the burly boy the captain of the juvenile football team, but he was also a fellow Sligoman. I learned from him during those first few weeks that the juveniles were confined to train in the top field, the juniors in the bottom field, and the 'new field' – the one that bordered Bothairbui – was reserved for the senior team. The inter-house leagues would be played in the top and bottom fields, which meant that the juveniles had to wallow in the mud between in-house league games during the wet winter months, which spanned just about the entire academic year, of course!

It was during one of those early training sessions that, covered from head to toe with that slithery slime, I came to know Fr. Gavigan, aka Sike. Everyone had a nickname in those days and it was not always complimentary. The Dean of discipline, however, was from my own nick of the woods, so I will take the liberty of divulging our nomenclature for him. We attended the same national school Castlerock, which was a three-teacher school nestled at the foot of the Ox mountains – a detail that I learned many years later when I met him at a reunion of the then famous school. He was sandy-haired and tall, with large sinuous hands – a feature that I became familiar with before my time was spent within those hallowed halls. You see, he used to clasp both my hands with his, and, with our fingers entwined, he would bend my wrists backwards until, with my back arched and my knees on the ground, I would have no choice but to answer truthfully and own up to whatever transgression I was guilty of at that particular moment. In addition, there were many such moments. However, lest you get the impression that this was cruel and unusual punishment, it was better in my view than the alternative. I always admired the fact that, when he caught me in the act, he dispensed his punishment there and then and the matter was concluded. I was more than capable of standing up to his enforced acrobatics, which we both knew was a better alternative than having to report to the President or some other fate which might be even worse, like detention for instance, which I considered a fate worse than death.

One evening, while making a b-line for the dormitory with mud dripping from every part of my body after one of those mud-wallowing training sessions referred to above, I was stopped cold in my tracks by the pronouncement, "It is far from indoor showers you were reared. Get outside and wash that mud off in the drain." I had to back-track out to the bridge at the entrance to the new field, which had about two feet of running water beneath, even in the month of June, and after getting into the drain, I washed off as much mud as possible. I instinctively knew, of course, that there would be a further inspection before I could re-enter the building, so there was no question of not doing a thorough job. Alas, what was I thinking? Even though I passed his inspection and was allowed to re-enter the building, I still got a chastisement to presumably memorise the occasion and remind me that, if in the future, should I contemplate a repeat of the performance, there was more where that came from.

The Crows of September

The first-year class of 1964 was bifurcated into class 1 (honours) and class 1A (pass). Class 1, of which I was a part, was assigned the class room next to the graveyard on the ground floor and, looking out the corner window, one could read the time on the cathedral clock, not that it was necessary to actually see the clock in order to establish what time it was because, after a few weeks of listening to that ding-dong, ding-dong, ding-ding-ding-dong, the time was indelibly imprinted on one's subconscious.

Indeed, it seems to me now, in retrospect, that the sound of that clock, which was reminiscent of the repeatability of a pendulum in simple harmonic motion, more than any other single entity represented the inevitability of everything that was St. Nathy's in those days. We did everything by the sound of that clock. For instance, at the very first decibel of the emitted sound, which signalled the end of study period on a Sunday morning, the ruailla-buailla could be heard in Gortaganny as everyone darted for the door and the sprint for the handball alleys began.

The same ritual took place at the end of a class period, with the exception that, in some cases, certain teachers took issue with the clock being the decision maker, rather than the teacher himself (I am intentionally being sexist here because there were no female teachers in St. Nathy's then), and would accordingly drag their feet at the culmination of class just to show the students who was boss.

The clock was not the only element of the cathedral that sticks in my memory. After football training there was 'first study', which commenced at 5.30pm sharp. In the month of September, it would still be bright outside at this time, but by the end of the study period at 7.00pm, it would just be getting dark and I have a clear recollection of a spectacular event that I witnessed for the first time as I looked out the window of that classroom in 1964. This event was the massive collection of crows that would assemble just above the Cathedral and continue to fly in seemingly endless concentric circles about the spire while, at the same time, creating an enormous din of 'cawing'.

I remember watching them for almost the entire study period once and wishing that, if reincarnation were in fact a reality, I would want to come back as a crow. Such was the desire I had to be free of the confines of that institution and, like the crows, be at liberty to fly away to whatever destination my heart desired. Is it not amazing that, when one is young, there is no limitation to the mind's ability to extrapolate the unthinkable? This is in stark contrast to one's ever-increasing lack of imagination as the years slip by, when the unthinkable becomes the impossible and the mundane becomes the unthinkable. I have often since reflected on this congruence of circling jackdaws and my ability then to visualise them as the ambassadors of everything that was desirable in that seemingly majestic world back then of unlimited adventure and unfulfilled ambitions.

A Special Relationship

There were two lay teachers in St. Nathy's back in my day. One was a rugby player who lived on Bothairbui; at least he used to walk to school and came from that direction. He taught me English in my last two years. I liked English and was reasonably good at it. Actually, come to think of it, there were just three activities at which I was content during my confinement at St. Nathy's. I say content because happy would be too strong a word. Those activities were, in order of preference, on the football field, in class, and in bed. I liked the football field because there I did not feel the confines of the institution and there I lived in a zone of complete dedication to mastering the art of catching and kicking a football. Mind you, I never envisaged the challenge of playing Gaelic Football as the ability to act in concert with fourteen other team mates in order to score more points than the other team, which was also comprised of fifteen team mates dedicated to the same objective.

As I look back on it now, I realise that the selfish view of the game as a personal challenge to master the mechanics of putting a round ball into flight was an acquired characteristic, rather than something one was born with and had its origin in the vacuum of no proper coaching as a young fellow. I suppose this all means that if I had it to do all over again, I would probably have done it differently and, who knows, maybe the outcome of some of those cliffhanger games might have gone in my favour as opposed to the alternative. Indeed, I sometimes wonder that it is perhaps the tradition in Kerry for youngsters to see the wisdom in team play, as opposed to individual heroism, and that it is this characteristic that is responsible for their domination of this heavenly form of adolescent recreation.

I loved the process of learning and above all else, I think, my curiosity was paramount in those days. I simply wanted to know everything. Of course, wanting to know and gaining the knowledge were two different things. In any event, I liked class and can truthfully say that there was not a single teacher in the school that I did not like, and I think the feeling was reasonably mutual. In bed, I felt I was free. In other words, the rules of the school could not penetrate me during my sleep and I looked forward to going to bed because it was, in a sense, a statement of defiance. I am not sure why I felt that way, but I think it had something to do with my non-conformist attitude.

Returning now to the rugby player, it was in my last two years at the school that I really got to know him. Prior to that, I thought that his view of the world was a bit harsh, as evidenced by his favourite declaration that the Primary Certificate, which at that time was the only evidence one had of having graduated from national school, was in his view "the bridge of asses", meaning that one only needed the brain of a donkey to pass that exam. He would sometimes ask a student who had failed to impress him if he had gotten his Primary Cert and, when the student in question would invariably answer yes, he would bark back: "Well, frame it because it is the only one you will ever get!"

Because our class was small in number, we occupied a small classroom just inside the main entrance on the right hand side of the entrance door for both of my last two years. I had the last desk beside the huge window that looked out directly at the gates, which guarded the entrance to the College. Directly beneath the window was a large radiator, which used to be warm and even hot sometimes. At the beginning of class, the rugby player would give out a class assignment such as reading an act of King Henry IV or memorizing one of the sonnets, and then he would lean his right elbow on the window, very close to the heat, and in whispering tones he and I would discuss football tactics. Especially before a big game, with St. Mary's or St. Jarlath's for instance, he would question me on my fitness and whether I thought we had a team good enough to win. I can truthfully recite that I cannot remember a single thing that we talked about concerning the English curriculum for the Leaving Certificate throughout those last two years, but I remember almost every detail of every conversation we had about Gaelic football and rugby. Oh, how I miss moments like those now. *Ar dheis De go raibh a annam.*

The Special Dinner

There were eight prefects chosen from the senior class each year and, in the words of Miheal O'Hehir, they consisted of two halves – the first half and the second half. You see, there was an unwritten pecking order attached to the prefects within which the first four were considered top ranking, which means I suppose that the second four were of a lower calibre. I offer no explanation for this other than to say it was one of those unexplained mysteries ,of which there were many in those days of 'do not ask any questions and you will not be told any lies'. The prefects would take charge of the classrooms during study period and the dormitories after lights out. They were sort of a 'management' team that helped to run the institution. In return for their services, they were rewarded with a special dinner. They got chips when we got bread; they got fish with their chips when we just got chips; and they got black pudding when we got dry bread. Oh, a special dinner really was a big deal back then.

It was the fall of 1968 and I had just returned from Croke Park, after having played in the All Ireland minor football final. I was let out of the College for the final under the watchful eye of one of my teachers, who happened to also be in charge of the senior football team that year and an old football mentor of mine going back to the days when I played under-twelve Gaelic football on the old pitch in Tourlestrane. He used to referee under-age games there when he was a Chaplain in Tubbercurry. Like me, he had arrived at St. Nathy's as a teacher in the same year that I did (1964). As a result of our extended relationship, we were good buddies both on and off the field. I was more than happy that he travelled with me for that great occasion because he was one of the founders of the minor board in County Sligo and, as much as anyone, was responsible for setting in place the fundamentals that led to our success in the championship run that year.

Incidentally and unfortunately, however, we lost by a single point. On my return to the College after the disappointing loss in Dublin, I was attending first study when the teacher on study-watch informed me that I was to report to the President's room. This, I thought, was decidedly bad news for me. The President and I were not cut from the same cloth and, accordingly, our respective views of the world were emphatically poles apart, which made me feel that maybe I was due a difficult time. Dutifully I made my way up those wide stairs at the end of the long corridor to the second floor on which his room was located, fully prepared to face the music. I knocked, entered and was told to sit down. The President gave me a long speech about responsibility and setting a good example. Eventually, he got around to telling me that I had been chosen as Senior House Captain, something that I was surprised at. You see, since I was passed up for a prefect, I felt that I was not one of the chosen few and, accordingly, had contented myself to focus on playing football and learning as much as I could before finishing the following summer. I became progressively ticked-off, though, hearing about all this responsibility stuff with no apparent mention of any corresponding beneficial collateral and, picking up a bit of courage when he emphasized that being captain of the senior football team was a more important job than a prefect, I chirped in saying: "Well, if it is Father, there is not much of a dinner out of it." Well the effect! That was a BIG mistake. Now the fat was in the fire. He became hostile; the tone of his voice became decidedly ugly and increased an octave or two. To make a long story short, he ordered me back to study and gave me a swift kick in the posterior as I walked out of his room. I remember thinking to myself as the sting of his shoe percolated from my tailbone up through the successive vertebrae of my spine, so much for the concept of the carrot and the stick. I still recall, however, snickering with my buddies back at study at the very thought of how he reacted to my failed attempt to negotiate the coveted special dinner. Notwithstanding my lack of success at gaining a place at the last-supper table, I felt that I had won that round and was delighted to cherish the small victory with my friends.

The Land of Opportunity

In a small village in the west of Ireland in the county of Sligo there dwelt a certain Austin O'Hara, his faithful and thrifty wife and their nine children – five sons and four daughters. The sole support of this family depended on the produce of a small farm of about fourteen acres. Weather conditions played a big part in the yield of this land, due to the lack of drainage and irrigation facilities. It was the year 1876 and poverty prevailed in many villages and hamlets in this rain-soaked region.

The O'Hara family was no exception to this tidal wave of despair that permeated the hearts of the villagers. One member of the family, James, a spunky lad of sixteen, decided to seek fame and fortune elsewhere, even though he knew that his education could not carry him far because he had not even graduated from grammar school. His big problem was getting enough money to take him from home to anyplace where he might get employment. James remembered that his mother had a small cash box with a large padlock that contained the very small family fortune. This he decided to break open and found one pound, a sum of great value in those days because it was enough to pay his passage from Ireland to England, with some left to spare. His mind made up, he left home for the nearest railroad station, which was eighteen miles by foot. If he were lucky, he might get a lift from a farmer on a horse and cart or a jaunting car.

Hours after his departure, the discovery of the missing cash was made and his failure to report home put the family detectives in motion. His father opined that he would go to England, but he would not reach the railroad station until the following day. He borrowed a horse from a more fortunate townsman, a tax collector, and set out that night for the railroad station. The first train left at seven o'clock in the morning and he wanted to be there before that time. He managed to get there in time and, sure enough, there was his son James waiting for the train. He talked to him kindly and begged him to come home. After much persuasion, James climbed onto the horse behind his father and rode home. There was great jubilation in the O'Hara family when the father returned with James, who told his mother how sorry he was and gave her the whole pound note he had stolen.

A month later, he left home again and his entire capital was one shilling. The family missed him, but did not worry because they figured he would be back soon when his funds were depleted. James, on the second venture, made up his mind that there would be no turning back. His die was cast to be the vanguard of a crusade or a hostage of destiny. After weary miles of travel, he found himself working for a farmer, some thirty miles from home, where he earned enough to take him to England. Here he worked in the coal mines for a few months. Being an opportunist and a man of great ambition, he fitted the pattern of a pioneer, so that one day he reached the goal of his aspirations by procuring a job on a cattle boat to Australia.

Now James was a young man in a new continent and he started work with a building contractor who gave him plenty of opportunity to advance due to his pleasing personality and progressive capabilities. In the years that followed, James amassed a fortune in enterprises that he used to very good advantage in educating a godson, who later became a priest, as well as other children to various professions. His first visit to his native Ireland was in 1912, when he sent nine nieces and nephews to college to be educated for various professions. On this first visit, he was fifty-two years old and his sisters and brothers did not recognize him until he introduced himself.

His death in 1915 climaxed a frugal life of a poor boy that made good in the 'Land Down Under'. Thomas F. Quinn, my paternal uncle, penned this account of the exploits of James O'Hara, who was his maternal grand-uncle and, therefore, my great-grand-uncle. My first cousin, Mary Joan Kelley (nee Quinn), actually typed the manuscript as my uncle, Tom, her father, dictated it to her when she was a teenager in their home in Boston, USA, and she is now the custodian of the original document. My uncle was one of the grand nephews who benefited from the money set aside by James to educate his extended family, and because of it, he was able to attend St. Nathy's College from 1913 to 1918.

Tom Quinn was a good athlete in St. Nathy's and subsequently at Maynooth College, where he studied for the priesthood. I had the occasion to visit him in the 1980s during the last days of his life in a Boston hospital. During that visit, I was astonished by two of his remarkable attributes. Firstly, since he was in his eighties, I was amazed by his clarity of thought as he took me through his recollection of the Easter Rising and his vivid accounts of his sporting exploits while in St. Nathy's. Secondly, I was impressed by his athletic accomplishments both at St. Nathy's and Maynooth College. In particular, he told me that he was good at track and field, having won the long jump and the hop-step-and-jump at St. Nathy's. In addition, he informed me that he was the senior handball champion in his final year. He went on to recount for me the three matches he played in that final handball senior league competition and could even articulate the ebb and flow of the score in the final game. I was particularly impressed with this degree of clarity of recollection since fifty-one years later in 1969 I too had also won the senior handball league but, unlike him, I could not match his blow-by-blow account of the final match.

Finally, as my tribute to the ingenuity of my great-grand-uncle, James O'Hara, I can report herein that he was responsible for putting in motion not only the education of a single grand-nephew at St. Nathy's College, but also a line of his descendants that has spanned almost the entire second one hundred years of St. Nathy's history. These were, starting with my uncle Tom Quinn (1913-1918); my cousin Tom (Dennis) O'Hara (circa 1915); my brother, also Tommy Joe Quinn (1954-1959); my cousin Padraic Maye (1954- 1959) and his brother Willie Maye (1966-1971); myself (1964-1969); and, finally, my nephews, John Quinn (1980-1985) and Michael Quinn (1982-1988).

1968 – A Year To Remember

The winter and spring of the 1967 to 1968 school year was wet. All the football pitches in the College were waterlogged. This was arguably the best year in the history of the College from a football perspective. I make exceptions for the years of 1957 and 1959 when, in the former, the College won the All Ireland Senior College's title and, in the latter, when they were a runner-up in the same competition. I am obliged to make these exceptions, if for no other reason than the captain of the 1957 team (Rev. Fr.) Eamon O'Hara, as well as the youngest member of that team, my cousin Padraic Maye, are both from my own club (Tourlestrane). The spring of 1968 was unique, however, because all three of the St. Nathy's football teams – Juveniles, Juniors and Seniors – were in contention for honours. In fact, it turned out to be the first time that all three teams won the Connaught title. The Juvenile team registered a spectacular accomplishment by defeating archrivals St. Jarlath's College, Tuam, by 10 points in the Connaught final. This was the first of the finals that year and it had a drag-along effect on the other teams.

I was the captain of the Junior team that year and my position on the team was centre field. We beat St. Muredachs, Ballina, and Summerhill College, Sligo, in the first two rounds of the competition. We were drawn against St. Joseph's of Galway in the Connaught final and the venue was Tuam stadium. It was a wet and windy day, and the game was a hard fought, very tight affair. We were down by two points (1-2 to 3 points) at halftime, after having played with the wind in the first half. The half-time score did not bode well for us, but in the second half we came alive and took it to the opposition with a vengeance. I can still remember that during second half, our lanky right full back from Castlerea, Noel Brennan, launched his patented rocket-like free-outs into the wind, which were a pleasure to catch.

Eventually, the match turned on a free kick, close to the end of the game, and that is still vivid in my memory. We were playing into the goals, which are at the end furthest from the stadium entrance, and the foul occurred at about the thirty-five yard line, but was very much to the right of the goal posts. This means that for a right-footed free taker, the angle is not well suited and, in addition, the wind was coming from the left. To make matters worse, the distance was just about at the outer range of my free-taking distance capability, all of which added up to a very high degree of difficulty. A single redeeming feature, however, which the opposition graciously provided, enabled me to convert the free. The opposition all fell back to the goal line as I stepped back to prepare my run-up to taking the free. Usually, well-coached players know that in this circumstance, at least one opposing player should take a position no more or less than fourteen yards from the placed ball and, with outstretched arms, create an obstacle in the path of a low rising free. This defensive tactic dictates that the free taker must hit a pop up that, in a stiff crosswind, is a total disaster. By falling back to the goal line, this allowed me to chose exactly such a low shot, which I knew was the only way that I could hope to cover the requisite distance between me and the crossbar. I was able to hit the low-rising shot with topspin and by starting the ball well to the right of target, the usual right to left trajectory, which topspin creates for a right-footed kicker, carried the ball over the crossbar with about two inches of elevation to spare. This was either the equalising or the go-ahead point just before the full-time whistle and, accordingly, it had a demoralising impact on the opposition. We went on to finish with a flourish and carry home the second Connaught trophy of the year on that day.

The Senior campaign was a drawn-out affair. We opened the competition with a demoralising loss to St. Muredachs, Ballina. This caused consternation in the camp because we were a focused lot and, thereafter, there was 'wigs on the green' at training each evening. Indeed, we had ploughed up the football pitches so bad that arrangements were made with some farmer on the outskirts of Ballaghaderreen to allow us to use his pasture field as a training pitch. I can still see the ditch that ran around this field, and visualize the line of bare lily-white butts arranged in a straight line along its banks as the team changed into our usual mud-wallowing attire. The net result of this outsourcing of resources paid off because we crushed Summerhill College in the next game, running out winners by seven points. The opposition in the semi-final was our nemesis, St. Jarlath's of Tuam, and the encounter was just as good as advertised. The game ended in a draw, 0-11 to 1-8, but I cannot now recall which team got the goal. The replay was a different story. Our team on that day was magnificent. Mel Flanagan, our team captain from Boyle, provided the leadership and, in co-operation with his counterpart at centre field, Sean Kilbride, they dominated the skies that day at midfield. At the culmination of play, we ran out winners on the score of 1-7 to 0-7 and broke a nine-year stranglehold by Jarlath's on the coveted Connaught title. The last remaining game in Connaught, the final, was against St. Mary's Galway and after beating Jarlath's, we were a cocky bunch. Indeed, I can remember the final being somewhat of an anticlimax; such was the impact of beating our archrival in the semi-final. We won the final in convincing fashion, even though the score line of 1-5 to 0-3 appeared to suggest that it was a close game. I had the good fortune, operating in a wing half-forward position, to be the one who crashed home the winning goal in this game, which, as I remember, was a source of bragging rights for a while back in the farmer's field.

By virtue of having defeated the best in Connaught that year, we travelled to Portlaoise to take on Colaiste Chriost Ri from Cork in the all Ireland semi-final. I remember on our approach to the pitch there that I was awestruck at the impeccable manner in which the field was prepared, especially in light of the fact that we had forgotten what green grass looked like. After a hard fought game, both teams finished with a score of 1-7, another drawn game. The replay was held in Limerick and the high scoring game produced a resulting score of 2-11 to 0-15 but, unfortunately, we were the ones holding the short end of the stick. Our opposition went on to win the All Ireland final, subsequently beating Belcamp of Dublin in Croke Park on a score of 3-11 to 1-10. I remember that we were all devastated after the loss, but looking back on it now, I hold this 1968 college football campaign high on my list of favourite memories.

A Unique Mentor

One of the most vivid recollections I retain of my time in St. Nathy's was the feeling in my stomach as I clawed my way through the mass of anxious football onlookers crowded around the bulletin board on a Thursday night to see if I had made the football team for the following Sunday's game. It was the practice then for the person in charge of the football team – usually one of our teachers and always a priest – to get together with the team captain on a Thursday or Friday night in his room and pick the team for the following Sunday. After the team was picked, it would be written out in handwriting and the captain would append it to one of the bulletin boards accessible to all students. I remember during my final year, when it was my turn to assist in the team picking, one such occasion in particular, when I went up to the room of the then Senior team mentor to pick the team. Since he was also my Greek teacher and it was approaching the Christmas break, I suppose it was natural that he happened to be working on his test questions for the Christmas exams when I arrived at his room. He was a serious man who, in order to stress a point, made a slight pause before and after the important syllable in a sentence and lowered his voice when he wanted to make a particular impression, rather than raising it. Accordingly, I quickly came to the conclusion that he was a man endowed with an unconventional mentality which, for some inexplicable reason, was a favourite theory of mine around that time.

You see, the concept of opposites was always running through my head in those days because I was continuously trying to improve my technique of kicking a football, which every free-taker knows calls for an opposite mentality. If you want the ball to go from outside to inside, you must kick it from inside to outside (draw in golf). Conversely, if you want the ball to go from inside to outside, you must kick it from outside to inside (fade in golf). This feature of putting a ball in flight always baffled me back then and I remember spending many long evenings in summertime, after we had finished cocking the hay, trying to understand it and, in fact, disprove this seemingly stupid characteristic of ball flight by repeatedly kicking the football first with my right foot and then with my left foot using the hay cocks as goalposts. I never did succeed in overturning this fundamental law of nature, but I got a few clippings from my father for overturning the haycocks that we spent all day grooming. On a more positive note though, a side effect of my experimentation was that I became ambidextrous, a characteristic that I used to torture more than one unsuspecting full-back before the sand ran out of the hour glass on the field of play.

Learning Greek, on the other hand, was a double-edged sword for me inasmuch as I enjoyed hearing about the strange goings on in Greek mythology, but that lexicon stuff, and translating those long passages that invariably contained the same syllables like the τους πολιμιους – which has something to do with horses I think – well I could take that stuff or leave it. In fact, there was one occasion when, despite the fact that I should have known better, my exploits with Greek translations and the unconventional mentality of our aforementioned mentor conspired to produce the only occasion when I received the formal punishment of six slaps of the cane on the outstretched hands. This was no big deal for me because I hailed form a national school where '*se cinn gan ceist*' was the standing order of the day, but in St. Nathy's, and especially with our Greek teacher, it was extremely uncommon. It happened during my third year when we were in the only classroom on the second floor that was directly over the one I described during our first year. Again, I occupied the desk in the back of the class which I shared with my good friend from Bothairbui who was a day-boy (that was our term for students who did not stay overnight in the College). Even though it was not my favourite thing to do, I usually had the translating thing under control, but my friend had the reputation of sometimes not coming to school fully prepared for a discussion of the Classics. In any event, on this particular occasion, as a reward for prompting my friend under my breath, I was ordered to walk to the front of the class and extend my hands for the aforementioned medicine. I knew instinctively of course that there would be an unconventional solution and, after the fact, I realised that I had experienced what was really meant by the expression η επιτηδεια.

Back in his room, there was little space available to work on picking the team because of the exam papers that were strewn all over his bed and on the floor. The priest's rooms back then were more akin to 'coach' rather than 'first class', and accordingly space was at a premium. As I attempted to assist him in clearing a space on his bed where we could start to layout the team on a piece of paper, I noticed that the test questions for my class were front and centre. Being ever vigilant, he noticed that I was trying to get a preview through my side-eye and, without delay, he pushed the pile of test questions under the bed out of my range of view, which was, for someone in my frame of mind, a provocative development. We finished picking the team and, as usual, I placed copies of the selection on all available bulletin boards.

However, on the following day, it was not within my nature to overlook the fact that the Greek exam papers were sitting invitingly under his bed, while at the same time my mentor was supervising the ongoing exams down in the great hall. It was not because I had any doubts about my ability to do well in the test – I always got a good mark in Greek – but more I think due to some inner force that compelled me to think that an opportunity like this should not be overlooked, regardless of their merit, that I decided after confirming that he was in fact on exam duty, to quietly slip into his room and strategically relieve him of a single test paper. Having successfully completed step one of the plot, it was off for the lexicon and step two, which consisted of going through each of the exam questions and ensuring that my answers were lexicon-proof. In addition, I concluded that I had better keep the information to myself lest my plot be discovered as a result of loose lips sinking ships. However, I eventually shared my secret with a class mate, who was a piper from Kiltimagh.

Notwithstanding all the shenanigans however, we won the match on that following Sunday, I did a perfect Greek exam the following week and, feeling full of myself and that everything was 'cool' (to borrow a contemporary word) I went home for the Christmas break. I was more than surprised upon my return after the Christmas break that I received the exact same mark on the Greek test that I had received in the previous exam. What went wrong? Did I not do a perfect test and had I not got every question correct? Why did I not receive a perfect test score of one hundred percent? These were the issues swimming in my head, but of course I could not ask for any explanation because of the delicate nature of the circumstances. Wisely, in retrospect, I put the whole episode behind me and turned my attention to the two major remaining objectives, which were trying to win a senior Connaught football championship and preparing to do my Leaving Cert.

On my last day at St. Nathy's, after we had finished the Leaving Cert exam and we were saying goodbye to our classmates and teachers in that long corridor referred to above, I decided to confront my mentor about the test results of the Greek Christmas exam. I was being conservative at first in explaining why I though that the mark I received was stingy at best, but in the end I came clean and admitted to what I had done. I suppose more than anything else I needed to get forgiveness before leaving the school and carrying the load of guilt with me for eternity. To my surprise, my mentor told me that he was aware of my transgression and that I should not worry about it any further. Presumably, he had the papers counted and, by a process of deductive reasoning – which was something he was particularly good at – figured out that I was the one responsible for the minus one computation or, in the alternative, my piper friend was using his lungs for something other than filling that wind-bag under his arm. In either case, I was floored by this response.

Many times, during the approximately forty years since this episode took place, I have reflected on what might have happened if my mentor had taken a different approach to dealing with what, even I would have acknowledged back then, was a serious breach of discipline. Indeed, violating the privacy of a teacher's room and stealing a test paper could easily be the basis for expulsion from the College. There were others in authority at the school then that would have certainly taken this approach. If that had happened, it could have jeopardised my Leaving Cert result and would certainly have had a major negative impact on my future. However, I was fortunate that my mentor was no ordinary teacher. He had the ability to overlook my childish pranks and put the well being of my future before all other considerations.

My experience since has taught me that it is the people we interact with more than any other single parameter that shapes our lives and determines, to a large degree, our success or failure. I have come to appreciate the extraordinarily important role of teachers and the enormous debt that a student owes to those who mould their future. If there is anything that I can convey to the crop of students who currently occupy the same desks that we did, it is that you should cherish your teachers because one day, like me, you too will look back and connect the dots just as I am doing now. For my part, I can only offer this, that the mentor whom I had for football and Greek, a seemingly unlikely combination, was not only a good teacher and an extraordinary mentor, but he was my friend when it counted most. It never entered my consciousness back then that one day, the Pope would pick him to lead the flock in the Diocese of Achonry. How appropriate!

The Science Lab in a Graveyard

During my time at the school, our science laboratory was that antique building that guards the graveyard on the right-hand side of the road as one takes the short cut to the College from the Charlestown road. To my knowledge, it is the only place on this planet where the science of the living is intermingled with the silence of the dead. Indeed, when I think about that place, I am reminded of the poem by Thomas Gray:

> The boast of heraldry, the pomp of pow'r,
> And all that beauty, all that wealth e'er gave,
> Awaits alike th' inevitable hour.
> The paths of glory lead but to the grave.

Because we visited the 'science hall' infrequently, it is a challenge for me now to recall from memory what it was like then. When I think back, however, certain unmistakable images of the place start to emerge from the fog. The entrance door was rotten and small pieces of wood had broken off so that it looked as though a hole had been created for a cat or small dog to use as an entrance – similar to what one would sometimes see in the houses of the more affluent segment of our society. Inside there was a blackboard with a track for holding the chalk, just as one might see in a large university auditorium of the day. The smell of hydrochloric acid permeated the entire place. This was presumably because it was just about the only liquid reagent stored there and was a popular item in whatever limited chemical experiments were conducted in that primitive scientific environment. There was at least one fume cupboard, possibly two, but I am not sure now. I often wondered what the purpose of the fume cupboard was. In my time, at least, the only thing we used them for was breaking stink bombs, which, in retrospect, was the closest thing to a chemical reaction we experienced there. Indeed, after the stink bomb scenarios, our clothes used to be saturated from the fall-out and, when we returned to the College to resume class in our usual classroom, the entire College wreaked of the stench of rotten eggs.

My most vivid recollection of these classes was the conduct of our teacher who, in addition to teaching us science, also taught us Latin. He used to come into our Latin class and, in a move reminiscent of John Wayne or Clint Eastwood, would draw two canes, one in each hand, from beneath his long black robes and in an excited voice proclaim: "*Disco aut dicere*", which, if memory serves, means 'learn or go home'.

There was a jar of Mercury that we had access to, and I remember we would spend the majority of class chasing the elusive heavy metal around the desk. Because of its wetting characteristics, a by-product of its angle of repose, it had a tendency to bead-up and run about a surface like a field mouse. Accordingly, the entire class would be engaged in what the seanachai would undoubtedly refer to as 'minding mice at a crossroads', as we tried to put the 'ball bearings' back into the jar.

Aside from preparing me for the reality of making my living as a lab rat, there is a more sobering theme that I would like to pass on to any future graveyard-trained, would-be scientist who might be inclined to follow a similar career path. When I first attempted to sign up for an honours course in mathematical physics at UCD, I was taken aside by the professor who, having determined from my application that I had attended what he inferred was a second-rate scientific curriculum during my secondary education, informed me that I did not have the necessary background to register for the course. I remember being furious at his audacity. Was I not entitled, having met the basic requirements, to enrol at the university to sit any course I wished, just like every body else? I politely told the professor that, since my father had contributed to the circumstances which lead up to the formation of an independent state and that, therefore, as his son, I was entitled to the best the Republic had to offer, I would be insisting on registering for the course. Under such uncompromising direct fire, he retracted and accepted my registration.

I cycled from Bellfield into Earlsforth Terrace and took my position near the back of the class during the first lecture, which is where I was most comfortable. There were only twelve students enrolled in the class and most were from prestigious secondary colleges like Clongoes Wood in Kildare and others, the names of which I cannot now recall. During that first lecture, the rest of the class were huddled together down at the first row of seats and were looking through what appeared as an important document and which I found out later was an excerpt from Newton's Principia Mathematica. The professor, most politely, asked me at the culmination of that first class if I was familiar with the work of Sir Isaac Newton. I embarrassingly responded in the negative. He said no more. He did not have to. I had received my first important lesson after leaving St. Nathy's. I was now swimming with much bigger fish in a much bigger pond than I was used to, and even though I was able to sign up for the pass course in the same subject and managed to pass the exam even, I never again made the mistake of second guessing the recommendations of a professor. Thereafter, I was content to build on the fundamentals that I did have. Even though the science hall in the graveyard adjacent to St. Nathy's left something to be desired, when stacked against some of the more advanced science curricula of the top-tier schools in the country, my training therein, nevertheless, has served me in good stead ever since.

The Last Hoorah

My last experience in the green and white jersey of St. Nathy's was a memorable occasion. It took place in the spring of 1969. Just as in the previous year, we had made it to the Senior Connaught final against St. Mary's, Galway. The game was played in their home pitch, which was in Pearce Stadium in Salthill. The playing conditions were terrible, with wind and rain spoiling the contest. The game was so bad that I am afraid I have almost no memory of it other than it ended in the dreaded draw and, of course, this meant there would be the inevitable replay. The run up to the replay was intense because of the huge progress of the previous year and the anticipation of getting a second bite of the apple. Within the College, there was a committee formed to produce small green and white flags that the supporters could bring to the match. Because the match was scheduled for Tubbercurry, the entire school would be travelling there by bus, which was an added opportunity to display the colours both on the way there and hopefully in triumph on the way back. We purchased a large quantity of white and green cloth from a vendor in downtown Ballaghaderreen and organised a chain gang to cut and staple the flags together. I remember, as a member of the chain gang, working incessantly to meet the deadline of having a flag for every student in the College by the Friday night before the game. We had permission to charge a nominal fee, which was based upon covering the cost of materials; and the distribution of the flags, as well as the collection of the fees, was completed at the last study the night before the game.

Everything went according to plan. On the morning of the game, the buses, idling back-to-back outside the College, were a remarkable sight, with the green and white flags intermingled, and the familiar smell of diesel adding additional ambiance to the already charged-up atmosphere. Unlike the first game in Galway, the day of the replay in Tubbercurry was very hot. It was a fantastic match and the ebb and flow of the game, together with the hot weather conditions, conspired to exhaust the players on both teams. Both were evenly matched and, once again, at the end of regulation time, they were deadlocked. Because this was the second time the teams finished in a tie, the outcome had to be decided in an additional half hour of overtime. During the overtime, players on both teams were dropping due to muscle cramps, but it appeared that we were more affected than the other side and it felt as though we were playing with a couple of players missing.

By the time the final whistle blew, we had come up short by a solitary point. I had managed to remain on my feet throughout the overtime, even though the expanse of ground I had to cover at midfield was evident in my gait. After I had cooled down, I was hit really badly with cramps. The trip on the bus back to the College was excruciating for me; I lay on my stomach in the centre isle of the bus and one of our teachers, the one who ran the basketball program – a particular favourite of mine, worked feverishly to disperse the muscle mass that had contracted into a dense ball in both my legs. Because of the intense pain of the muscle cramps, I did not have much opportunity to reflect on the devastating loss on the day of the game. It was during the next several days that the reality of losing the game slowly sunk in. I remember feeling low during this time. Thereafter, St. Mary's went on to the All Ireland final, but were beaten by St. Brendan's, Killarney. During the following years, I had the privilege of playing with and against many of the players on that St. Mary's team and became a team mate at UCD of the famous eight All Ireland medal holder Kerry man, John O'Keefe, who was a stalwart of that winning St. Brendan's team.

Concluding remarks

Spending five years of one's teenage years in an all-boys boarding school may not be the ideal environment in which to do so. One can succumb to what sailors often refer to as cabin fever. In addition, there are many challenges other than simply mastering the academics. For me, the concept which the call to 'tog out' came to represent was most important. It provided the mechanism within which I could change, grow and attain fulfilment. Most importantly, it has provided continuity of purpose for me these many years hence. I can only recommend to those who may follow in the next two hundred years of St. Nathy's history that they find their 'tog out' equivalent and hope that it will bring as much fulfilment to them as mine has for me.

Is mise le meas,
Aodh O'Chuinn.

• 30 •

Forewarned!

Patsy McGarry

LC 1970; Religious Affairs Correspondent Irish Times

S t. Nathy's College has educated – or attempted to educate – three generations of my family to date, with a fourth being preparing in the wings. My grand-niece Saoirse has just started playschool in Ballaghaderreen.

I cannot say for certain when our association with the College began, but it was in the month of February and in either 1930 or 1931. I can be certain of the month, but not of the year. My late uncle Sean was born in September 1917, the year after the Easter Rising and the year before the end of World War I – those two pivotal events in the life of twentieth century Ireland.

He attended primary school in Mullen, near Frenchpark in Co Roscommon, which is about seven miles from Ballaghaderreen. My grandmother was determined that her two boys – Sean and my father – would get more than a primary education. There were also two girls in the family, my late aunts May and Baby (Winifred), who were arguably both brighter that either of their brothers, but no one thought much about educating girls beyond primary level in those days. The argument went that it was the men who would have to support a family.

My grandparents did not know when the secondary school year began as neither had progressed beyond primary level. So it was in February, almost co-incident with the beginnings of the calendar year, that my grandmother brought Sean to St. Nathy's in the ass and cart. He remembered the month, but not the year. He had to be around 12 at least, he speculated, so it might have been 1930. Arriving at St. Nathy's they met the president Canon Roughneen, and my grandmother persuaded him to take on Sean as a day-boy.

He brought Sean to one of the first year classes where he was introduced as: "This blessed fellow who has neither Latin or Greek, but neither had Shakespeare*." For the following five years, Sean cycled a round-trip of 14 miles a day from Mullen to St. Nathy's and back, six days a week – there was a half day on Saturdays. He remembered many things from those days, but one that has always stuck in my

Dean Connington,
First Priest President of St. Nathy's College

1889 student photo, taken outside Cathedral

Students from St. Nathy's College at
Liturgical Festival 1956

Macbeth, 1952

Julius Caesar, 1956

1957 Team, All Ireland Senior Football Champions

1908 Football Team

1968 – Connacht Juvenile, Junior and Senior
Champions

Outdoor handball courts. C.1960

Playing courts with handball alleys in background

Collage of Sporting Heroes

Stone from St. Joseph's Convent

St. Joseph's Convent

St. Joseph's Convent staff c.1990

Vocational School staff members with students and their projects

mind was of how he studied Shakespeare by candlelight at home. The house had no electricity, even in my own childhood many decades later.

Sean never lost that sense of great privilege at being the first child from the town of Mullen to receive a secondary education. He never lost his sense of gratitude to St. Nathy's either. Not long before he died in 1999, then a retired civil servant from the Department of Agriculture, he spoke again of those days with tears of gratitude as he was sure the fees for his education were never paid because the family had no money. He could not be certain because his parents' pride would never allow him to ask, and because in all those years at St. Nathy's neither Canon Roughneen nor anyone else ever brought up the subject. He could not be sure, but he always believed those fees were never paid.

St. Nathy's played a central role in my own family's move from that house in Mullen to Ballaghaderreen in 1962. We children were coming to an age when secondary school was on the horizon. My father decided to move to Ballaghaderreen because of St. Nathy's, St. Joseph's convent secondary school and the Vocational School, all of which had a good name where education was concerned. There were six of us by then, eventually seven, and we would attend all three schools.

I spent six years at St. Nathy's, having repeated the Leaving Certificate after a pretty disastrous performance first time around. All of our teachers at the time, apart from the late Bill O'Reilly and Jimmy Flanagan, were priests. Conditions were spartan, discipline was strict and academic standards were high.

I was the first person in our first-year class to get a 'wiggin' from Bill O'Reilly, or 'Billy' as we called him. He had also taught my uncle Sean all those years before. In fact, as I discovered later, he had taught every other teacher then in St. Nathy's. He taught us English in my first year and for one class we were asked to write an essay. He told me to stand up and read mine out loud. I stood up and could not make out my own handwriting. I fumbled and mumbled, and he gripped what passed for my locks and the' wiggin' commenced. My handwriting has not improved.

Of course certain things stand out from those years – such as the late Fr. Michael Giblin's regular accounts of the journey of a much-discussed German film factory to Ballaghaderreen. Over many weeks, before commencing our Irish class, he would painstakingly trace that factory's journey through Germany to Belgium, across the English Channel, through southern England to Fishguard and from Rosslare until, as he said, it got stuck at the old Lung bridge about three miles from Ballaghaderreen.

"It cannot get through. They have to widen the bridge and God knows how long that will take," he said. Of course, and as we all knew would be the case all along, the factory never came to Ballaghaderreen. The same Fr. Giblin got the highest number of honours in Irish at St. Nathy's up to then in our class's Intermediate Certificate examinations. There was also the late Fr. Tom Lynch, who taught us history, English, and football. He trained the St. Nathy's team that won the All Ireland College final in 1957 and he tried, tried and tried again. He loved Gaelic football. His variation of that hoary old trinity went: "Lads..." – we were always 'lads' to him, he would never denigrate us by calling us 'boys'.

"Lads," he would say, "rugby is a hooligan's game played by gentlemen. Soccer is a gentlemen's game played by hooligans, and Gaelic is a gentlemen's game played by gentlemen." At which point we would all laugh.

Fr. Jimmy Colleran, who never used a cane or any instrument of punishment – rare in those days, taught us about basketball and the great outdoors, and helped us build a swimming pool in the Lung River, where we would later spend many lazy summer days. He also taught us geography, a subject I would later take to degree level. (The two others I took were history and English). He was the man I asked to be patron of a youth club we local kids set up in Ballaghaderreen.

Fr. (now Bishop) Tom Flynn had the impossible job of teaching us Greek. He was patience and perseverance personified. He even gave us grinds in his own spare time. He and his successor as President of St. Nathy's – Fr. (now Canon) Andy Johnston – were both very kind to me when doing my H.Dip in Education at the College and, later, in giving me teaching hours there in the grim 1980s. I also had hours teaching at the Vocational School when Eddie O'Reilly was Principal. Teaching hours were then as rare as profits in a recession. Another man I remember from those days, though he only taught at St. Nathy's for a short time, was Fr. (now Monsignor) Joe Spelman. We had him for English in our Inter Cert year. I cannot remember what the title of an essay he gave us was, but I do remember his reaction to what I wrote. It was around the time that Charles de Gaulle, then President of France, visited Canada and provoked an international crisis by saying in a speech there: "Vive le Quebec libre" (Long live a free Quebec). This was at a time of great tension between English- and French-speaking Canadians.

There was a line in my essay referring to this, which began "And talking of long noses..." before going on. It was a pun on de Gaulle's sizeable nose and his interference in Canadian affairs. Fr. Spelman laughed out loud at the line, was impressed by it and said so. This made a very strong impression on me at the time. All these years later, I still remember it and how chuffed I felt at his spontaneous reaction. For all I know, it might be a reason why I chose the career path I am on today.

Then there was that poor man Fr. (now Archdeacon) Paddy Kilcoyne, who was a new arrival in my later years at St. Nathy's, while also a curate in nearby Carracastle. Three or four of us 'bloods from Ballagh' were marooned after a dance in Charlestown one Sunday night and, having no choice, set off walking the 10 miles home. As we approached Carracastle, one of our number (not me!) had the bright idea of calling in on Fr. Paddy and asking him to give us a lift home. There was a furious debate about doing such a thing at that hour of the morning, but the same 'one of our number' would not be stopped and, as we debated, the deed was done. Fr. Paddy was graciousness itself and, if annoyed at all, he showed no sign of it. In fact, he seemed to be just very amused at the situation we had got ourselves into and took us home.

My brothers Sean, Pearse, Declan and Douglas also attended St. Nathy's. It survived. Since then, so have my nephews Sean, Tommy, Garry, Declan, and my nieces (who would have believed it when I was there?) Niamh, Aoife and Mary... and it is still standing!

But the question troubling all of my family just now is whether such a sturdy institution, despite its extraordinary history, can survive Saoirse?

Can the experience gained in 200 years of educating all those generations through such momentous events as the Battle of Waterloo, Catholic Emancipation, the Famine, the fall of Parnell, World War I, the 1916 Rising, the War of Independence, the Great Depression, World War II, the Cold War and the Collapse of Wall Street prepare St. Nathy's to survive our very own white (sometimes) tornado? We worry. Let us pray!

* Scholars now believe Shakespeare was taught Latin at elementary school.

• 31 •

'Twas like Emigrating at Thirteen

John O' Mahony

LC 1971; TD; Manager Mayo Senior Football Team

Going to secondary school in the 1960s was similar to entering a whole new world. Boarding at secondary school was like emigrating at 13 years of age, and it was a massive shock to the system. You were leaving your family, your primary school friends and your neighbours behind you for the first time in your life.

You were entering a world where you had to look after yourself (except if you had an older brother to look out for you – in my case Dan O'Mahony or Donal as he was known then). New friendships were formed, many of which would last a lifetime. I sat beside Donie Brennan from Chaffpool, Curry, on my first day. At that first meeting, many things were discussed such as family, getting a TV at home for the first time and of course Gaelic football – we are still talking about such things 40 years later!

You were certainly outside your comfort zone in those first few weeks. The classrooms and desks seemed bigger, the dormitories and refectory were massive, one followed the crowd so as not to get lost, the food was (being diplomatic) hard to get used to. Let us just say it was not an al a carte menu and you could get a bit of the Western People stuck along with the bread pudding!

Much has been written and said about the harshness of boarding school in all secondary schools including St. Nathy's. Coming back after Christmas was especially difficult. Will I ever forget the early freezing mornings and the long weekends with nothing but study, study and more study? Despite this, the overriding memories are all good.

Sport – whether it was handball, basketball or the major one, Gaelic football – provided a wonderful opportunity to play the game you loved, to wear the green jersey you were so proud of, and to get an occasional day away from the hum drum of college life. The football and sport kept some of us going from week to week. The guidance and coaching of Fr. Tom Lynch, Fr. Michael Joyce, Fr. Tom Flynn (now retired Bishop) and Fr. Pat Lynch was outstanding, and we hung on to every word they said. They were our Mick O'Dwyers or Alex Fergusons. Later on, if you were lucky enough to be captain, you, along with vice captain, got a say in team selection before the big matches. As well as this new responsibility, the tea and fruit cake and the hour off study were more than welcome.

Then there was of course the aftermath of the match, where you had to report back to your class or dormitory with a blow-by-blow account of the match; and, if there was a report on the match in the following week's Western People or Roscommon Herald, the class would try and persuade Fr. Michael Giblin to read it at the beginning of the lesson. He often pre-empted the request, pulling the paper out from under the soutane and proceeding to read the report, often embellishing it with many descriptions of exploits that may not have been in the paper at all. This added considerably to the entertainment!

It was my privilege to go on and teach in St. Nathy's for many years and to develop a bond of friendship and loyalty with thousands of pupils and all of my teaching colleagues over the years. I also fulfilled a dream of being involved in the All Ireland B Winning 2000 Senior Football Team, bridging a gap of 43 years when Fr. Tom Lynch led the College to Hogan Cup success in 1957.

Thanks for the wonderful memories. Congratulations to all on 200 years of education – academic, spiritual and sporting.

• 32 •

The Collection by
One of 'The Nine'

Tom Jordan

LC 1972; MD and founder of Linbawn Ltd, HR Consultants

The ongoing loss of Ireland's intellectual power, particularly to the UK and the US, started to dwindle in the late 1960s, especially after Ireland's accession to the EEC. In the west, Abbot Laboratories, Hollister and Travenol established facilities where there was a good supply of available labour, and new houses started to sprout up again across the landscape. Our generation of students attending St. Nathy's no longer had to move to Dublin, join the Gardai or Civil Service, or emigrate to London or New York.

During this period, civil rights in Northern Ireland became a huge factor that would take twenty five years of bloodshed before peace was eventually restored. In St. Nathy's, after the awful atrocity of Bloody Sunday on 30th of January 1972, we the senior students set up a collection on the morning of the 31st of January. This money was to support the families of those who lost their lives. Nearly every student gave what they could to this collection. The generosity of the boarders, day-boys and staff really impressed me. God knows we had little, but we gave it all! Twenty five years later, while leading a group of business people supporting deprived communities in Belfast, I heard John Hume tell a story about a sum of money that arrived to him from St. Nathy's College, Ballaghadereen, some days after this horrific event of Bloody Sunday and how much this gesture was appreciated. This ethos of St. Nathy's with its example of reaching out to those in need very much influenced my future life and thinking.

During this time we had the Beatles, Woodstock and Top of The Pops, and in St. Nathy's we were encouraged to enjoy this new wave of music. In the big hall, where we all sat our Inter and Leaving Cert exams, facilities were available to play our rock music and dance with no inhibitions. I remember Louis Walsh from Kiltimagh, and now famous in the music industry, cutting his teeth in this area, coming to terms with the new Irish bands that he would later manage. I can recall in 1970 our own former pupil Doc Carroll of the Royal Blues, whose pop song

Old Man Trouble was at number 1 in the charts for weeks at that time, visiting us and dishing out free cigarettes, which were consumed happily by those in fourth year and onwards in the infamous smoking shed. Probably, looking back, the smoking shed was one of the few privileges that should never have been allowed, but we enjoyed it.

When social historians write about Ireland in the twentieth century, particularly between the 30s and the 70s, a cloud will hang over the religious, particularly those who were in institutions of care. During my five years at St. Nathy's, we had two lay teachers and the remaining teaching and catering staff were priests and nuns. From my own experience and that of my peers in St. Nathy's, I would like to state categorically that at no time during this period did any priest or nun act inappropriately. Yes, a few of the priests were occasionally a bit excessive with the cane, but I am sure the same could be said of the lay teachers. Overall, I remember to this day the kindness of some of these men: namely, Fr. Colleran, Fr. Giblin, Fr. Duffy, Fr. Finan, Fr. Tom Lynch, Fr. Hannon. They were men of vision who empowered us to take responsibility at an early age.

One of our lay teachers then, who is still a member of the academic staff at St. Nathy's, is Alex Mc Donnell from Kilmovee. He was of tremendous help to me personally. Alex taught me agricultural science. In 1978, as I was presented with Mayo Person of the Year Award for community work, a telegram from Alex was read out and in it he spoke of his pride at seeing my potential being realised.

Every morning at St. Nathy's we were awoken by this awful bell, which somehow and surprisingly was never was stolen. We had twenty minutes to get washed, make our beds and get to the church for prayers and mass. Breakfast does not offer any fond memories; indeed, no meal brings me any fond memories. It consisted of a small amount of porridge, with tea in a teapot, with milk and sugar already added – whether one took milk or not was non-negotiable – and thick slices of bread from Duff's. Towards the end of breakfast, a prefect would bring a tray of bread and roar: "Do you want any more?" The amount you needed was dropped on the table like a missile. There was a fellow from Foxford who used to eat a rather large amount of this bread twice a day. He was a baker's son, so the quality of the bread must have been good.

Classes were of forty-five minutes in duration and there were eight each day, although we had a half day on Wednesday and Saturday. Before lunch, we went to the oratory to recite the rosary. This only whetted the appetite. Alas, for me, lunch, like breakfast, did not draw great satisfaction. I will never figure out how the slice of meat served six days a week, which I believe was the best of beef, managed to look like something mined from the ground. There was the massive bowl of potatoes for each table. For desert, we were treated to the famous bread and butter pudding, rice, semolina or tapioca. My mother-in-law will almost have a seizure if she is offered leek and potato soup. This is because she was in hiding in the mountains of the Basque country for two years during the Spanish Civil War. During this detention, she had leek and potato soup every day. I have much the same reaction when I see bread and butter pudding on the menu at my favourite restaurant, and this desert is becoming more and more popular!

Between 4.00pm and 5.30pm each day there was training for football, handball or basketball. St. Nathy's excelled in all three sports. In 1968, we got to a replay of the All Ireland College's Senior semi-final, which we lost by a point to Colaiste Chriost Ri from Cork, who went on to win the All Ireland. It was a shock to all to lose this match as we had a fine team. In handball, an All Ireland win was a regular event, but such was the standard of handball that internal competition was hugely supported. There was often up to one hundred students over the stairs of the alley watching games with great interest, with the referee marking each score in Roman numerals into the concrete on top of the back wall using a sharp stone.

Study periods were three hours per night, with extra hours of study at the weekend. There was a prefect supervising all ten classrooms, with a priest supervising the corridor. Before heading to bed, prayers were held once again in the oratory. At night, 'lights out' was the duty of the prefect and on nightly duty, after 'lights out', the Dean would appear with his big torch, checking for contraband, which was mainly sweets and fruit that had been smuggled in.

Visitors were allowed for one hour per week between 4.00pm to 5.00pm on Sundays. They had to park at the side of the College, facing the Charlestown road. If you attempted to bring in a parcel and were caught by the Dean, it was confiscated. The theory behind this was that those boys who did not have visitors would feel deprived.

The more I look back and the older I get, the more I appreciate some of the skills I picked up and the experiences I had in St. Nathy's. Over the years I have met many fine men who came through St. Nathys and who have made a major contribution to society, both in Ireland and abroad. It is worth noting that in the past thirty-five years, nine past pupils from St. Nathy's have been selected as Mayo Person of the Year.

• 33 •

This Sporting Life

Oliver Feeley

LC 1973; Deputy Principal St. Nathy's College

"Can you play football? Have you any sisters?"

These were the two questions most asked of me when I entered St. Nathy's as a first year in 1968. The questions were put to all first years to test their mettle. The first question was deadly serious; the second was a typical macho question from a senior student in all boys' boarding school.

Football, handball and, to a lesser degree, basketball occupied a huge part in the lives of St. Nathy's students in the late sixties and early seventies. The era 1955 to 1974 was when sport in the College was in every student's cognisance. The senior house captain had a very influential position and was looked up to by all students, especially those in Junior year.

I remember distinctly the Senior House Captain in the 1968-1969 season, Hughie Quinn. He came from Annagh in Toulestrane, and starred for Sligo Minors in their one and only run to an All Ireland Final in 1968. He visited all the classrooms during study and wrote up the words of the school song on the blackboard for students to commit to memory. You dared not turn up at the practice in the yard outside the old toilets without knowing the lyrics. The tune was 'McNamara band' and the whole thing has stuck with me ever since. Practice was carried out after 7.00pm tea, and on match days the song was chanted vocally from one end of the game to the other.

Leading up to the match days, which were either Saturdays or Sundays, the team trainer selected the team with the help and advice of the team captain. The team and subs list was put on the notice board at the end of the 'red' hall and students rushed to the board at the end of the first study to see the team selection. Knowing the team by heart was a necessity to avoid a clout or a kick from a senior student for not showing sufficient interest.

Match days were special. In my first year, all home games were played in Tubbercurry, and all students travelled to Senior games. Busses were organised, money was collected and students were happy because they were free from confinement for a couple of hours. Racous songs about 'the old woman who lived in the woods' or about what would happen to De Valera when the "Red Revolution cometh" filled the bus.

Igoe's in Tubbercurry or J.J Cassidy's in Ballymote were the shops that benefited (some might say otherwise) from the customs of throngs of students who had not seen a shop for months. Big crowds attended the matches as college football was enjoyed by many neutrals for its skill and purity.

On match days, players were given special treatment. The long table was prepared for them in the refectory and their diet included largesse of food selection that was the envy of the ordinary mortal who sat at their tables of four in the refectory. For matches, togs and socks were handed in by the players on the Tuesday before matches so that they could be laundered before match days. New laces were given to players to avoid any frustrating breakages that might occur as a result of rotting laces subjected to very wet and muddy conditions of the school's pitches. The laces were symbolic of the frugality of the pre-EEC Ireland, and yet at the same time were symbolic of the generosity of a school that was itself being run on a shoestring budget!

The staff were engrossed in the whole sport culture. Prior to a big game, professors would engage with their students in lengthy discussions on the merits of the football team during classes when 'points' were not the be all and end all. After matches came a post-mortem analysis by the same staff members. They saw it as a 'quid pro quo' for academic co-operation and progress in the days when match fever subsided. It also gave them a chance to recall when they were students themselves. Everybody benefited. They reflected on the glories of All Ireland victory in 1957 and the near miss of 1959, when the late Micksie Clarke missed a penalty enabling St. Joseph's of Fairview to squeeze home. Thus the legend grew, and the feats of former days engendered in the hearts of current wearers of the jersey a burning desire to emulate and even surpass those greats of old. It created a bond among players and a fierce pride in the school for whom it was an honour and a privilege to represent.

My first year saw St. Nathy's win the Connacht Juvenile 'A' title and heartbreakingly lose the Senior 'A' final to St. Mary's of Galway in a replay in Tubbercurry on a score of 2-12 to 0-17. The game went to extra time and afterwards everyone, players and spectators alike, came back shattered.

After lights out in the dormitories, the major games would be replayed over and over again. When discussions of the fortunes of the school team came to an end, equally heated debates arose as to who was the better forward, Mickey Kearins of Sligo or Joe Corcoran of Mayo. A flash of the Dean's torch, who stealthily entered during the animated discussion, usually put such matters 'to bed' for another night. But the debates lived on... sport was meaningful; sport was life in the College.

After my third year, the St. Nathy's song had a much more trendy 'Yellow River' as its tune. Jarlath's, for their part, adopted the Beatles tune 'Yellow Submarine' as their anthem. Battles between the two football nurseries saw rival fans on either side of Tuam or Charlestown roaring themselves silly in support of the blue or green. During my five years in St. Nathy's, Connacht titles were won every year, but alas the blue Riband of Connacht College's Football, the Aengus Murphy Cup, never rested on the sideboard of St. Nathy's during my time.

Ironically, the year before I came to St, Nathy's, the College swept the boards in Connacht. Juvenile, Junior and Senior titles were garnered for the school and the greatness of those teams became the yardstick for the teams that followed in their immediate aftermath.

Interestingly, while football dominated as the great team sport, handball was the sport that everyone played. Races for the alleys after mealtimes led to the risk of accidents in the school. The first lines allowed from the refectory were in pole position, but prefects on duty along the main corridor could regulate the flow to suit their particular favourites. Once in the alleys, the first four had their time in court, while next in line had 'winners on' to console them.

One of the great mysteries for the first years was the 'goings on' in the back alley. This alley was the domain of third years and any ball that strayed into it from a first- or second-year court was mysteriously gobbled up. It rarely returned, and so another half solid had to be purchased; six shillings for a new one available from the Dean, or less on the black market. Sometimes an unfortunate student ended up buying his own ball back from some extremely mercenary third year who, with a few deft strokes from a compass, altered the initials engraved on the original ball. Keep in mind that students have very little money in the late sixties, and in some ways such antics provided the first of many entrepreneurial lessons for the future tycoons. Business at that time was not a serious subject in the College!

Handball successes were many in my time in St. Nathy's. Constant practice brought the cream to the top. Provincial and All Ireland titles were won on a regular basis, but the most meaningful competitions were the 'house' championships held during last term. A milling crowd at the top of the steps at the back of the 'front alley' provided gladiatorial witness to some amazing battles. In my third year, Kevin Geraghty from my class created his own niche in St. Nathy's handball folklore. In that year, he won the Juvenile, Junior and Senior 'house' singles titles – a feat never achieved before or since. In the context of the standard at that time, it was truly an amazing feat.

Athletics and soccer leagues took place during the final term, but important as they were, they paled in comparison to the sport that consumed the minds and bodies of the students in the months beforehand.

Sport helped people to survive during those years. It gave some students status and self-worth, it gave others a hope and a dream, but for the entire student body it enriched their lives. It made past glorious and the future interesting. My mind is teeming with anecdotes that could fill a book, but this recollection is not about individuals or their feats, it is about the ethos of sport and how it permeated the lives of everyone in St. Nathy's during my student days. My life is all the richer for having been involved. Two Connacht college medals are among my most treasured possessions.

Some of my abiding memories are of the generosity of staff who brought players to matches in their own cars. They would give pocket money to their passengers and that gesture meant so much that it created a lasting impression.

Sport was good for mind and body. In my years as a student in St. Nathy's it provided a lasting buttress. I am forever grateful for it and wish that it could do the same for the current generation of students. They could do worse. To identify with 'Mc Namara Band' or 'Yellow River' was good and wholesome. It provided a legacy for living.

Memories from St. Nathy's

"Up going home in 4 weeks, 3 days, 7 hours and 33 minutes!"

This was the most commonplace graffiti to be found around St. Nathy's when I was a student during the late sixties and early seventies. Every boarder counted down the time before the next break – and there were not many of those. November was a two- to three-day break. Christmas holidays lasted a full month. There was two weeks at Easter and then full release for the summer.

Once a student entered St. Nathy's as a boarder, one really had two homes. St. Nathy's became one's home for the best part of five years. It may have been a fairly regimental home, but it was a home nonetheless where care was taken of students. Frameworks for good living were created and students learned to live without the trappings and comforts of some homes.

Life was regulated by bells. A Leaving Cert student had the responsibility of ringing the bell for rising in the morning. Fifteen minutes were allocated for dressing and washing and making one's bed. From there, the journey was to the oratory for morning prayers and mass. Breakfast followed. Then the cathedral clock, which sounded every fifteen minutes, determined the beginning and end of classes. Rosary was at a quarter to one, followed by dinner. Afternoon classes followed this, then recreation. At half-past five, first study started, followed by tea at 7.00pm. Second study began at 8.00pm, night prayer at 10.00pm, and finally lights out in the dormitory by half-past ten. This was the regimentation I referred to earlier.

So what made life interesting for a boarder in St. Nathy's? What cheered people up? It was many things. It could be looking forward to a letter given out by the Dean at dinner, or after school 'bread, milk and syrup time'. It could be library book night. It could be sport or a game of chess or draughts during recreation. It could be table tennis. It could be a game of push penny at a window. It could be a good conversation going around the 'walk'. It could be talking about teachers. It could be looking forward to a film shown on the end wall of the recreation hall. It could be the College shop that opened for business on Saturdays, Sundays, and Wednesdays for 45 minutes at a time. It could be visitors on a Sunday. It could be an interesting class. It could be a food parcel or 'caffer'. It could be the three-day retreat. It could be the night before going home.

Life may have been regulated, but there were always surprises. The greatest surprise I got during my first year was brought about by the 'ASTI' strike of February 1969. We got three weeks off school even though our school had only two lay teachers. For the few weeks leading up to the strike we were full of questions on the issue. Some teachers talked, others said nothing, but eventually we were all sent home and thanked God for the College's solidarity with their ASTI colleagues, even though we had no notion of what the issues that occasioned the strike were.

Classes were somewhat different back then from what they are now. Curriculum was one thing, but many classes were spent talking about things that had nothing to do with the curriculum, such as sport and the performance of the school teams. Our geography teacher had a wonderful habit of discussing at length what he would do to improve the College if he was President. All that he needed was the leading question and someone could always be counted on to provide that.

Our science teacher had the unenviable task of teaching us the facts of life. The title for such a lesson was a 'spiff'. 'Spiffs' coincided with a feast day of 'Our Lady', and these were the most listened to classes of all. Human reproduction was the starting theme and from there the lessons centred around respect. There was plenty to be discussed going around the walk after these lessons, which would not have been the case when physics, chemistry or plant biology were on the agenda.

During my second year, the teacher that I had for civics devoted the entire year to reading extracts from John B. Keane's works and various ghost stories. It had nothing to do with the prescribed course, but it was very entertaining and had the added benefit of keeping the class interested. During the same year, my religion teacher read the play 'The Righteous are Bold' to us, followed 'Riders to the Sea'. Those were compelling classes and stayed with me for years afterwards.

French classes were full of diversions. Early on we intuitively knew that our French teacher loved to get sidetracked. He himself would create the opening for the diversion. The chat might be about French culture or films or sports or just about anything. And yet, French was taught remarkably well. I consider it a privilege to have been in those classes because one learned much more than the subject and that was what an 'all round' education was all about.

It is said that 'bread is the staff of life'. If that was so then we were well 'staffed' while living as boarders in St. Nathy's.

Monica Duff's freshly baked bread was the cornerstone of all diets. Eight slices were placed on each table at the start of breakfast in the morning and tea in the evening. Eight slices were divided between four hungry students, and the seventh and eight prefects came around with extra bread later on during the meal. Bread was also on offer at 4.00pm with a syrupy concoction to spread on top, which was washed down with a cup of milk. Present-day sport's dieticians would no doubt raise many eyebrows about such a proliferation of carbohydrates, but it filled tummies until the next visit to the refectory. Fair play was paramount at every table. A pad of butter was placed on each table, which was about one-tenth of a pound of butter. This had to be cut in four, so a knife had to be put into the teapot in order to cut the butter into four triangles. To avoid any controversy, the butter dish was then spun so that no favouritism could be shown by the hot knife user. The triangle that faced you was then yours. That triangle had to do no matter how many slices one consumed.

Mealtime was interesting. The Dean walked quickly up and down between the rows of tables to make sure that order and decorum was maintained. He also kept a sharp eye out for 'imported' foodstuffs. Banned substances such as 'sandwich spread', jam, 'proper' marmalade, 'lemon curd' and tinned meat were often smuggled into the arena. The Dean's job was to detect and confiscate such contraband. The student's mission was to smuggle in on their person such condiments as might improve overall food taste without detection. Getting it to the table without detection was the easy part. Using it and passing it on to a table companion was the tricky part. Jam had to be put on the underside of the bread, tinned meat had to be disguised, and all had to be achieved in seconds. A rapid change of direction by the Dean meant ruin. The offending item was confiscated and the user was removed for that meal. Yet the risk was worth taking.

During my first year, I sat at a table with three students who hailed from the Tubbercurry-Toulestrane region and they were very kind to me. Perhaps the fact that my father had a country shop meant I had the potential of bringing in niceties, or maybe because I seemed vulnerable in my first days in the College, entitled me to a place at their table, but it was an enjoyable experience. I also learned some harsh lessons about minding my own business. Beside the table where I sat, four 'townies' took up station. Two of them hailed from Swinford, one from Foxford and one from what seemed like a metropolis – Ballina. They were musically minded and would harmoniously belt out tunes by Marmalade or the Beatles during breaks in mealtime. One evening 'Fox on the run' was the tune in vogue and I innocently looked on at their efforts, only to get a clatter across the face reminding me to never look in at their table again. I never did. Two of the group at that table live near me now, but I doubt if they can recall that lesson in chastisement. I certainly can.

At nearly all times there was a rhythmic regularity to life in St. Nathy's, but sometimes routine was interrupted. Every October a retreat was held. This involved three days of complete silence. It began on a Monday morning and continued until Thursday morning. There were no classes, no recreation and no study periods. It was a time of introspection. An order of priests conducted the retreat. It involved liturgy, mass, confessions, talks, and meditation. It was geared towards giving strong roots to any students that had a vocation to the priesthood, but to those that had not, it was a welcome island of time to themselves. I remember a story of one student who had no notion of priesthood in his head but decided to go along to the visiting priest to say he had. His prime motivation was a cigarette given to each visitor if they needed one to settle their nerves. It was said his nerves needed a fair bit of settling!

Another time life was different was when there was snow. Everyone was 'encouraged' to go outside during break time. There pandemonium reigned. Seniors took on Juniors in snowball fights, which the Seniors invariably won. The would isolate groups of first years, as hunting dogs would corner helpless sheep, and cover them in snow. Some students would suffer the ignominy and misfortune of being rolled in the snow in the football fields. One can only imagine the state of students coming back in for study or class after that. But all the chaos was kept to outdoors; clothes were changed and normal service resumed once indoors. The clothes were shoved into the student's laundry bag and sent off to be washed, returning within a few days to be collected outside the refectory.

Ascension Thursday was a sport's day in the College. This was a great day. Races and field events were conducted on the football pitch. Fr. Colleran had spent ages preparing an eight-lane 400-metre track for the day. This was also the only day in the year that there was an ice-cream shop with no fridges or freezers! Full blocks of ice cream were purchased and had to be eaten with rulers or set squares while sitting on the grass. Removal of cutlery from the refectory was a serious no no! But the novelty of the ice cream and the day itself allowed students to be happy in the knowledge that the countdown to going home for summer was close at hand, fewer weeks, fewer days and fewer hours left for the graffiti merchants. Three long months in your other home were close at hand and thoughts of the following September were far away. Your character training for that year was at an end, but the indelible imprints of St. Nathy's were becoming more marked, and after your five years you were a Nathy's man, a trait you carried with you for life.

• 34 •

My Memories of St. Nathy's in the 70s

Eugene Toolan

LC 1974; Head of Education Department St. Angela's College, Sligo

As we passed the Four Altars' Penal Monument in Monasteraden on that glorious September evening in 1969, that sinking feeling came over me. We had spent the afternoon stooking oats but, despite the glorious sunshine, my mind was not on the task in hand. Indeed, my feelings fluctuated from trepidation to excitement at the prospect of becoming a border in St. Nathy's College, Ballaghaderreen.

On arrival, my case was taken by a second-year student, the first gesture of kindness from our mentors. The goodbyes were short, with no outward tears! I was led to the dormitory, selected the bed with the least hollow in the middle and started to unpack. The prefect outlined the rules. Like many others, it was my first night away from home and I heard most of the Cathedral chimes that night. When the bell rang at 7.00am, I joined the silent queue for the washroom with my fellow first years; a new towel on my arm, and new toothpaste and toothbrush in my wash bag.

Bishop Fergus (R.I.P.), Bishop of Achonry, celebrated the morning mass. He anticipated my feelings and spoke on how he felt on his first morning as a boarder. He wanted to run home, but decided to give it a go and try it for at least a week before giving up. I took his advice and I stayed for five years.

While the subject content prepared us for University and work, it was the incidental comments and personalities of various teachers that were influential in preparing us for the 'University of Life'. Geography subject knowledge was interestingly interspersed with discussions about scuba diving, life saving and reflections on basketball matches.

I remember the many famous historical quotations that were frequently quoted in French class, some of which I later re-articulated while a primary teacher, including: "Never in the annals of human endeavour did so many do so little, in so long a time!"

The philosophy learned in Greek class was not always classical, much of it was suitably related to contemporary society, which I feel will remain with me forever. I learned that true education is not just the imparting of knowledge. Effective education broadens and opens a person's mind, generates and cultivates inquisitiveness, excitement and critical interest, promotes positive attitudes, is life-related and, above all, is about the individual pupil's self-worth, talents, qualities and holistic development, as well as the betterment of society. I was fortunate that most of my teachers in St. Nathy's ascribed to this philosophy of education.

The food provided was supplemented by the 'caffer', which was smuggled into the dormitory from the visitors on Sundays or by dayboys working on commission. Various ploys and 'trafficking' routes were used to outwit the authorities; it was a highly organised collaborative effort. I wonder if a certain Curry councillor's wife make a porter cake as good as his mother's; or is a certain well-known publican in Loughglynn still fond of milk choc goldgrain and Fanta orange, and does he remember the times we locked ourselves in the tower house to enjoy our clandestine feasts?

Extra-curricular activities, especially sport, were a major part of our life in St. Nathys'. We were encouraged to participate in a wide variety of sports and I proudly cherish my Connacht Juvenile Gaelic Football medal. The Gaelic Football matches were major occasions. If they were played in Charlestown, we normally got to attend; and for the particularly important ones, we held rallies the night before the match to practice our chants and singing. However, for the 'away' matches that we did not get to attend, it was the duty of the prefects to give a blow-by-blow account of the proceedings. In the case of the second-year dormitory prefect, this blow-by-blow account and astute match analysis always ran into the early hours of the morning. One could almost feel they were watching a video replay of the match. It is no surprise that this student from Kilmovee subsequently became a famous inter-county GAA manager and RTE pundit! Then, of course, there was the selling of forecasts for these matches: "As many forecasts as you like for 10p; and twice as many as you like for 20p!" The fostering of a dubious entrepreneurial spirit was in evidence at times.

At the time there was a farmyard attached to the College. One day while clandestine darts were being played, a dart became embedded in the ham of one of the pigs. It created quite a rumpus around the College, much to the bewilderment of a certain Science teacher who was very fond of these animals. On another occasion, a pupil who had become disillusioned with college life decided to bring the donkey inside. He was met on the corridor by a certain unruffled teacher, who was alleged to have casually remarked: "Please take your brother outside."

We were not allowed out at weekends and longed for the holidays. We literally counted the days, hours and minutes; 'Up going home in 16 days, 12 hours and 35 minutes' would often be found written on a copy or inside a book cover. We had a film on the night before the holidays to keep us out of mischief. However, there was usually very little sleep that night as dormitories had to be raided and beds 'skied', sing-songs held and general carousing. Next afternoon we headed home after a morning of 'free' classes. It always took me sometime to readjust to the smallness of my bedroom, to the absence of my friends and of the Cathedral clock chiming away the hours.

• 35 •

Handball in the 70s

Leo Henry

LC 1975; Academic Staff St. Nathy's College

St. Nathy's College boasts a rich tradition of success in college handball. The early 1970s enhanced this tradition, with St. Nathy's winning all Connacht titles and two All Ireland titles in 1973 and 1974. Jeremiah Walsh, Paddy Noone, Ollie Burke, Aiden Henry, Kevin Geraghty, Anthony Cogan, Michael O'Hara, Damien Griffin, Fergal Geoghan, John O'Connor were some of the top players of that era.

Handball was second to football in terms of popularity as an extra curricular activity, but courts were always sought after. Games and challenges were taken seriously, none more so than the handball title each year and the senior, junior and juvenile house league titles. These games generated great interest and usually had large numbers of spectators.

Fr. Gregory Hannon was our handball coach and mentor. He was assisted by Fr. Michael Joyce and Fr. Pat Lynch. Fr. Greg unsparingly gave of his time to oversee the development of the game of handball in the College and the success of his teams in all college competitions.

Training in earnest began in November and often required travelling to Charlestown and more often to the indoor court in Ballymote for training sessions. Connacht college competition usually began in January and there was always the treat of a supper at a restaurant on the journey home. The real treat however was the trip to Dublin and to Croke Park for the All Ireland finals. We travelled up on Friday afternoon, booked in to our B&B on the North Circular Road, then off to Croke Park for a practice. We then had our evening meal before we retired. The semi-finals were played on Saturday, with the All Ireland finals staged on Sunday morning. The college's handball final was always played on the morning of the National League Football final. Thus we were always given complimentary tickets in the VIP section of Croke Park for the league final.

In 1974, we won the All Ireland Handball College's Team Championship, beating St. Macartan's, Monaghan, in the semi-final, before defeating Presentation Convent, Castleconnor, in the decider by 109 to 84. Our team was Kevin Geraghty, Michael O'Hara, Noel Griffin, Damien Griffin, Fergal Geoghan and myself. Kevin Geraghty achieved a unique double by winning the Senior Single's Title on the same day.

To promote College's handball, the Handball Council, with Joe Lynch as general secretary, had arranged with RTE, who were televising live the league final between Kerry and Roscommon, to have the presentation to the All Ireland College's Handball Champions before the league trophy presentation to the winning league captain. As luck would have it, Kerry scored a goal in the last seconds of the match to draw level and force a replay. Therefore, there was no presentation to the winning captain of the league trophy and our moment of television glory faded.

After an evening meal, we set off west for Ballaghaderreen. Fr. Jimmy Colleran met our cavalcade at Lung Bridge and requested that we wait for ten minutes before resuming our journey into town. Fifteen minutes later, when we arrived in Barrack Street, we were greeted by all of the boarders from the College. When we alighted from our transport, they carried us shoulder high up through the Square to the Fairgreen in front of the College, where a large bonfire had been lit to honour our success. After words of congratulations from the President, Fr. Tom Flynn, we retired.

This truly was a remarkable event in the student life of St. Nathy's College and in the welcoming home of an All Ireland winning team.

• 36 •

A Trip Down Memory Lane

Frances Dunne

LC 1979; Basketball Coach St. Nathy's College

It is with fondest memories that I look back on my days at St. Joseph's, both as a student and as a basketball coach. My student days began in 1973 where Sr. Agatha was my first Principal. Those days were, as the saying goes, 'the best days of my life' – as long as there was a basketball match or training session incorporated into the day. In its earlier history, netball was the main sport played in St. Joseph's but, with the arrival of Sr. Eileen Scanlon in the early 70s, the sport of basketball took off.

It is to Sr. Eileen that I owe so much, as she instilled in me a great love for the game that I still have today. Basketball plays a great part in my life and it is with a great deal of pleasure that I have passed on and continue to pass on this love and knowledge of the game to the students of St. Joseph's and St. Nathy's.

In my own school days, I look back on my teachers with great memories and see what an excellent academic institution that they had built up. Sr. Athanasius and Sr. Anne were also Principals during my student days, with Mrs. Moran as Vice Principal. Miss Maureen Smith was my science teacher, with whom we had the pleasure of dissecting many a rabbit. Mr. Tommy Davey, our French teacher and school tour organiser, took us on many a trip to France; and many were the green faces after the long ferry journey. Sr. Dolores, with her motherly instincts, always kept a loving eye on us and even made sure that there was a spare uniform for any student who had got theirs wet coming to school. Other teachers, including Sr. Declan (now Sr. Nell), Mrs. O'Flaherty, Mr. John Lynch, Mr. John Reid, and Mr. Seamus O'Connor, all added to the great memories that I have of St. Joseph's.

On the basketball courts, which incidentally were outdoor, unlike today's modern sports halls, our matches were played in all sorts of weather. We won many an honour under the guidance of Sr. Eileen, whose attention to detail in every game is still etched in my mind; she bounced, passed and shot every ball. The we being: Sinead McGarry, Denise McGovern, Evelyn Cunniffe, Sandra Regan, Geraldine

Flynn, Martina Casserly, Mary Tighe and Jean Gannon. In order to improve my basketball skills, each summer during my school years was spent at Dungarvan Basketball Camp; surely the sign of a fanatic! On our first trip to Dungarvan with some of the above mentioned, we missed the train home and the Teddy Solan express had to be sent for to rescue us.

When Sr. Eileen moved on, success for St. Joseph's seemed less frequent. Memories of losing many Lonleitros finals and the tears that were shed still stand out, but as they say, "time is a great healer", and it is not till later that one realises that losing makes us stronger and helps us accept life's ups and downs, as well as to cherish those winning moments. As I entered my senior years in school, I had the opportunity to coach junior teams under the guidance of John Reid. One memorable match sticks out in my mind, the local 'derby' match with Swinford. Some of the Swinford team included boarders who were from Ballaghaderreen! The atmosphere at this game was made all the more intense by the large number of parents supporting their respective schools. In the end, the St. Joseph's girls' nerves held out and we came out victorious. It was then that I caught the coaching bug. The team that day was Noeleen Kelly, Ann Cunniffe, Eileen & Anne O'Grady, Alison& Ann Spelman, Irene Gallagher, Maura Mahon and Pauline Feeney.

I left St. Joseph's in 1979 and went to college in Galway where I continued to play basketball. Mr. Reid and Miss Geraldine Newcome commissioned a new team of assistant coaches to help train the school teams. They were Jacqueline Egan, Mary Geever, Eileen O'Grady and Ann Cunniffe. I spent a further two summers in Dungarvan getting my coaching qualification and a third to acquire my referee's badge.

In 1982, I returned to St. Joseph's as a basketball coach, an opportunity given to me by Sr. Anne Cuffe. Success did not come instantly on the basketball court, but when it did, a winning tradition soon built up. Every trophy we took back to the school was special, but by reaching the final stages of six All Ireland Championships we definitely put St. Joseph's on the map. My most memorable All Ireland outing was the first, held in Tralee, where we reached the final after defeating a fancied team from Macroom of Cork. In the final we were desperately unlucky to lose out to a strong team from Killiney, Dublin, despite having a seven-point lead at half time. The team was Karen Cafferky, Emma Kilcoyne, Kathleen Flynn, Jackie Keegan, Martina Caulfield, Margaret Gallagher, Karen O'Connor, Dearbhla Quigley, Karen Brennan and Catherine Freeman.

The school received its greatest honour in 1996 when Nicola Farrell was picked for the Irish U16 basketball team. Nicola lined out for her country against Iceland and also in the Four Countries Championships (England, Scotland, Wales and Ireland). Nicola was not St. Joseph's only international as Grainne O Mahony lined out for her country in no less than six international events in the long jump.

As I come to an end of my trip down memory lane in St. Joseph's, it is with a great deal of pride and affection that I look back on my association with my alma mater. The buildings may be gone, but the fond memories will always live on.

The amalgamation of St. Joseph's, St. Nathy's College and the Vocational School meant that I have moved on to coach basketball in the new school. Sport, but in particular basketball, still continues to flourish in the new school.

No longer do teams have to train outdoors with the provision of a state-of-the-art sports complex in the amalgamated set up. Thankfully the success in basketball has continued in the new school. The school has won three All Ireland titles since the amalgamation, in 2001 with the boys, and in 2004 and 2007 with the girls. Another great honour bestowed on the College was that Michael Higgins, a student in the school, was chosen for the Irish U18 team and played for his country against Scotland, Luxemburg and in the European Championships in Belgium.

Thank God for sport. Next to the weather, people probably talk more about sport than any other topic. We discuss up-coming games with anticipation and afterwards replayed the excitement of the winning goal or basket. Some people believe that winning is everything, and possibly it is to some; but maybe, in sometimes losing, we develop better as people, more able to accept the ups and downs in life. Sport demands a combination of physical skill and strength, an alert mind, enthusiasm, purpose and more often teamwork. Many friendships are formed through sport. Sport helps a person adjust to daily life; and the ability of people to use their leisure time properly is more important now than ever before.

• 37 •

To School Through the Streets of Ballagh

Sinead Mangan

LC 1979; Principal of St. Attracta's N.S.

St. Joseph's Secondary School opened in September 1933. The Irish Sisters of Charity ran the school until the summer of 1971, when they were replaced by The Mercy Sisters from the Diocese of Achonry. Extensive renovations were carried out, Sr. Agatha Durkan became Principal, and John Hanley's (our caretaker extraordinaire) work began in earnest.

I started in Saint Joseph's in 1974 with all my friends from primary school, which at that time was called Saint Francis Xavier. Sister Regina was the Principal in the primary and after two years with her in fifth and sixth class, we were ready for the transition.

Dare I be so boring as to say that I loved every minute I spent with that lovely class of girls from Ballagh, Lisacul, Kilmovee, Loughglynn, Mullaghroe, Frenchpark, Tibohine, Derinacartha and Monasteraden. We had a reunion in 1995; it was great to see everyone so well and so happy. I had a job trying to get a word in edgeways!

While the infrastructure of Saint Joseph's at that stage left a lot to be desired, our education was of the highest standard, both academically and socially. It was ahead of its time; it was broad-based, varied, integrated, including sport, art and not to mention Mr. Davy's *ceol, craic agus dramaiocht*.

Having shared all my school years in the same class/seat as Frances Durkin, you can imagine the great commitment we had to her passion – basketball. Lord, we were fit! We seemed to spend most of our time running; if it was not after a ball, it was uptown to school in the morning, home at lunchtime, still running, and back up in 30 minutes. At four o'clock, we would be off again, only to return often for basketball training or a match before study.

A great influence on us was Sr. Eileen Scanlon, who brought us to a basketball college in Dungarvan to improve our skills. It must have worked as we won many honours for Saint Joseph's. Fr. Colleran, the then President of St. Nathy's, also encouraged us, even allowing the St. Nathy's basketballers to shout for us at many a Longleitros final.

As a student at St. Joseph's, I always felt cared for by the teachers (too numerous to mention) who were sincere and relaxed in their approach to us. A significant factor in their successful delivery of the curriculum was their sense of pastoral care and their general rapport as a staff. They were always open to suggestions and treated us like adults, especially in our Leaving Cert year.

In the Christmas of 1978, Mrs Moran allowed us to cook a full traditional dinner. Her state-of-the-art kitchen was a hum of glorious activity and savoury delights… Nigella eat your heart out! There again, I was lucky with my cookery partners Denise McGovern and Francis Dunne for cooking and Georgina Lynch for presentation. Washing up and sampling the goodies always being my forte!

After we completed the dreaded exams, which as an academic class we took very seriously, the teachers, at St. Euthanasia's suggestion, met us on a beautiful summer's evening for a little soiree at the convent. It was my eighteenth birthday and a great treat to be brought around the convent. I can still smell their highly polished floors and always appreciated their attention to cleanliness. That evening the teachers told anecdotes about our five years with them, all of them complimentary! As a Principal/teacher, I realise that these are the memories that remain, the thoughtfulness, the many acts of kindness, the sense of security and belonging.

Looking out my office window, I can see what is now all that remains of the convent buildings i.e. St. Attracta's National School, as well as the church where we enjoyed many spiritual moments of reflection before we were let out into the world. I feel humbled and honoured to be playing a part in carrying on the excellent tradition of education started here so many years ago. June 1995 marked the end of St. Joseph's Secondary School.

In the 1970s, we were lucky and did not have the many extra challenges imposed on schools today. In spite of this, I continue to model our school on St. Joseph's. Our staffroom is similar, democratic and fun. Our pupils are more culturally diverse. As has been said, we are so popular that the children are coming from Pakistan! However, like our predecessors, through tolerance and compassion we have managed to make the arrival of newcomer pupils a positive experience. They are a joy to teach, hardworking and respectful of teachers and classmates alike, just like we were in St. Joseph's!

Mar scorfhocal, ba mhaith liom buiochas a ghlacadh d'fhoireann Naomh Iosef. Go n'eiri le scoil Naithei sa todhchai, muinteoiri, daltai, agus Priomhoide, go momhor sa bhlian spesialta seo. Le dea ghui i gconai.

• 38 •

To the Staff of St. Joseph's

Imelda Greene

LC 1982; Academic Staff St. Nathy's College

Leaving the security of Lisacul primary school and entering secondary-level education in Ballaghaderreen in the late 1970s was a major step, and so it was with a mixture of excitement tinged with apprehension that I entered St. Joseph's Secondary School. The school was run by the Mercy Order and several members of the teaching staff at that time were religious sisters. My first encounter was with the then Principal Sr. Athanasius (R.I.P.). I remember her kindness to the students, her gentle manner and her firm expectation of co-operation from all. Her tenure as Principal was followed by Sr. Anne, who always had the good of her students at heart. In particular, she guided her Leaving Cert students through their career choices with great insight and interest.

I am greatly indebted to Sr. Dolores, who taught me French in my junior years. To her I owe a great debt of gratitude for engendering in me a great love of the French language and culture, which I retain to this day. Others from the Mercy Order who influenced me in my formative years include Sr. Emmanuelle, who taught maths; Sr. Veronica, who taught French and religion; and Sr. Joachim, who accompanied us on piano in singing class and reminded us that "to sing is to pray twice".

Of no less importance during those years were the lay teachers on the staff. Vice Principal Mrs. Moran taught us the arts of cookery, needlework and embroidery, and impressed upon us that long after we had forgotten our history and geography, these were skills we would still use. Mr. O'Connor introduced us to the delights of Mark Twain's Huckleberry Finn and Shakespeare's Merchant of Venice, which he arranged for us to see staged in a Dublin theatre, while his analysis of poetry was always insightful.

I thank Mr. Reid, whose belief in the total immersion method of Irish in the classroom may have concerned us somewhat initially, but bore fruit long term and left me with a lifelong love of the language. In my early years in St. Joseph's, Ms. Smith and Ms. Reid were the dedicated staff in the science department, and both endeavoured to show that science did not only belong in the biology, physics and chemistry section of the science book, but had a real relevance to everyday life. I recall a class spent dissecting a rabbit, only vaguely however, since I had passed out before the demonstration ended. Subsequently, Sr. Anne kindly suggested that perhaps a career in nursing was not for me!

Ms. Naughten later joined the science department and continued the good work for Leaving Cert biology. Cashbooks and ledgers were the order of the day for the commerce class. Rarely did the trial balance work out for us, but, under the watchful eyes of Ms. O'Flaherty or Mr. Lynch, we eventually got there.

Having the same teacher for three subjects for Leaving Cert is probably quite rare, but so it was for me when Mrs. Flatley taught me English, French and geography. I recall studying the short stories of Maupassant in French class and world hunger featured in geography. In English class we enjoyed the novel Silas Marner and endured a Shakespearean play. Has anybody ever heard of Cariolanus? I remain indebted to Mrs. Flatley for guiding me successfully through almost half of my Leaving Cert course.

I have nothing but very fond memories of all of the staff in St. Joseph's. They always went out of their way to do the extra bit for their students, to impress on them the importance of life skills, and to raise their self-esteem. They brought the kindness and compassion of Jesus Christ to countless students and for that we, their former students, are very grateful. I returned to St. Joseph's as a young teacher some years later and once again experienced the kindness and support of the staff towards me starting out in my career.

The five years spent in St. Joseph's offered us a great sense of security. Outside events impacted on us now and again. I remember the excitement of Pope John Paul's visit to Ireland, the tragedy of the stardust fire and the death of Republican prisoners on hunger strike in the Maze prison. But for the most part we existed in our own cocoon. We knew where we were and what we were doing. Then after our 'Grad' in the Lough Gara Hotel and as the Leaving Cert approached, I recall the sense of unease as the uncertainty of the future beckoned. The Ireland of the eighties had little to offer its Leaving Cert students. Unemployment and emigration were rife, but we maintained a sense of hope. So the Leaving Cert came and went and we embraced the future, whatever it might hold.

Lasting friendships were forged during my five years in St. Joseph's. I recall my classmates from that time with great affection. Many of us became reacquainted at a class reunion in recent years, and a few I have not seen since we left school. I remember in a special way Maria McCann and Barbara McCann, who sadly have passed away to their eternal reward. May God grant them eternal rest and console their families.

The old Irish proverb goes: *'Is aoibhinn beatha and scoláire'*, and I have to agree with that. I hope the students of St. Nathy's College agree too and that they enjoy their education and, even though we are once again stricken by recession, that they will be positive and hopeful about the future. *'Ní bhíonn in aon rud ach seal'* – because this too will pass.

• 39 •

In Memory of St Joseph's Secondary School

Anne Doherty

LC 1982; Academic Staff St. Nathy's College

It was 1977, the year in which we paid our final tributes to legends like Elvis Presley and Charlie Chaplain, but for me and many of my classmates, this year and the subsequent five years were symbolic of the most memorable and enjoyable experiences of second level education in Ballaghaderreen. It launched a new step for me in my school days as I headed into St. Joseph's Secondary School for the first time.

The months prior to my entry were filled with enthusiasm, anxiety and suspicion as to what may lie ahead for me as a student because I was leaving the somewhat secure and cushioned environment of the adjoining St. Francis Xavier primary school. As a sixth-class student, we were often delegated certain little 'posts of responsibility' from time to time, which would take us across the connecting bridge between the two schools and up into the convent proper. On such visitations, we obtained sneak previews of the school and all the nooks and crannies that we could later use as 'hideaways' in time of trouble.

Sr. Athanasius (R.I.P.) was Principal in my first year. An inspiring, dedicated and charismatic leader, she encouraged and enthused every student and teacher under her leadership. Those days we were most fortunate to be educated by the Sisters of Mercy, who gave selflessly of their time working with us on circular and extra curricular material during and after school hours.

Whilst resources were somewhat limited, we were never disadvantaged in areas such as sport, drama, musicals, religious retreats or school trips. Sr. Anne Cuffe took over the reins in 1980, having previously taught history and geography at the school. She taught with enthusiasm and zeal, and had an in-depth knowledge of her subject areas, while at the same time she was always approachable both as a teacher and as school Principal. She gave us career guidance at senior level and always came to class armed with an array of literature on college courses and career choices. She arranged guest speakers for classes, mock interviews and supervised aptitude and interest tests, and took a keen personal interest in each student's career path. She was in every way a leader ahead of her time, predisposed to her dual role as Principal and classroom teacher.

Religious education formed the backbone of our civic and moral instruction. Each class year had a retreat and we regarded those days as 'treats' away from the banal routine of the classroom. Occasionally, retreats were celebrated outside the environs of the school at Banada Abbey. At school, every class commenced with a class prayer in either English, Irish or French – the latter we can thank Sr. Dolores for. This prayer set us up for each class in a spiritual and disciplinary sense of the word. Each month we looked forward to our class mass that was read by Fr. Tommy Johnson, and every student was afforded a chance of partaking in the liturgy.

As we progressed into senior cycle, a new vibrancy was added to our masses as some students had learned the guitar, under the leadership of Sr. Evelyn. I was fortunate to be among the members of the first guitar group founded at the school in 1980, the legacy of which I have carried to the present day with my classmates Anne Carmody to the Cathedral Fold Group. Hours of practice went into those guitars; tuning, retuning and exchanging songs during lunch in the P.E. hall and on the front lawns of the convent on fine sunny days. Time never stood still for us and boredom was a word undiscovered in our vocabulary as we embraced every opportunity afforded to us.

Music, song and dance were integral parts of our daily school lives and connected us to St. Joseph's in an extraordinary way. The Annual Christmas Concert was no exception. In 1980, we preformed the Music, Song and Dance of Stephen Foster under the direction of our music teacher, Mr. Tommy Davy.

The true story behind the show was not really to the forefront of our minds. We just wanted to sing, dance and act, whether or not we were really able to do so! It was our Broadway and many of us showgirls were kitted out in costumes from Finn's of New Street. We existed on a diet of excitement, fun and thrill at the expense of Mr. Davy's patience and tolerance, but we truly admired and appreciated his professionalism, sense of humour and the endless hours of rehearsals he endured with us.

New subjects like business studies, science and home economics added depth and variety to the curriculum. We were afforded the opportunity of developing our culinary and sewing skills under the watchful eyes of Mrs. Caron and Mrs. Moran. If stitches could speak, they would recall some stories, the tears and blood-stained fingers that went into the manufacture of those pillowcases, aprons, gingham blouses and pinafores. While the task given seemed laborious at times, we learned so much through trial and error, and indeed, a few fellow students progressed to be Rachel Allens in later years.

The science laboratory also opened windows of opportunities for students at St. Joseph's Secondary School. Nestled on the second floor overlooking the main convent road, it was a room bustling with young budding and innovative scientists. Numerous dissections of dead rabbits took place, often on a weekly basis for the benefit of the faint hearted among us who may have missed previous episodes. We had total disregard for miximatosis and were oblivious to health and safety rules as these action-packed experiments and dissections brought biology and science alive to us. The annual science room clean-up was looked forward to in great anticipation by all students, as burettes and pipettes fluttered across the science room like jumbo jets preparing to take off. Those not directly involved in the clean-up operation would cast a watchful and pitiful eye over the two white mice in the cage that we earnestly longed to free on too many occasions.

Other students were superlative in the gaseous fields as they turned on the gas taps in an attempt to stifle, if not suffocate, the rest of us. In a true sense of the word, we were the founders of the 'Young Scientist Exhibition' – we were scientists ahead of our time and indulged in a 'Young Scientist Exhibition' on regular occasions. Nevertheless, we were privileged students to be exposed to such a child-centred curriculum, and while fun and frolics may have come into play, the important thing we recall is that we enjoyed and remembered what we learned.

Any excess energy stored was later utilised to full advantage in our physical education classes under the instruction of Mr. John Reid. We did not need Addidas, Reebok or Nike to enjoy a game of basketball or volleyball. Lunchtime school leagues whet our appetites with healthy rivalry against the senior girls, whom we always regarded as role models.

The main highlight of the sporting year was the student-teacher match at the end of the school term. It was our annual chance to surpass them, and, while at times we succeeded, thankfully nobody ever needed CPR or first aid. A great sense of camaraderie and sportsmanship always existed among teachers and students alike, while at the same time we upheld our dignity and respect for our teachers, as we were too aware of the jury that might face us if we did otherwise!

Mr. Reid also taught maths and Irish. As my Irish teacher, he imprinted a profound love of the language, oral and written, in me and impressed upon us all the uniqueness and importance of our culture and heritage. He regularly supplemented and enlivened the curriculum of our time with scealta, paidreacha and piseoga, and brought a unique vibrancy and vitality to the language. With such an inspirational teacher behind me, it is little wonder that I later embark on studying Irish as one of my degree subjects at University College Galway.

In this year of 2009, we are still very fortunate to have Sisters Dolores, Emmanuel and Kathleen in our midst, and are proud and delighted that they are still actively involved at community level. The former students of St. Joseph's Secondary School are indebted to the Sisters of Mercy in Ballaghaderreen, who provided the finest calibre of education and curricular programmes to students who would have be unable to afford a private education otherwise in those days.

To the Sisters of Mercy and the former teachers of St. Joseph's, you are true ambassadors of education and I salute and thank you all for the wonderful years I spent with you.

Ar scath a cheile a mhairimid.

• 40 •

Concert for Ethiopa

Joe Egan

LC 1985; Chairperson of St. Nathy's Parents' Association

When I was asked to put a few words on paper of my memories from St. Nathy's, my initial reaction was that I am too young to write anything with a hint of the memoir to it. Reality soon bit when I had to admit to myself that it is a quarter of a century since I sat my Leaving Certificate. Having reluctantly realised that I could not disqualify myself on these grounds, the next task was to decide on content. Some matters might best be left unexamined until after the Freedom of Information Act brings them into the public forum in only a few years, some items are only of interest or intrigue to yours truly or a small cohort of friends and some lose colour in the telling.

My first memories of St. Nathy's go back before I entered those halls where the essence of floor wax and perspiration was intended to inspire. At approximately three years of age, I have a memory of my two older brothers in their black school blazers and being struck with the notion that these two striking figures of men looked markedly different from the two boys that only minutes earlier had been involved in full-scale warfare in our bottling store. Sometimes the clothes indeed maketh the man. It did strike me as unusual that I had brothers who disappeared for what seemed like months on end.

Some years later, I remember my Grand Uncle Mick telling me tales of daring do when he and my Grandfather John V attended there in the twenties. Again, discretion and legal implications would determine that some of these anecdotes remain out of the realm of the printed word. My next memories involve attending concerts in the school that my brothers were taking part in. Yet again, my siblings were almost unrecognisable and that was probably a good thing. The next striking memory is of going to football games where St. Nathy's competed against old enemies. It always struck me that the attendance of a few hundred always appeared to be in the thousands, such was the atmosphere and the volume of support generated.

In the mid-seventies, St. Nathy's turned me into a smuggler and a latter day Bluebeard. Bottles of Miwadi orange had to be spirited up through side doors, bags of chips from the soup bowl secreted in through the 101 window, more elicit contraband was concealed in the handlebars of my Raleigh Chopper which conveniently had a grip which easily slid off. This contraband could be bought singly rather than in packs of ten or twenty, and sometimes the booty had a serious bend on it after almost traversing the bend in my handlebars. The reality was that once the bottle of Miwadi was out of the sleeve of my jacket and safely into the hands of my brother, a group of other lads had gathered willing to pay me to challenge the trade winds, detect the shoe-tipped footsteps, run the gauntlet and ease the pain until the end of term.

Everything geared up towards mid-1979 and sitting the 'Broderick'. It seemed as if hundreds were doing this exam to an impressionable twelve-year-old. There followed a summer of expectation and eventually the transition was made from the Brothers to St. Nathy's. It was an all-male preserve, bar an energetic nun who seemed to do everything at a pace. There was Saturday school and Wednesday had a huge emphasis on sport. We had no uniform, yet we all appeared very similar. There was something Darwinian about the place because it definitely was survival of the fittest.

I was surprised a few months ago when discussing memories of St. Nathy's with a close friend. His memories seemed to have taken on a very different slant from mine. I had to agree with him that an all-male institution could indeed be a very tough place. There were incidents that happened which I have a vivid recall of, sometimes the velocity and ferocity of the blow still rings hollow in the head, and those were just the ones meted out by mere fellow students. There were times when the machismo and masochism was just a wee bit too evident. I could never understand why the movie selected for showing before a break would be a gritty western or a martial arts movie. I remember the aftermath of one martial arts movie resembling down-town Taiwan after the Triads had gone on a spree, with broken beds, fractured limbs and bloodied noses ensuing.

Rural myth and urban legend were the stuff of life in the early 1980s. I am not sure whether anyone actually walked along the façade at the front of what has now become A Block, but I do know one lad who sat on the sill of a window that had been nailed down and there was no sign of hammer and nails around. Some islanders did take to the top of the 'Box Alley' for their afternoon stroll. The 'Back Alley' was the place where the boys became legends or limped away with tattered leg ends. Pinball machines do not make a good substitute for a bed. The shrapnel from a toilet bowl could indeed kill a person. A rabbit with rigor mortis can only appear to be attempting to steer a car. The only thing that attempting to dry banana skins on the roof of the smoking shed did was to create an awful smell and mess. Some stories grew legs; you just had to be there to witness.

My happiest memory of my time in St. Nathy's is a concert put on pre Live Aid to raise a few quid for the crisis in Ethiopia. The producer/director and the musical director are still members of the staff and would probably prefer to remain nameless. The fact that they brought such a disparate and desperate bunch of lads together and produced such a fine concert is indeed testament to their genius and willpower. To get so many teenage boys on stage for the first time in their lives was an achievement in itself. These lads went out to their future careers steeled by the memory of a night in front of an audience of hundreds when they overcame fear and nerves to take to the stage. Hundreds have appeared on stage down through the years, some fine productions have graced those boards, yet I will always remember that young priest and that musical director, only a couple of years older than some of their charges, marshalling such a memorable night.

It is hard to fully convey in words the main attribute that St. Nathy's has. St. Nathy's has a 'connectedness' that goes beyond words. Earlier this year in the National Basketball Arena in Tallagh, St. Nathy's competed in an Under-16 All Ireland Final; that afternoon, the team which won the Under-19 Final, was coached by a past pupil of St. Nathy's and a former classmate of mine. Even twenty-five years later, we could still talk animatedly about incidents that had happened and our peers whom we could chiefly remember by their 'slag', yet, we had to dig deep to remember their actual name.

I am truly proud of my connectedness with St. Nathy's; the tales from the Twenties, the pictorial evidence of the Sixties, my own foray there in the late Seventies, being a member of staff in the Nineties, my children attending there in the Noughties.

Nathy's is very much part of me. I studied texts in 1984, which my brother studied in 1976, and which my son will study in 2010. There were days when some teachers called me Dinny, John, Tom, Joe as they worked their way through the chronology to find me. I was aggrieved then, I am glad now. We all look forward to the bicentenary of St. Nathy's and we know that it will be marked fittingly so that connectedness can reach forward.

• 41 •

'Nathy's' as it might have been

John M. Regan

LC 1987; Lecturer in Political Science at Dundee University

I remember the manner of my leaving St. Nathy's better than the arrival. That departure was on the 27th of June 1986, the day of the first referendum on divorce. Hitching a lift to Frenchpark, I registered a vote for the first time before leaving for a summer job near Dundalk. Mine was no distinguished academic career and I am often reminded of something the late Liam Caron used to say. Liam, who attempted to teach me something about agricultural science, wryly liked to make the distinction between getting an 'education' and getting 'pieces of paper' (i.e. examination results). Remembering Liam nowadays, I encourage my own students not to confuse these very different outcomes.

St. Nathy's had much of the sterile austerity of other religious houses I knew. Convents and presbyteries, hospitals and seminaries seemed to me to be built around the same oversized rooms, resonating corridors, and clinically polished floors. All this made for me the familiar and mildly oppressive ambiance of institutional Catholicism. My first visit to St. Nathy's was for a short interview about, I cannot be quite sure, Easter 1983. It was during the holidays and the corridors rang empty.

Returning the following September to a full house, what impressed the 'new boy' were the sounds and noises of this new school. The badinage in the form of wise-cracks and 'slagging' seemed relentless, where boys jibed with anecdotes and shrieked taunts and 'slags' at each other. Mostly this was well humoured and a good deal of it, as I thought at the time, witty and sometimes sharply observed. All of it sounded very different to an English school.

The new boy arrived from Manchester as a sixteen-year-old dayboy from the country. The last detail is significant because country dayboys were a distinct group. Bussed home each evening, country dayboys played a lesser part in St. Nathy's life. In contrast, many dayboys from the town attended evening-study, returning home to eat and to sleep, and this made their routine similar to the boarders'. Boarders at that time were still the focus of life inside St. Nathy's, and they appeared a little more self-assured than, and sometimes aloof from, the dayboys. There was also an impression that St. Nathy's was more theirs than ours and this was the source of a silent grievance. Borders looked out for each other; defending, for example, vulnerable boys against dayboy thuggery.

Dormitory-life, the daily rituals of eating and washing together and long hours of study placed much of the borders' life outside of the dayboys' experience and knowledge. There were other associations and cabals, both secret and open. The 'non-nationals' formed an unobtrusive group. These, who were the accented English and US sons, born of the 1950s and 1960s emigrants and returning to Ireland late, enjoyed free association, while the others attended their Irish classes. There were also 'repeats'; smokers; mitchers; 'dossers'; 'swots'; footballers; handballers; and basketball players, but by-and-large the important distinctions were to be found between boarder and dayboy, town and country.

Immediately there was a new vocabulary to learn. Until recently, I assumed that the strange new words were Gaelic in origin, but as it happened more often they belonged to an unfamiliar English unspoken outside Ireland. A word familiar to the Irish ear like 'Cogging' (to copy or cheat at school work) is now unknown in Britain. Originally meaning 'to cheat at dice' or 'otherwise to engage in underhand dealing and deceit', it is an example of Elizabethan English surviving in our schools. Having similar origins, 'mitching' (to truant) means 'to shrink or retire from view; to lurk out of sight; to skulk', and this was practiced with alacrity by some collegians on 'Ballagh's' court and fair days.

These words are common enough in Irish schools, but there were others more specific to St. Nathy's. 'Buffer', a mild term of abuse in my own time, is a seventeenth-century word meaning originally 'fellow' or 'man'. 'Buff-man' (I never quite understood the precise meaning of this borders' phrase) meant, at the beginning of the nineteenth century in Hiberno-English, 'boxer', and likely derives from the pugilist term 'to stand buff', meaning not to flinch. Derogatory in its intent or not, 'buff-man' was often applied to country boys, perhaps identifying someone similar to a 'hard chore' or just a 'chore' pronounced 'chawww'. 'Wigging', as in 'he got a severe wigging for messing in class', is an obsolete English slang-word originally meaning 'a rebuke' or 'scolding'. Country boys might have said 'he got a good skelp' (to strike, beat, smack'), which word is middle-English in its derivation, not Gaelic. These and other words were institutionalised inside St. Nathy's and formed part of the college's language, which is impossible now to fully recreate. And, against a lively and varied 'sound-scape', not infrequently I was reminded that I sounded different too.

The St. Nathy's where I started was in transition from diocesan seminary to an ordinary secondary school. Until the early 1970s, as we were sometimes reminded, it was not unusual for twenty or more novitiates to go to study for the priesthood each year. But by the mid-1980s, that number dwindled into single figures, and in some years to none. This presented a significant problem because St. Nathy's was losing the larger part of its founding raison d'etre as a seed-bed for vocations. In response to this, the regime had relaxed markedly by the time I arrived.

Radios were permitted and earlier prohibitions on newspapers and tobacco were relented, while boarders began to go home weekly instead of at the end of the long terms. All of this reform was enlightened, but it indicated two subtle changes in the deferential relationship between the boys and the college authorities. If students now went home on Saturday nights, partly this was because it was becoming difficult to stop them climbing from windows and attending discos. That kind of disobedience had been a lesser problem, when in earlier years the college's authority had been more daunting. Other reforms belatedly reflected those introduced at Maynooth and other seminaries coming in the post-Vatican II liberalisation, but St. Nathy's nevertheless struggled to keep up with a rapidly changing society alongside the changing expectations of its students.

Compared to Catholic schooling in Manchester, perhaps surprisingly, religious observances in St. Nathy's were often more discrete. Attendance at Mass was compulsory, but infrequent at least in dayboy hours. Classes in religious instruction on the other hand witnessed robust exchanges where students challenged doctrine (this was the era of Garret FitzGerald's 'liberal-crusade') and the President, Fr. Andrew Johnson, stoically as I thought, refuted the suggestions of anomalies and fallacies in Church teaching. The challenges to, and sometimes wholesale rejection of this theology, were of course outward expressions of youthful rebellion, but they were no less sincere for that. This again spoke to that breakdown of deference, which was accommodated with notable forbearance on the side of the priests.

Though some complained about the regime, as schoolboys do, to the newcomer St. Nathy's was in fact more liberal than expected. Formal punishments were rare, bullying among the boys (in the upper-school at least) was unusual, and generally – and this is a strong memory – students were civil not to say generous to one another. The divisions between boarder and dayboy, as among town and country, lapsed significantly during my three short years.

Over that period, greater efforts were made to include dayboys in College life, with priests and teachers driving them home to outlying parishes after sporting and other evening activities. When in 1985 the disparity between the number of boarder and dayboy prefects (seven border prefects to the dayboy's one) was raised as an issue, the President appointed five new dayboy prefects. History records with a sense of justice that the upstart, drawing attention to this discrimination, was not among the new appointments! But at the same time, this minor victory for equality also identifies the College's subtle reorientation away from boarders and boarding, toward dayboys and the day-school.

There was of course pressure to succeed academically, but most often this was self-induced, with the studious signing-up for extra-study, and the truly ambitious working through lunch-times and every other available hour. For some, a university degree and ultimately a profession were realistic goals. Third-level education was encouraged for all and was made achievable to boys of varied and different economic means. Boarders, because of the still admittedly modest fees, were drawn largely from the sons of shop-owners, middling and substantial farmers, and less often from the higher-professional classes.

During my time, no medical-doctor's son attended the College. Town-boys often shared the same social backgrounds and advantages as boarders, but country-boys came from a spectrum bridging the unemployed and the significantly wealthy. Reinforcing a sense of difference, country-boys often spoke the idiom of their countryside and sometimes this was ridiculed by their classmates into silence. For this reason, one suspects more than a few of those lads sat out their education without saying so much as a word when that is they could help it.

Admittance to the College came with expectations of formal educational advancement, and the basic environmental conditions to achieve this. From the advent of free secondary education in 1967 (but prior to this too), the College offered an opportunity to local boys. In this respect alone, Ballaghaderreen and its hinterland benefited from the College's proximity. Not because it was the only school sending students to universities and later to the RTC's and IT's (though for much of its existence it provided the lone opportunity for Achonry's boys), but because it carried within it an older ethos of creating an educated Catholic society where earlier this had been absent or at best horribly deprived. This aspiration was neither as pronounced nor as overtly class-centred as found in schools run by the Jesuits or the Loretto nuns, but it did exist in St. Nathy's. For a time, this quietly overtook its diminished mission as a feeder seminary.

St. Nathy's had academic aspirations for all of its students. Despite anything that critically might be said about the College's provision, this was important because it offered a choice to be seized or, for those who wished it, to be left well alone.

This choice contrasted very favourably with aspects of an English schoolboy's education. In my own family, three sons spanning three generations benefited from the advantages that St. Nathy's bestowed. With and without fees, St. Nathy's helped shape more than a few lawyers, doctors, teachers, building-contractors, agricultural-economists, journalists, scientists, farmers, pharmacists, bishops and ironmongers; and, without prejudice to any of them, sometimes they came from very modest clay. It is then for a reason that the College stands as an achievement of a materially impoverished people who, after 1810, rose out of something short of subsistence. This observation should invite reflection on the enabling power of even the most restricted education in a society striding the Great Famine.

Recalling the College of 1903 to 1909, William O'Dwyer (1890-1964), lawyer, judge, ambassador and sometime colourful mayor of New York wrote: "In this isolated oasis of learning... doors were opened for us." (William O'Dwyer, Beyond the golden door St. John's University Press, New York, 1987, p.61.) O'Dwyer's recollections of College life, though mixed in their sentiment, in this one respect still rang true eighty years after he entered the College.

History was initially my preferred subject at St. Nathy's and in September 1983, Fr. Tom Towey organised his honours class much as a university seminar, with prescribed readings and roundtable discussions. The innovation was welcomed.

Also offering a vista on an enticing world of ideas and contention were Fr. Andrew Finan's English literature classes. In these we ventured far away from the curriculum and once liberated were exposed to the New Yorker, Time, the London Review of Books, British broadsheets and to what was then seen as a curiously exotic publication, the Irish Times.

One day in Fr. Finan's class, news arrived with some obscure periodical that the Soviet Union, no longer able to feed herself, was importing reserves of grain from Canada. Could this be true? What did it mean? We could not answer these questions in 1985, nor comprehend their enormous significance, but there was quiet excitement that we were discussing them at all. More than a few have since expressed their gratitude for those classes, not because they primed them for examinations, but because they provoked them to think and to think independently. In this respect, one is forced to reflect on the narrow Catholicism of St. Nathy's the seminary, and the numbing textbook-led curricula were sometimes weak in promoting individual expression.

It is now impossible to re-imagine the limits of our imagination just twenty-five years ago. In reality, our minds were too often bound by a few newspapers (the 'Independent' or the 'Press'), and the limits of RTE radio and television. Ballaghaderreen had cable access to British television, but few of us, dayboy or boarder, had access to or money for cinema. While the curriculum offered gems like Gus Martin's celebrated anthology of mostly dead poets Soundings, it remained difficult to access new books by living writers.

On Barrack Street, the town's then modest library was well provisioned with romances and detective novels, but held little for the more curious reader. There was little enough library provision in the College apart from the devotional literature bequeathed by past-teachers. (I am told back-copies of Rolling Stone magazine were later anonymously deposited.) At the time, none of this was a vocal complaint. However, it begins to explain the novelty and influence on impressionable minds of visits by the Druid Theatre's touring productions of Tom Murphy's Famine and J. M. Synge's The Playboy of the Western World and, ultimately, our own attempts at performance. All of these were bursts of colour on a sepia landscape.

There existed respect, sometimes healthy sometimes grudging, for boys who really 'hit the books'. The examination results of some of the teaching-staff (all save two were St. Nathy's educated, most had boarded before becoming seminarians for long or for short) provided impressive benchmarks to be measured against.

But for many, the curriculum inspired only greater fascination in anything extra-curricular. St. Nathy's offered opportunities on the sports-field and in the sports-hall, as well as in theatrical productions, quizzes, and my own distraction (alongside Brosna's Felim Regan) debates. Given the chance for free expression, some shined brightly.

Among those opportunities was the Christmas 1984 concert, appropriately enough aiding relief for a catastrophic famine in Ethiopia. We raised £1,000 in one evening. That concert has special significance for me now framing other bitter-sweet memories of the mid-1980s which should briefly be recalled here. The economy neared bankruptcy in 1984, and good employment in Ireland seemed doubtful for many of us.

By the end of that year, the burst of the 1980s having long eclipsed the boom of the 1970s, our generation was emigrating in their thousands. We were let know the craic, like the work was plenty in London and New York, and this was the sweet. But the bitter was tasted in the pessimism many then had about any future at home. In the few this reinforced a strong instinct for survival through examination results.

Neither were we immune to the malaise overlaying the economic depression. This was the era of the Kerry babies' tribunal and vitriolic and confused debates surrounding the unborn child's constitutional right to life, as well as marital divorce. Closer to our life experience were the deaths of schoolgirl-mother Anne Lovett (15) and her infant-boy, following her attempt to give birth outside a county Longford church. The pregnancy's concealment ended soon after the mother went into labour inside a Marian grotto. As the tragedy emerged through the media during the first week of February 1984, it sketched, then as now, an appalling low-point in the transition from one society to another.

Our Christmas concert was a joyous diversion from our studies and the gloom outside. The Inter Cert students adapted Michael Jackson's music video Thriller in a brilliantly mimed song and dance routine. There was a rich and memorable performance of scenes from William Shakespeare's The Merchant of Venice, followed by readings from the work of some living writers. All of this was engaging and great fun, but what happened next marks a now obscure achievement in the College's cultural history.

The finale was provided by College band 'Making Faces', with Gallagher twins Jarlaith and Turlough providing lead vocals, Michael Moylett on lead guitar, Joe Geever on base guitar, Fintan Judge on keyboards, and Seamus Geever making a rare appearance on drums. They opened with the Gallaghers' and Judge's composition 'Party in the Bay' (a live-recording from the night is available on the website 'YouTube'), followed by Rick Springfield's 'Jessie's girl'. In squinting retrospect, it is the original composition that remains the night's enduring creative achievement, but it was the band's cover of the Doors' 'Riders on the storm' that burnt so deep into my consciousness that it has remained the defining memory of those years at St. Nathy's. Does anyone else now remember the audience's rapture as the band picked-up the lyric after Judge's instrumental? What those six young men did that night transcended our surroundings, showing us what could be done by our own people. Momentarily they connected us to a world just beyond our reach, but one beckoning us and promising life in all its pain and all its glory. And, in all its misery and joy, so it has been.

Riders on the storm
Into this house we're born
Into this world we're thrown
Like a dog without a bone
An actor out alone
Riders on the storm

Dr. John M. Regan (Class of 1986) lectures in political history at the University of Dundee, Scotland.

• 42 •

St. Joseph's

Marie Staunton

LC1987; Consultant Radiologist, Toronto

It is quiet outside. Sunday night. Snow is falling steadily, muffling the sounds of traffic and people going about their lives. The city of Toronto stretches before me, lights twinkling, touching the inky blackness of the chilly night – minus thirty I remark; another cold one.

I am pacing, not knowing quite where to begin. A lifetime and the Atlantic now lie between me and St. Joseph's, but even so, I am easily transported back to a time when a navy procession made its way daily up and down the Convent Road. Yes, a navy uniform with knee-length socks of course, no dangly earrings and absolutely no runners! If I close my eyes, a kaleidoscope of sights and sound in no particular order jostle for attention. Inwardly I smile as I dust them off and peruse the memories that lie before me.

What has St. Joseph's meant to me, a former pupil? The thing I value most are the friendships that were forged in our secondary school that have stood the test of time. I still count among my close friends the select few who knew everything about me back then; the girls you told when someone said "Do not tell anybody"; with whom I still laugh until I cry.

How lucky I was to meet those girls!

I received a fine education in St. Joseph's. I was allowed to think, to formulate opinions and to have a voice. I was challenged both academically and as a person, and that helped me shape the adult I am today. I learned that hard work was rewarded and that I could achieve anything I set my mind to. Look where this has taken me! The marvellous adventure that is my life to date: medical school in Galway; sub-specialist training in Dublin; and continuing in Toronto where I am now a consultant radiologist in one of the largest hospitals in Canada.

I look back fondly through my rose tinted glasses. I will admit that from here, those days look golden. I remember the hijinks and hilarity that were in abundance all those years ago – aching for experiments to explode in Miss Smith's science class; the obsession with basketball and how good Noreen Byrne and Teresa Hanglon were at it; the amazing school support for the team; musicals practiced, perfected and performed; how amazingly well Ruth Coleman sang; the inspector's car and the shaving foam; romance; boys; St. Nathy's; discos; school retreats; Christmas tests; Sr. Dolores – all part and parcel of that time.

On a recent visit home, I happened to pass up the Convent Road. I was astounded by the fact that where St. Joseph's once stood is now an empty field that stretches to the convent orchard. I was somewhat indignant that someone had bulldozed my school to make way for progress; somehow I just assumed it would always be there.

In a way, it is as in my mind's eye, I will always see that dilapidated old cream-coloured building with the peeling grey door where I began to grow up, to have an opinion, to speak my mind and to find my way in this world from where I now look back with fondness, gratitude and pride.

• 43 •

Basketball in the 80s

Micheal Cormican

LC 1987; Member of Staff, Higher Colleges of Technology, UAE

There are 12 seconds remaining. St. Nathy's are up by one against St. Pat's Armagh in the semi-final of the inaugural schools under-19 Cup 1987. The winners were to play North Mon from Cork in the final. An offensive foul gave St. Pat's the opportunity to go to the free throw line and win the game. Silence fell upon the crowd in the Inchicore Hall as the Northern lads equalized. The second shot followed with both teams wishing and hoping for the opposite result.

Basketball was a central part in the life of most boarders in the 1980s. St. Nathy's teams throughout the decade were the dominant force at both Connacht and national level. This fact was all the more impressive in that most players did not learn to play until they started first year. The strong bonds formed between players both on and off the court ensured that St. Nathy's teams performed well at all age levels.

My introduction to basketball was when I welcomed home the under-15 and under-19 teams on winning the All Ireland in 1982. This was the first time the double was achieved by the same school in the same year. The first basketball game I watched was when Ballinamore travelled to play us on the outdoor courts at under-15, under-17 and under-19 in the LonLeitRos competition. Shane Morley, Paul Lowry, Colm Wallace and I stood in the perishing cold watching the games, longing for the opportunity to be playing ourselves. These games culminated in probably the biggest school's sporting event in Connacht, held annually in Roscommon sports centre, the LonLeitRos Finals.

The countdown to basketball training began as the last class finished at four. From there it was straight to the refectory where we consumed the 1980s version of sport nutrition and energy drinks – jam sandwiches washed down with cups of milk. A mad dash up the terrazzo stairs to the dorms to change followed. The sport trends of the time included singlets, hooded tops and Adidas top-ten or converse boots. Our enthusiasm was a little too much at times for Fr. T. Johnston as we tried to take the basketballs from him as he walked along the red corridor to the outdoor courts. Often he would throw the balls in front of him to disperse us. First and second years trained on the mossy court adjacent to the football field. I believe practicing our dribbling and driving skills on such a surface stood us well when we travelled to our competitor's indoor courts. After an hour training, it was time to tog in and do what we were there for in the first place, study. Tea at 7pm was followed by scrimmage games and games of 21 on the outdoor courts under the floodlight until study again at eight.

Basketball became more that just a sport; we got an appreciation for Perry Como music while travelling to and from games in Fr. Joyce's Peugeot. It afforded us the opportunity to travel the length and breadth of the country playing in gyms from Belfast to Crosshaven. Basketball and football were a natural compliment for each other in St. Nathy's, as is reflected by the number of top players down the years that were equally successful at both disciplines. This was only made possible by the great understanding among the various coaching staff in the College.

And by the way, St. Pat's missed their second free throw to send the game into overtime (which we narrowly lost).

On behalf of all the players who picked up a basketball in St. Nathy's, I would like to take this opportunity to thank both Fr. T. Johnston and Fr. M. Joyce for the years of hard work they put in – coaching, refereeing, mentoring and character building all of us on courts across the country. Thank you for the memories. *Go raibh mile maith agaibh.*

• 44 •

The Blonde, the Professor and the Nervous Stammer - Notes on a Liberal Education

John Joe Callaghan

LC 1989; Director of Native Speaker Language School
and Summer Camp Ireland.com

When given an essay to write while a student in Nathy's, a succession of long-suffering English teachers drilled one thing into me – in essay writing there has to be a beginning, a middle and an end; basic rule, most important thing, core principle – ok, ok, I get it... just not necessarily in that order. So you will forgive me if twenty years down the line I continue the habit of a lifetime and, to quote Tom Waits, "lead with my chin".

I will start somewhere in the middle. After I left Nathy's I got a place studying arts in Maynooth. Well I actually got a place on the prestigious Hal-al Scholarship programme – I spent a year on the killing-line and in the belly-room trying to scrape together fees and cash to help fund the big adventure. Bu, when I eventually got there, part of the degree in Maynooth involved studying the Classics – Greek and Roman civilisation. Now before I go too far into this, let me assure you this was something I sort of crash-landed into. It was one of the choices in first year Arts and I had wandered round the campus sampling various lectures, like a wedding crasher at the buffet – and just as shifty looking. I had stumbled into an economics lecture earlier in Freshers' week and had briefly entertained notions of fiscal edification, but scuttled out before the end with a piercing headache. So I found myself in more humanist territory – the Classics. The reason I was more at home was due in no small part to having studied the Classics in Nathy's, and apart from the epic scraps that I now think inspired many re-enactments out in the box-alley, I felt I might have an aptitude for it, that and I may have thought it might be a handy number as they did not have anything in civics at the time.

Although I only had to do Classics for a year – with good behaviour – it turned out to be a bit more challenging than I had thought. In the Roman section, there was a lecturer who was a priest of mature years who had a pretty fearsome reputation for not suffering fools – and first year Classics students – gladly. One of the tasks set to us as part of his course was to write an essay on the subject of liberal education.

I do not really remember much about it – something to do with Cicero. At the time, it did not sound so bad really. I thought I would throw in a few opinions on letting it all hang out and hey presto: '*Robert c'est votre oncle*' as they say in Gaul.

In those days, you went to the office of the lecturer who had corrected your essay, you would knock politely at the door, pick it up, jump on the bike and continue being a man about town. Some professors were kind enough to leave it on a special shelf or box on the wall of the corridor outside their office and you could pick up the good or bad news yourself. Not so with the black-robed professor of Classics. I skulked around the corridor for a bit, checked the box – no joy. A second fly-by was not able to fully establish if he was in his lair or not, but that question was about to be answered – as he suddenly burst out of his office and began to shuffle apoplectically with papers at the box shelf – a cross between Dracula and Yosemite Sam. I suddenly got a rain-man like fascination with the paint work on the opposite wall of the corridor until he had swept back in, his black professor's cloak swishing behind him. I shuffled over to the box and discovered the familiar scrawl of my masterpiece sticking out of its plastic sleeve. From a glance, I could see a lot of red marker slashed all over it. Well... he had been liberal with that anyway.

Just then, one of the prettiest girls in all of Maynooth sashayed down the corridor on a similar mission to mine. The place filled with a heavenly perfumed aroma and Barry White music. A golden aura emanated from her blonde hair. She was in my Classics class and I would stare suavely at the back of her head in lectures. I had entertained impure thoughts about her and, as with all boys who grew up in an all-male school environment, I could only manage self-assured gazes at women when they were not looking. My nervous fumblings at trying to avoid meeting old Professor Death were now compounded with Porky Pig impressions as she deigned to smile at me. You see, there had been no girls in St. Nathy's in my day and discos were still affairs where opposite genders lined out across from each other in the Midnight Club, more in an atmosphere of suspicion, loathing and repressed lust... ah, good times.

Anyway, this particular Venus De Milo was a nice girl from somewhere in Dublin. Affluent by the sound of her accent. Today she probably gets all the groceries in farmers' markets, drives an SUV and has got even younger looking. She had none of the wily prejudices of those of us up from the country. She granted me a smile the way the fairy godmother would wave her wand over rags to make the dress for the ball.

I had a quick peek at the mark on my own essay and put it back quickly into the plastic sleeve – you do not need to know the gory details, but in a savage scrawl under the offending vowel was written, "This rambling drivel touches on many things, but SADLY NONE OF THEM TO DO WITH LIBERAL EDUCATION!" I was sort of expecting it, but I had expected at least a consonant for a mark.

Her nibs, who normally would not even step on me, suddenly became interested in my academic progress. "How did you get on?" she asked. "Mumble..., yeah, no, grand... mumble well, maybe not great mumble..." I answered with a debonair glance at my feet, and a panicked attempt to put it away. Oblivious, she gave a cursory glance at the box and, as there was no aroma of lavender and happiness, she assumed it was waiting inside with the big guy. Gloriously unaware of the danger, she knocked at the door and from within the minotaur bellowed to enter. She opened the door and I was momentarily caught in the gaze of the professor. I made a Scooby-doo style attempt to go one way and then the other as he enquired what she wanted. "Sorry," she said, "it's just that I cannot see my essay here in the box." I started to lift my legs and move out of his stare and down the corridor before I turned to stone. As I moved off, I noticed a little plastic rubbish bin with papers sticking out of it. "Did you try the bin?" he thundered. She staggered back from the affront and glanced distractedly at the bin full of liberal education. She bent down to retrieve something and I quickened my pace, feeling a little better that, despite having got a mark well into the alphabet, at least my masterpiece on Liberal Education had made the box on the wall.

Jump forward to the present and my mind goes to the topic of liberal education once again, but with the benefit of 19 years to ponder. So now I can say something about it – minus the blonde, the professor and the nervous stammer.

The St. Nathy's experience taught many things. It prepared its many sons, and eventually also its daughters, to go out into the world, and speaking from my own experience it allowed us to grow in an environment that prepared us for the world. As you can tell from my stellar performance with the blonde, we were not exactly given classes in sophistication and urbanity and I would even go as far as to say that many of us, including yours truly, left St. Nathy's still pretty naive.

What I feel was ingrained in us by the St. Nathy's experience was the philosophy of the landscape – stay with me, I will go back to talking about blondes in a minute.

The west of Ireland has always necessitated that its children adapt to and ultimately endure the trials and tribulations that it throws at us (and for some of its elected representatives, even the odd tribunal). So, in an almost evolutionary process, we have been conditioned to anticipate adversity, then adjust and ultimately overcome it. For generations, graduates did so on local farms, building sites around the world, banks and corporations in many, many walks of life.

The men and women that St. Nathy's produced as students – and those who eventually returned as teachers – were as much a product of that environment as anybody. But their role amplified something that they transferred to us. You see, what I now think is important about a liberal education is not necessarily knowing, but more importantly understanding. Our teachers passed on an almost spartan sense of 'you can do this'. Actually, let me elaborate on that; it was more a sense of 'get up outta that and feckin' do it and never mind yer whingin or I'll hop yer head of that wall' kind of thing. And that is the crux of the matter. We were naturally curious, but the staff gave us a sense of confidence... in their own 'I'd hop your head off that wall" kind of way.

I can say this with a bit more experience than some of my generation because I was one of the 'fortuitous fourteen', (ok, not a great title but the 'dirty dozen' was taken, ok!). This was the rag-tag bunch of fourteen ne'er do wells, who were to become the first ever Transition Year Class in St. Nathy's. Transition Years (or 'ty' as it became know amongst the dude sections of the school) had been around in Ireland, in limited supply since 1974, and saw an increase in provision in the late 1980s, though they were still not exactly mainstream until the mid-1990s.

I cannot tell you exactly how anyone convinced me to spend an extra year in secondary school without failing the Leaving Cert, but they did... not the brightest button in the box, sez you.

But the thing was, we did some really interesting things and I can tell you we spent a considerable amount of time on the roof of the College doing them. We built a bee-hive, started a company, took up rugby (yeah, on school time!), started our own radio station (hence being up on the roof so much), staged a pretty ok version of 'Philadelphia, Here I Come' and planted a load of flower beds round the place that are still going strong today. Learning how to do all this stuff was good, but do you know what I remember after all these years? The array of teachers who rolled up their sleeves and dragged us through it like the brave young lieutenants that they were (most of them were younger then than I am now... don't ask). I will not embarrass them by mentioning them, suffice it to say that they jumped into the trenches with us and roared, "Come back with yer shield, or on yer shield," and led the charge from in front. When assailed by doubt in our abilities to rise to some of the challenges that lay ahead of us, most of them would respond by always telling us in a matter-of-fact manner: "Ye can do this." When we needed their advice, they were like Michael Caine in the Italian Job ("'Ang about lads, I 'ave an idea"). When we planted the flower beds, Fr. Joyce (go on then, let's name and shame) drove us out in his car to our bog in Lisine to get turf mould for the flower beds – I can still see the wheels spinning and us pushing his new Peugeot, trying to get him out of a soft spot that he had backed into, giving a new slant to the definition of 'getting stuck in'.

I remember being down in Shannonside with Ollie Feeley getting pallets to build up part of the stage for the play we were producing – which had a very formative influence on me and started a life-long love affair between me and pallets – you would be amazed what you can use them for!

I remember Fr. Joe Caulfield walking round with a pliers and a screw-driver cheek by jowl with us setting up the radio station, and Fr. Andrew Finan standing in the cold hall night after night with his battered copy of Brian Friel's collected works, patiently waiting for us to come down from a fit of the giggles and helping us explore drama and expression. Hollywood's loss was our gain.

Fr. Leo Henry, introducing us to 'To Kill a Mockingbird' and numerous other texts that we would otherwise have never had time to cover in a time-sensitive Leaving Certificate and gave us a love of reading and not just regurgitating.

Tom Fahy, teaching us how to run a business, lodge money in the bank, do accounts, order fruit for the shop and sell shares to raise capital "Leave a line and draw a line, this account is now closed." Great words of advice that Tom never intended to stray beyond book-keeping, but which served me well in putting any bad thing behind me later in life.

Man, those guys and anyone else I have left out were like Spartans. You know, the word 'laconic', which, for those of you at the back, means 'to be of few words' comes from Lakonia / Lakedonia – the region in Greece of which Sparta was the capital. These boys were known for being hard chaws and not having much to say. In a bit of a shindig with the Macedonians, Philip of

Macedon threatened them with: "If I enter Laconia, I will raze Sparta to the ground." The Spartans' reply was: "If."

That is my memory of the men and women of St. Nathy's, of few words, but always spoken well. They engendered a laconic but steely attitude to getting things done, a stern self belief and provided the gentle reminders that nothing is beyond us; that self-pity is poison and that it is adversity that shapes us. I wonder if Obama was a St. Nathy's man?

So, thank you St. Nathy's. You were sometimes a dark forbidding place, an unsympathetic witness that told me to get up and keep going. I do not always miss you, but you have implanted yourself firmly inside me and I think although you aimed your boot a bit lower, you may have ended up somewhere in my spine.

And so I conclude this essay by saying categorically and indubitably that the definition of liberal education is to plant a seed of never-ending curiosity and to nurture it with the idea that nothing is beyond us… that is mine, by the way, if you want Cicero's, get thee to a library.

• 45 •

Memories of St. Nathy's College

Declan Moran

LC 1990; Software Engineer

Quiet corridors of stately dark brown panelled walls
Sustain a serene silence that permeates
The old school halls. Containers of peace.
Only the surrounding town adds a dreamy distant
Murmur to the background of timeless tranquillity.
It has no meaning here.
An occasional closing door five corners away
Echoes fading steps from high-set ceilings
And an impervious cold stone floor.
Of some anomalous wayfarer, errant on his lonely way
Out of place the footfall soon abates,
Swallowed by some secret darkened passage
Beneath the brass capped wooden stairs.

Then a chair moves behind a door
A single sliding rubbery squeak
Momentary harbinger that signals forth
A roar of countless heaving chairs
A thousand thumping feet
Burst through all doors to feed
A massive swelling wave of green and blue
That thunders down the hall
Quiet now hides behind a trembling wainscot
Along a beaten stone tiled floor

The beast breaks through the pale
Grey blue hanging doors,

Pours unawares its zenith past.
Patient phalanx of lockers now lines the way.
Cannaen forms that feign a pass
Bestow lateral bolts of individual consciousness
On bobbing heads that swirl and eddy from the mass.
Sturdier shoulders walk straighter lines
As padlocks spring open a welcome click
In master's half forgotten hand

Friends' faces emerge and pass
A trotting straggler catches up
To groups of twos and threes
Making their way slower than necessary
Across the yard by the handball alley.
Toward a new school of cream rectangular bricks,
Double glazed windows in white pebble-dash
And a curiously intangible atrium.
Where every teacher has a suspicious metal closet
A modern green blackboard
And an on the whole pleasant view
Of rural Ireland.

Letters with numbers in Maths for big boys!
An alien alphabet with squiggles and bars
Pythagoras' legacy cosine rules
Cubic equations and natural logs
First derivative integral curves.
Exercise no movement – gymnastics for the brain.
Thus armed with variable incertitude
We became confident adolescents
Capable of answering not just one question
But infinitely many.

101 English starts with a laugh
Expert instruction incipient on impressionable minds
The class that was one becomes the many.
History, philosophy, psychology,
Social studies, allegorical fancy.
The queen of tongues soon shows her face,
Letters to characters, pages their lives.
Turning keys and building bridges
'Twixt the space that measures day and night,
Cerebral caverns measureless to man.
Hotspur, Eppie, Miss Havisham,
The miller sailing to Byzantium
You have burgeoned our banks of youth.

Schubert's trout and three gypsies stood
Inside lofty iron gates a sheer granite façade.
Day boys demur to the servant's side entrance
Where concrete bicycle stands mediate
Between sagging grey patio slabs,
With their characteristic pattern of puddles
To be avoided on rainy days,
And an overgrown ancient graveyard.
Two stories of the corner dedicated
To teaching our *teanga naisiunta*
Tuiseal ginideach, cead diochlaonadh,
And the saga of Peig

Crisp winter mornings outside the woodwork shed.
A hazy grey shroud of half fallen dew
Imbues the air with a soft stasis,
Reassuring blanket of unchanging foreverness.
Over the swimming pool long-since drained
Where spectres of past pupils frolic and swam.
Was the weather so much better then?
Sizeable set squares for technical drawing
Brass tipped rulers – Mjolnir in the hand.
Blunt 8mm chisels bite dovetail joints
Planed over steadfast battle beaten benches.
And the vice held fast. Fashion a handy
Scissors holder for your home kitchen.

Bunsen burners, table of the elements
And the whitest taps I have ever seen
Equations of motion, Ohm's Law
And the reassuring comfort
Of Newtonian predictability.
Trendy jackets and the latest basketball boots
Tea breaks (in groups) on the walk
Dire Straits, the Cure, U2
Catechism, retreat and the Ten Commandments,
Young high-strung bodies vibrate in the chapel pews.

Passé compose, plus que-parfait
Past tense of avoir, Je m'appelle.
A polished mosaic staircase in the west wing
Pours incongruously up into the study hall.
Etched words on antique benches,
White sash windows rarely open
Afford a glance across the fields
To a regular row of mature evergreen trees

That seems to mark the edge of the world.
Where does that door in the far corner go?

Zenus, Apollo, Aphrodite
Noble Hector, Perseus and Ajax the great.
Hephaestus in empty stomachs at five to one.
Borders converge on the refectory
Teachers glide across the quadrangle
And day boys descend upon the town.
The mysterious case of the disappearing desks
Found half sunken in the lawn outside.
Mitochondrion, Krebs cycle, cytoplasm.
Hyphenated abbreviations chalked on the board
String together a web of life

Four o'clock infused us with oxygen.
All weather outdoor basketball courts
With precariously scattered loose chippings.
Layups, double dribble, swish.
The click-clack march of the football boots
Outside the changing rooms.
Shower cubicles and muddy legs.
The weight room up the narrow steps
Past the prefect in the tuck shop
And the hidden smoking shed.
The indoor court was seldom used
Except for assembly, rules of the house,
The Plough and the Stars,
And the Bishop's blessing – last class off!

Points, preferences, career guidance.
Was ever a subject so hard to teach?
Yet so admirably taught?
A glossy prospectus from Manchester polytechnic
Sails slowly round the class.
Arts in Galway, medicine in UCD
Dentistry, law, tool-making.
Picture yourself in a decade or more
Unborn futures with a mind's eye see,
When does one know what one wants to be?

• 46 •
Robur Nathaei …
The Strength of Nathy
Tomas Surlis

LC 1990; Studying for Doctorate in Ecclesiology,
Gregorian University Rome

Resplendent in my new uniform, I will always remember, or perhaps I should say I will never forget, the night I arrived at St. Nathy's College. There was a knot in my stomach that announced the dreaded moment had finally arrived! My father had accompanied this fledgling as he haltingly flew from the nest for the first time, and another 'Father' welcomed us at the front door – the formidable-looking person of the Dean. It was early January 1988 and my parents had decided (and I was informed!) that the time had come for me to go to boarding school to better prepare for my Leaving Certificate exams. To declare that I was horrified would be an understatement. Suffice to say that I had often passed through Ballaghaderreen and wondered, fleetingly, what the interior of the rather grand looking building was like, but now here I was, about to have my worst fears confirmed. It was bad enough to be going to boarding school, but to be sent there after Christmas was a humiliation beyond description. How on earth was I going to fit in? All those lads who had come here in September would be well established by now. What were they going to make of this newcomer in their midst? To make matters even worse, I had forgotten my quilt and no amount of pleading with my father would convince him to go home and get in for me. The other 'Father' said not to worry and that he would sort something out. The 'something' he sorted out turned out to be two blankets of questionable vintage which served as bed covering until my quilt duly arrived.

I waved goodbye to my father from the steps of the College and then forlornly headed indoors, following the Dean, Fr. Peter Gallagher, to my new quarters. Let us just say that the dormitory was not exactly what I expected. I was now the proud possessor of a bed and locker that were rather fittingly positioned on their own a little distance away from the other beds and lockers in a large open-plan room. As the litany of disasters grew in my near-traumatised mind,

I silently cursed my parents and wondered what sort of devilry had prompted them to inflict such torments on their innocent and heretofore loving son?

How on earth was I going to survive all this?

Well, survive I did. Indeed, after a month had passed, I looked back on that first night and had to ask myself what all the fuss was about. St. Nathy's College was not so bad after all. It was not all horrors. In fact, there were quite a few blessings in the mix too. Chief among them were the friends I made there; friends whom I am still proud to number among the best I have ever known in my life. It was they and the comradeship we shared that made life in St. Nathy's not only bearable, but even to a degree enjoyable. As time passed, I found my place in the well-established hierarchy. I began to do a little better at my studies, although, despite valiant efforts, I never mastered theorems and trigonometry! I never became proficient at football either. I found athletics more to my liking and did reasonably well... well enough, that is, not to disgrace myself!

Names such as 'Study Hall', 'Ref' and 'The Walk' became so familiar as to pass almost unnoticed in the medley of conversation that formed the quasi-musical background to each day.

Many were the blessings and challenges during my time in St. Nathy's College and I am grateful for them all because they helped me to become the person I am today. I still remember with gratitude the teachers who cultivated the sometimes hidden talents within me and who helped equip me for the choices I would have to make as the hour of my departure into the wide, wonderful world edged ever closer. Some of those teachers later became colleagues and friends when I joined the staff of the College not long after my ordination in 2003.

Now, when I pass through Ballaghaderreen on my way to or from Tubbercurry and look up at the once formidable-looking buildings, I no longer wonder what the interior looks like. I know every inch of it. Its grey wall now inspire many and great memories of people and events that have marked my life forever. Robur Nathaei... in the strength of Nathy, we were formed to become persons for others. In the strength of Nathy, may all who celebrate the Bicentenary of this great institution of learning for life be inspired to give thanks for all that we may have received and all that we have been enabled to give.

• 47 •

The Pontoon Boarder/Dayboy

John Geary

LC 1994; Solicitor Dublin

It came as no shock to me when in the summer of 1988 my parents informed me of my impending departure to secondary school in Ballaghaderreen and boarding at St. Nathy's College. After all, my two older brothers, Michael and Brendan, had been there ahead of me and they turned out ok. That September, when the Olympics were just getting underway in Seoul, Korea, I was shipped off on a five-year package holiday to the local Diocesan Boarding School in Ballaghaderreen.

Looking back, the five years passed very quickly and I have to say that overall, the experience was a good one. It was difficult being away from home at the age of 12, but it helped toughen me up for what lay ahead.

Education, sport and discipline were the hallmarks of the St. Nathy's tradition. There were some brilliant teachers. Fr. Michael Joyce was a masterful science and biology teacher. He captivated his audience and was passionate about what he imparted.

James Flanagan from Ballymote was an incisive teacher of maths and, although he would on occasion put the fear of God into you, his results did speak for themselves.

Paddy Henry from Tourlestrane was a legendary Irish teacher who made the subject both interesting and fun. I also had him for French and his 'joie de vivre', at teaching lads from Lisacul and Loughlynn the ins and outs of French grammar and vocabulary, was a beauty to behold.

Throughout my time in St. Nathy's, most boarders just could not wait to get out of there. There was something very restrictive about being holed up and not being able to do what you feel like doing. You saw the dayboys head out of the iconic gates everyday at 4.00pm to a relative freedom, whereas the life of a boarder was to stay inside the confines and dream about escape another day.

The end of daily class at 4.00pm heralded a stampede to the canteen where the Dean, Fr. Gallagher, had a long table of Charlestown's finest 'All Fresh' white bread pans lined up for us, together with fresh milk and gallons of it. Along with jars of strawberry jam, we would tuck into the bread like as if it was going out of fashion. Growing boys had a tendency to be famished at that hour of the day, and the wise Dean always had plenty of bread ready and I can safely say I never remember it running out. Three or four slices would be some lads' lot, whereas others would easily do half a loaf, and one boarder I remember in particular could do a full loaf of bread with ease.

Sport was a great focus of life at St. Nathy's. Geography teacher John O'Mahony trained the first years twice a week after school and, as one of a few Mayo students in the class, it was a great thrill having the Mayo Senior Football Manager of the day train us. Fr. Joyce was our Basketball coach and was responsible for encouraging so many students into the game. Fond memories of trips to St. Mels in Longford or taking part in the Lonleitros competition, when the school day would be shortened with Fr. Joyce rounding us all up on the bus. He was a very generous man and he would regularly stop off and treat us to burgers and chips or some chocolates. I have no doubt this generosity came straight out of his own pocket and the students always appreciated him for this.

Fr. Martin Jennings was a terrific member of the teaching staff at the College during my time. He was our career guidance teacher and the 'Quiz Master' at St. Nathy's. Fr. Jennings worked tirelessly for the students and his boundless energy made him one of the top handball coaches in the West of Ireland. The College had one main ball alley, or the 'box alley' as we knew it. Off that, there were three other alleys that were occupied by students in different years, and these walls were the source of many hours of distraction and fun.

Other priests at Nathy's during my time were Fr. Andrew Johnson, who was the College President; Fr. Tommy Towey, who was another great football coach and superb history teacher; Fr. Andrew Finan, who was an ever-present during my tenure in Ballaghaderreen – his love and passion for English literature and poetry ensured me a good honours result in the Leaving Cert; Fr. Leo Henry was also one of the corner stones of the College during my time and taught me Classical Civilisation and English up to the Inter Cert. When I was preparing to leave St. Nathy's, fresh-faced Fr. Martin Convey arrived to St. Nathy's to replace Fr. Joyce, who was elevated as Parish Priest of Curry. Fr. Convey became the science and biology teacher and later took over as President of St. Nathy's.

These men gave great dedication to the thousands of students who passed through their classroom and sporting fields. Although we were often the bane of their life with our cheekiness, juvenile behaviour and the general high jinx that boarders would get up to, behind it all every student appreciated what they had done for us and the part they played in helping to form us into the good men we are today.

The make-up of boarders was diverse. In every year, there was a solid base of County Roscommon lads. They hailed from places like Castlerea, Ballintubber, Roscommon town or Elphin. The Sligo crew usually came from towns and villages like Tubbercurry, Ballisodare, Collooney or Sligo itself.

The Mayo lads were usually in the minority, but there were always a few from Swinford, Charlestown and the Foxford area. Add into that a sprinkling from other corners of the West of Ireland and a handful from Dublin, and you got a mix of students that you could only find in St. Nathy's.

These territorial divisions often continued on the football fields and the basketball courts. Competition was fierce at times and pride in the county colour would always be to the fore. Us Mayo students took comfort in the fact that most of Ballaghaderreen classified itself as more red and green than saffron and blue, and so we were on relatively safe ground.

The supervised study in the study hall every night was something that most of us dreaded. For the Leaving Cert, the daily three and a half hours probably was not enough, but for first and second years, the time tended to drag.

The first session between 5.30pm and 7.00pm was not too bad. A break for tea and perhaps a stroll around the 'walk' brought you up to 8.00pm, when study resumed until 10.00pm. That was a long stretch every night, but in hindsight, it gave us no excuses for not having our homework completed.

After study each night we would assemble in the oratory for nightly prayer. I used to enjoy the twice-daily visits to the College oratory for morning and night prayer. This oratory was constructed in the late 1950s by my grandfather, P.J Kelly from Westport. I used to imagine him working and building the chapel on many a frosty night as I gazed up at the Dean belting out a decade of the rosary.

There was a perception that the food we as boarders got in St. Nathy's left a lot to be desired. The reality was that the food was pretty good. Imelda Towey, along with Patricia Cafferky and Mrs. Corrigan, ensured that what was served up to us was healthy and wholesome. For my first few years, the food was plated and served on rings on each table. Later we queued at a hot plate and this was a real test of your charm. If you could soft talk the lady dishing up the food, it might entitle you to an extra scoop of mash potato or perhaps a breast chicken instead of a leg. The desserts are still some of the most vivid memories I have of St. Nathy's. Custard was top of the list, which on Mondays was served with fruit cocktail; on Tuesdays we would get apple crumble with custard; on Thursday a slice of sponge and jam was served with custard; and finally on Friday, a repeat of fruit cocktail and custard would be enjoyed. Wednesdays would be the only 'custard free' day, when rice pudding was the dessert of the day.

Students used to gamble. We would play a game of 21 on the basketball court and would bet a dessert on the outcome of the game. If you lost the game, your opponent would get your dessert. Often this would lead to a must-win 'double or quits' game, where the result was either pure disaster or a sigh of relief. If you lost your apple crumble and custard, then the wounds would take a while to heal!

There is no doubt that life in St. Nathy's took some adjusting to. The rulebook, the law of the jungle, applied. It was a melting pot of characters. Some were jovial and funny; others were on the look out for chinks or weaknesses. The key to survival in boarding school was to 'fit in' and, if you could achieve that, you were halfway there. If you stood out from the crowd, for whatever reason, then slagging and ridicule were never too far away. All of this is typical of daily life in Irish schools across the country and St. Nathy's was no exception. Your time in Nathy's certainly toughened you up and, if you got knocked down, your resolve would ensure that you got up again just as quickly. This was a great life-skill to acquire and one that takes on even greater resonance upon leaving St. Nathy's.

The foregoing is just a snap shot. There are lots of other great stories still fresh in the mind some twenty-odd years later. Planned (and successful!) escapes downtown; midnight raids on dormitories; the rivalry and the friendships. I also remember the day Fr. Johnson caught Stephen Joyce and myself in Morelli's takeaway; we were just about to tuck into a tasty burger and chips when we were nabbed.

The Dean, Fr. Peter Gallagher, was some character. I got to know him much better after leaving St. Nathy's when he became administrator in the parish of Foxford. He ruled the roost in St. Nathy's and you messed with him at your peril. His skills of interrogation and information extraction were legendary. He had an inner resolve to get to the bottom of a prank that I have not seen displayed by anyone since. He was also very fair-minded and if you had a genuine request, he would try and accommodate.

My five-year boarding stint came to an end in June 1993. However, I ended up repeating the Leaving Cert as I was still only 17 and there was further room for improvement with my results. I managed to convince my parents that if I was to repeat my Leaving Cert, it would be financially better for them if I stayed in Spellman's Motel on the Dublin road on a B&B basis, and had my lunch and tea in St. Nathy's. I remember calling to see John Spellman and asking him what he would charge me if I were to stay four nights per week. The princely sum of £9 B&B was agreed (which in 1993 was a steal). So, for my repeat Leaving Cert year, I stayed in Spellman's and ate my lunch and tea in St. Nathy's, as well as attending the nightly study sessions. It worked out surprisingly well and my two older brothers cannot believe I pulled off that stroke.

So the five-year package holiday actually ended up as a six, and then I was ready to leave the nest in Ballaghaderreen and go to university equipped with all the life skills I had learned in St. Nathy's. A number of us St. Nathy's boys now regularly meet in Dublin for a night out and we spend hours reminiscing the great times spent and the characters we encountered along the way. As the years pass, those stories and memories become more treasured.

• 48 •

Vocational School

Alex McDonnell

LC 1963; Principal of Vocational School, 1986-1995

Vocation education classes commenced in St. Brigid's Hall in October 1935 with an enrolment of 32. The school on its present site opened for classes in October 1939. Up to 1967, students followed a two-year course leading to Group Cert. Free post-primary education was introduced in 1967 and the school commenced presenting students for Intermediate Cert. In 1969, students started the Leaving Cert course.

I began my teaching career in 1967, having little knowledge of the various courses being presented and the facilities available. I knew it was a distinct second level system with manual expertise in a core area. I was conscious of some teachers who taught there; in particular, I knew two teachers of science in whose footsteps I was following – they were Professor J. B. Ruane, the Head of Agriculture who lectured me in UCD, and Oliver Hynes, who was a CEO in Galway.

Being an early arrival on my first day, I was observed entering the school, from an upstairs window, by Mamie Woods, the caretaker. A warm Ceid Mile Failte was given to me and this was the beginning of a marvellous friendship from a motherly figure, which only culminated 41 years later with her death at the ripe old age of 101.

Of particular interest to me was the home school garden, which involved first-year students. The school had a vegetable garden that was painstakingly managed by caretaker Gerry Reid. Of course there were times when Gerry's colourful language best described the havoc created by marauding arthropods. Students cultivated their own garden. Here they encountered triumphs, setbacks, obstacles and disappointments. The mistakes and failures encountered were valuable lessons learned. No prescribed text could make the connectedness with nature that growing these plants fostered or educate people to the vagaries of the carrot fly, slug, caterpillar, turnip, flea beetle or cabbage root fly. Students competed for the prizes awarded and no doubt in some cases Granddad lent a helping hand. Even the adjudicator learned new ways from students of tricking and trapping a slug.

The Christmas concert on the day of the holidays was an event to look forward to, with the contribution of students in verse, song and dance loudly applauded. The endeavours of one staff member to involve students in ceili dancing at these events involved considerable effort, with the outcome not always to his liking. For those not eager to tread the boards, a film filled the vacuum.

The school had many memorable productions in concerts, musicals and dramas. One such memorable production in 1980 was 'Our Town', directed by Edward O'Reilly. There was much success in quiz competitions, debates and public speaking. Both individual awards and group project prizes were won on many occasions in history, thanks to the tutelage of Ms. Bernie Jordan.

Sport played an integral part in the life of the school, with Gaelic football to the fore. The school won many County titles at both junior and senior level. Prominent footballers included Pat Doory, who later played for Roscommon seniors, and Noel Durkin, who starred for Mayo, as well as John Joe Hunt, Philip and Tom Callaghan, Dan and Tom Finn, Michael Moffitt, Kieran Farrell, Laurence Frain, Brendan and John Duffy, Seamus and Padraic Cassidy. I recall teachers versus a strong student team match, with the students carrying the tag of strong favourites. The teacher's team, which had a number of club players, emerged victoriously and I still remember the disappointment etched on the faces of the students.

The laying down of a taramacadam court heralded the arrival of the basketball in 1981. It was played mainly by girls including Cathy McCann, Tracy Hough, Ann Casey and Rachel Casey; they competed successfully in various competitions. The occasional student versus teacher game always resulted in the girls being victorious.

With the building of a 40x20 indoor handball court in 1985 on the school grounds, there was a new emphasis on handball. Students competed at all levels and won many County and Connacht titles. Prior to this, it was a one-wall affair against the gable wall of the school, with teachers frequently having to dodge the path of the ball. No health and safety issue there! Among the outstanding handballers were John Flynn, Gerry O'Gara, John Mangan, John Clifford, Eugene and Barry Mc Donagh, Noel and Adrain Boyle, David and Dermot Greene, David O'Gara, Adrain Regan Ted Moore, John Roddy, Kevin Keegan, Thomas Calter, Neill O'Hara, Laurence Frain and the extremely dedicated Sean Jennings.

After a November break, a student joined the PE class. He was successful in convincing the teacher that he had just enrolled. Much to the amusement of the class, he proceeded to cause serious disruption as he decided not to comply with any instructions given. A very agitated and irate teacher only cooled down much later on learning that this 'new student' was an impostor. The following day she turned detective in identifying the miscreant.

I also recall the student, who obviously did not like science, and who, during the course of a class, broke a thermometer and said he had swallowed the mercury. Later, in the doctor's surgery near his own home, he retracted his statement, much to the relief of all.

The Vocational School produced many educated and inspired men and women who distinguished themselves; people who became educators at second and third level, who pursued civil service careers, who excelled in technical expertise, who became involved in property development at home and overseas, and who played a distinguished role in the life of their own community and further afield.

The school was renowned as an adult and continuation education centre, providing many and varied courses including extra mural courses. I am very proud to be associated with the school, which achieved much for the students and the community.

We think of the people who built the school, those who taught in the school and those who studied there. We remember the many staff who made a huge contribution to the running of the school and who impacted positively on the lives of so many.

For me, it provided a very satisfying, happy and rewarding career. I cherish the continuing friendship provided by colleagues and students. I can honestly say if I was at the starting blocks again, I would choose the same path.

• 49 •

How Many Handball Titles?

Dessie Keegan

LC 1999; Project Coordinator Youth Work Ireland

In the autumn of 1994, I walked through the dayboy's door for the first time. I still remember how nervous and frightened I was. The sheer size of the buildings, the vast number of students, the subjects I was going to have to learn, all the new teachers – how was I going to cope?

Within days of starting, I was in Fr. Jenning's car being whizzed off to Headford for a handball blitz. What great joy! I began to think yes, I can survive in St. Nathy's. I became very determined to improve my skills and become a top-class handballer. Fr. Jennings was to be my inspiration, motivation and coach. Along with Campbell Brennan, Paul Flynn, Vincent Moran and Brian Tansey, we trained most days with the encouragement of Fr. Jennings. We travelled all over Ireland playing in competitions and met many people who were to become lifelong friends. We eventually had a path worn to Croke Park for All Ireland finals. We won so many that we have lost count. I am very fortunate to say that to date, I personally have won 61 All Ireland titles, four World titles, four American titles and three European titles.

There are two incidents that stand out in my memory from my handball exploits. The first was when I was training for the All Ireland Hardball Championship. I was alone practicing in the St. Nathy's 60x30 court one Saturday evening. Fr. Jennings appeared and gave me some advice about different shots. Jokingly I said to him: "Why don't we have a game?" "Righteo," he replied, "I will be back in ten minutes." Ten minutes later he was back with his Puma tracksuit on and in runners. I was in disbelief. I had never seen him togged out before or to play handball. Now playing handball is one thing, but playing hardball is another. Hardball is like a golf ball and most players use gloves and goggles. Fr. Jennings had neither. He insisted we play and I must say I took it easy on him. He struggled but he would not give in. His hands even bled. Such is the determination and self sacrifice of the man that he would do even that to help another.

The second incident occurred when Brian Tansey and I were due to play in an All Ireland final. We were under pressure to study for our exams. This we explained to Fr. Jennings. "No problem," he replied, "I will pick you up at seven in the morning and will have you back home in time to get ready for school."

Finally, I would like to thank all the staff for putting up with me and for making my school life so very enjoyable and meaningful. I would especially like to thank Fr. Convey for the leadership he showed, for providing us with access to the handball courts and for recognising our success; to Paddy Mulligan, my English teacher, who always spoke for the heart, who always listened to my views and opinions, and whose encouragement enhanced my self esteem and confidence; to Bernie Jordan, my history teacher, who was a most dedicated teacher and who always went the extra mile in providing me and my peers with the support we needed; and to Sr. Kathleen, who provided me with extra tuition – her kindness will never be forgotten.

• 50 •

Sporting Memories of School Life

Joseph McCann

LC 2000; Scientific Services Process Specialist, Abbott Ireland

Three aspects of school life in St. Nathy's College stand out in my memory from my five years there. The life skills needed for self-discipline, a healthy interest in sport, and some very helpful teachers dominate my mind's landscape. Students of my class concerned themselves mainly with issues involving their timetable for classes, whereas my main priorities revolved around training times for handball, basketball and football.

My first day in St. Nathy's set the tone for the next five years. An ability test to give an indication of a student's academic potential was timetabled for all first years on that day. I had to miss the test as I was competing in the National Finals of the Community Games. Delighted with my alibi, I was shocked to find out on the following day that my great handball mentor, Fr. Jennings, had made arrangements for me to sit the same tests. Thus, a valuable lesson had been taught. One had to embrace the academic side of life in St. Nathy's no matter what your prowess was on the sporting fields.

Throughout my years at St. Nathy's College, I had the privilege to play under outstanding coaches in all of my three chosen sports. John O'Mahony was my football manager during my first year, a year in which we captured the Connacht First Year title for 1997. He also trained the junior team which won the Connacht Title in 1999 with largely the same set of players. Then, in 2000, he led us to capture the Connacht Senior B Championship, the Connacht Senior B League, the Flanagan Cup and the All Ireland B Championship. Frances Dunne coached our basketball teams and had the distinction of leading us to All Ireland triumph in 2001. Fr. Jennings was our inspiring coach on the handball courts where he gave unselfishly of his time. In my senior years, he was succeeded Alex McDonnell, who carried the baton of coaching handball in the College. At all stages, they were assisted by that handball legend and enthusiast John Gaffney, R.I.P., who brought players all over the country in his pursuit of excellence.

I was fortunate to have come under the influence of such enthusiastic and knowledgeable mentors.

During my time at St. Nathy's, I had the good fortune to win six All Ireland medals in handball, and the days of finals have a special place etched in my memory. Fr. Jennings would have all the handball squad in for mass at 7.30am in the College oratory. He maintained that morning mass was worth eight aces in any game – a theory hard to prove or disprove – but it put us all in a positive frame of mind. After mass, we would set off for Croke Park by car or minibus and our minds would be focussed on doing battle for All Ireland honours. Many of my opponents are good friends of mine today, which is one of the positive sides of taking part in sport.

Sometimes my participation in three sports caused organisational difficulties. In my first year, I was lucky to be selected for the Northwest Regional basketball team. The competition we were involved in was held in Limerick. We got to the final but unfortunately I could not play in it because it clashed with the All Ireland handball finals. Fr. Jennings stepped in to the rescue. He collected me in Limerick at 11.00pm on Saturday night and brought me home so that I could rest in my own bed. His parting that night was that he would see me at 7. 30am for morning mass – the routine was so important. It must have worked because I won the final and that qualified me to represent both St. Nathy's and Ireland in Blackpool at the Eton Fives handball competition, which was a great singular honour for me.

The pinnacle of my football career at St. Nathy's was reached when I was in my fourth year. I was always aware of the proud football tradition of college teams of the past and that year saw a significant extension of that tradition. We captured the Connacht Senior League and Championship titles, the Flanagan Cup and the All Ireland Senior B title in that wonderful 1999-2000 season. Everything came together for us that year, which was not surprising considering we had a coach of John O' Mahony's acumen and football nous leading the charge. He brought sheer professionalism to the squad and instilled in each player the sense of commitment and preparation necessary to achieve at the highest level. We trained in rain, hail and snow. No training was missed. Even if you were injured, you had to be present to lend moral support. If you had to be absent, you did an extra session. If you were not giving it 100%, you were told about it. Part of the preparation was a test of your ability to represent your school with honour and distinction, and to be polite and pleasant while doing so. Early morning sessions at 7.30 were held so as not to interfere with class time. Training was scheduled for holiday times so as to maintain levels of fitness. "What makes winning so great is what makes losing so bad," was a phrase John used during one of our victorious homecomings. The positivity of that comment stayed with us all though the year as we embarked on a remarkable clean sweep of titles. After winning the All Ireland, the people of Ballaghaderreen put on a huge homecoming for us. For two days we were treated as celebrities. It is great memory to carry from my time at St. Nathy's.

During my Leaving Cert year, I concentrated all my energies on basketball. I was chosen as captain of the senior team, an honour I was delighted to have bestowed on me. Frances Dunne trained us expertly each evening after school. We were small in stature but big in heart. We bonded well together as a team and our preparation for the All Ireland final appearance was meticulous. The night before the final, we stayed in St. Patrick's College Maynooth. The final against Oatlands of Dublin in the National Basketball Arena was really exciting, made all the more so by our busloads of support. We held a commanding lead at half time and just held on to win by two baskets, with Sean McDermott winning the MVP award. It was a great finish to my sporting career in the College.

During all my time spent on various courts and football pitches, one thing remained a constant. I was never allowed to miss any more class time than was necessary and all the time that I did miss had to be made up. Teachers gave me and all my peers tremendous encouragement. One comment from my Religion teacher, Ms. Egan (R.I.P.), has always remained with me. Standing in the middle of the canteen one day, she said to me: "Sport will cover most of your life, but an education will cover all of your life." It was so true. Many other teachers echoed the same sentiments in different words. St. Nathy's was indeed full of leaders.

Being chosen as 'Student of the Year' in my Leaving Cert year was a particularly gratifying award for me. It could not have had much to do with my academic prowess! My photograph was placed on the wall the year I left St. Nathy's and that tribute inspires me more than any other. When I walk down those hallowed corridors, I am humbled to be part of the great tradition that is St. Nathy's as a sporting institution. I am proud to have played some small part in the enormity of it all.

• 51 •

Formation

Patricia Giblin

LC 2002; Occupational Therapist

When I started to attend St. Nathy's College, it was like entering a melting pot of people and subjects, where my horizons suddenly expanded and any dream was possible. I remember the first day of school and the nervous tension that buzzed in the air as we bewildered first years gathered together in the canteen. We scanned the crowd for a familiar face and eyed one anther warily, wondering who would become our firm friends, and if we would ever get to grips with navigating the maze of corridors and classrooms. To suddenly be catapulted from a small national school, where you knew everyone and sat at the same desk in the same classroom day after day, to the bustle of a large school with different teachers, classrooms and peers was daunting, but quickly faded to a distant memory as it soon seemed that I had always been walking through St. Nathy's corridors. I can still almost hear a teacher shouting "Hello Padraigin" down the corridor, the laughter of my classmates and I at some now forgotten joke, and the enchanting echo of Christmas carols in the halls as the singers rehearsed for the annual Christmas carol service.

St. Nathy's was the place where help and support was always at hand, where the ethos of the school inspired you to strive to achieve your goals, and guided you as you selected your future path in life.

Although my school days may now be over and my time in St. Nathy's gone, St. Nathy's will always be part of me. And, whether I bump into a former teacher, am catching up with an old school friend or am simply reminded of some funny incident from my school days, I will look back on the time that I spent there with fondness and respect for the contribution it made in shaping the course of my life.

• 52 •

Personal Reflection

Joseph Mitchell

LC 2005; Law Graduate UCD

It is funny to reminisce about St. Nathy's from such a short remove. I last set foot in St. Nathy's in the summer of 2005, having arrived in 2000. Taken in the context of 200 years of college life, it is only a moment ago. Therefore, my recollections may be familiar to many of the current students.

The school leavers of my era emerged from the rigours of 'the Leaving' into an Ireland experienced by few others who left the insulated environment of secondary education – an Ireland of almost full employment, a free education system which was considered one of the best in the world and a truly multi-cultural society where everything seemed possible. We took our first tentative steps into adulthood knowing little of tough times, unlike many previous generations who faced war, unemployment, emigration and wholescale uncertainty. Sure, we were a generation unencumbered by major obstacles, but maybe burdened by levels of expectation previously never experienced.

A great sense of history pervaded our school days and one would have to be oblivious to the surroundings not to realise that St. Nathy's was a school like no other. For the first few weeks, the old building held particular fascination as it offered up new staircases, rooms and layers on a daily basis. The décor of the intricate fine wood panelling and the team photos stretching back through the ages that lined the corridors, reminding us of the illustrious sporting traditions of the school and of the great and of the good who had walked these same halls. The black and white faces that peered out at us from those old frames were an ever present reminder of the proud heritage of the College and their eyes spoke to us of the same optimism and hopes for the future we shared. Yet, I think that we walked past them every day without ever really looking at them.

From the excitement of the first week to the glory of completing the final exam, my St. Nathy's years were both eventful and mundane, a simple time of routine and of hard work, but above all a time for forging friendship, building character and acquiring knowledge and values in equal measures. This feeling of routine was best exemplified by how we passed our spare time, walking in groups of threes and fours around the C Block, surely thousands of times over the years.

On hard winter days, we bumped and jostled each other to warm ourselves against the tall radiators at break time, after the habitual lunchtimes spent at the meeting point outside the boarded up Lough Gara Hotel and the Friday lunches spent in the coffee shop on the Square.

Some of us watched the football matches taking place early in the morning, sheltering by the Complex against the bitter wind coming in from over the Brusna Hills, and while the conversations have been lost in the mists of time, I am sure they concerned some of the characters who we listened to in class every-day, each with their own unique style.

Paddy Henry, who despite teaching me every morning, laboured under the impression that my name was James (or Seamus); so much so that this became a running gag among the other lads. Yet, despite this botŭn, his energy and enthusiasm instilled us with a great grà for conversational Irish.

Fr. Finan, a great character whose love of the English language was infectious, his famous word power exercises, his many catchphrases and his dry wit are often recounted by his past students.

Billy McGee, whose arrival in our fourth year after the untimely death of Ms. Egan, R.I.P., brought a youthful breath of fresh air and whose anecdotes often had the class in stitches – something of a novelty in a religion class.

Roof ball, a game with a unique twist on handball, became an addiction. It involved hitting a tennis ball against the roof which overhung the walkway between the old and the new building (A and C Blocks). This was a game that was tolerated more than encouraged by the teachers who risked walking through our alleys, indeed they were often relegated to taking a detour out through the rain rather than risk the wrath of those whose games they would otherwise disturb. Shouts of 'How many bounces?' 'Bad serve' and 'Game ball' were the battle cries of the fierce competitors as the hordes of onlookers waited impatiently for their turn. On wet days, when the courts resembled a mud bath and the ball was barely recognisable, we played on regardless of the mucky hands and the mess. Those who could utilise the element of surprise offered by the overhead ledge and the unpredictable bounces off the jagged stones of the facing wall to defeat their opponent were considered masters of the game.

Each alleyway seemed to mark a progression through the hierarchy of the school and in some respects an attainment of maturity. Once you had reached the prized single corner alley, you could rightfully claim seniority. While the attraction may not be apparent to some, it was immense fun, and the craic among the lads was always ninety.

As Patrick Kavanagh remarked in Epic: "Gods make their own importance"

Similarly, we had our own epic contests with single games lasting all lunch, thoughts of food were forgotten until the bell tolled and we were brought back to reality by the urgings of an impatient teacher to be on our way.

Our class has not been together since the balmy summer of 2005 and the graduation night in Bundoran. Some now have third-level qualifications, jobs and trades, a select few have county championship medals, some area married or engaged, others have children, some have gone to seek their fortune overseas, some by choice others by necessity, yet, thankfully we can all keep in communication much easier than our forebears through the medium of the internet.

While no two will share the same memories of their time in St. Nathy's, as the spectre of emigration once again returns to rural Ireland, it is a common experience that unites us all, no matter where the future takes us.

St. Nathy's was a huge part of our lives for five of our most formative years, and so perhaps its greatest legacy will not be measured by the number of Leaving Cert points it garnered for us but by the strength of character it instilled in the students who passed through the gates.

After all, as someone once said: "Education is what remains after one has forgotten everything he learned in school."

• 53 •

Will I Stay or Will I Go?

Aoife Bruen

LC 2007; Studying Medicine UCD

I left St. Nathy's just over a year and a half ago, having spent the best part of five years within its halls. But when I started thinking about writing this, it made me realise that it has never left me. That is why I decided against writing about one of the funnier one-liners tossed into the midst of some half forgotten biology lesson, or even about the day a dog wandered into the school and taught me a lesson about live animals, but rather I would write about the day I realised that there was something special about St. Nathy's in comparison to other schools, and that was the very last day I spent there as a student.

The last day I spent in St. Nathy's was an ordinary day. There was the usual rushed conversation, peppering the stolen minutes between the day's nine classes, the usual food and semi-ignored VHI music videos playing on the TV's in the packed ref halfway through the day. The surprising thing was that during each class we were given a full lesson. We were still hushed when the omnipresent chatter in the classroom evolved from a dull, pervasive humming into an entity of its own. Each at the draw, our teachers were still trying to give us one last piece of information that might help us through the exam, and a few tales from their own college experiences to make us a little wiser once we had cleared the looming hurdle.

Then the final bell rang and everything seemed to be the wrong way round. Although that may well have been because we had put our chairs on top of the desks. We walked out of the classroom into the hall and that is when we realised we did not really want to leave. We walked to lockers we no longer had the keys for; talking about all the other days we had done the same thing. We just kept walking, all the way through the school and I could not help remembering how I had felt when I walked the same way on my first day there, how small I had felt next to the big wooden stairs in the A block, the neatly stacked tower of lockers, how my tummy had felt, full of fluttering insects when faced with the prospect of speaking to the tidal wave of people I had found myself caught up in walking to my first class.

Now, with some of those same people standing at my side, I felt like the stairs in the A block were just stairs, the row of lockers did not dwarf me where I stood. One of them was mine. It was strange, I was not a frightened 12 year-old anymore, I was comfortable. But now I had to leave.

Walking towards the main exit, we ran into Fr. Convey, who shook hands with us and wished us all luck in our exams and our lives afterwards. Walking through the door, we stopped and looked back. That was the moment we realised that this would be the last time we did so, and then came the surge of nostalgia and the strange, unexpected feeling that maybe we were not ready to leave. Or maybe we just did not want to. I might have spent the best part of five years in this College, but it might have been St. Nathy's College that was the best part of those five years of my life.

• 54 •

Ron Barassi Medal Winner

Pearse Hanley

LC 2007; Professional Footballer with The Brisbane Lions

What do you want to be when you grow up?

For me, there was ever only one answer to this age-old question. My one interest, often times my only interest, was football and I wanted to be a professional footballer. To this day, my mum claims she knew from the day I could walk that I would become a footballer. If I was not playing it, I was watching it or talking about it; anywhere I went, I took my football. Some kids had comfort towels, others teddy bears, not me though, I had my trusty football.

As the years passed by and I got older, my love for football grew. I can vaguely remember other parents discussing with mine, after underage games years and years ago, how I was a "natural talent", just "gifted with the ball". But what they did not see were the hours I spent each day and night with my older brother Andrew practising in the garden. Games and tournaments a plenty, these I would have given anything to win; we were very competitive! This often led to tears at the end of the night, but this was to be expected, just part and parcel of it all. We were very much in it to win! It was at home in my back garden that I firmly believe, under the tutorship of my dad and after many a defeat to Andrew, that I developed my fundamental skills, my respect for practice, but most importantly my motivation to succeed, which I believe has since stood me in good stead.

Primary school was not long passing and I soon found myself in St. Nathy's. This was great; it meant even more football, playing with the school teams. We had some great battles over the years with the usual rival schools, some of which remain my most satisfying victories. It was these games, or merely the thought of these games, that got me through sitting at the school desk. The books were never my strongest point, but I kept the head down and tried my best to stay clear of trouble, which I did quite well for the most part.

During my time in St. Nathy's, I was fortunate enough to have represented the Mayo minor team over two consecutive years. Defeated by Down in the All Ireland

Final culminated 2006. Far more satisfying was captaining the Mayo Minor team to a Connaught title the following year. Coupled with that, I was blessed to have followed in my brother's footsteps and made the final selection to represent Ireland in the Under 17 Compromise Rules series against Australia. This was an amazing experience. I got to travel Australia and represent my country doing what I love! To top that off, it was an honour to win the Ron Barassi medal of excellence for being 'The best and fairest'. All in all, football and the memories it has left with me remain the highlight of my time in St. Nathy's. I will always remember the school, the friends I made there and of course the staff for keeping my feet firmly on the ground at a time when I could have allowed my sporting endeavours to blow me off course.

All clichés aside, I am currently in Australia living my dream of playing professional football for the AFL Brisbane Lions Club. I was Dublin City University bound on a GAA Scholarship, but I suppose the lure of stardom got the better of the books again. It turned out that my performances with the Irish Under 17 squad did not go unnoticed in Australia. The Brisbane Lions Club tracked my progress for six months afterwards, before landing on my doorstep in Ballaghaderreen bearing a two-year rookie contract.

I am now in my second season with the club; I made my debut for the first team last year 2008, which came as a huge surprise to me. I am training hard and making the most of this opportunity, and I am hoping to be a successful first team player.

Down the road, I hope to resume my studies in Dublin City University, and more importantly, I hope to bring the Sam McGuire Cup across the Shannon and home to Mayo.

People might say that I am dreaming, but so far so good.

I would like to thank Fr. Leo Henry for the opportunity to put my career profile this far on paper and to wish him and everyone in St. Nathy's the very best for its bicentenary.

• 55 •

The Carol Service, Social Awareness and Much More

Rachel McDonagh

LC 2009; Student of French and English TCD

As the young first year ran off gushing thanks, I could barely contain the ironic grin threatening to erupt on my face – not too many years ago, back in 2004, I had been the newbie, with a kilt down to my ankles and a bag the size of Mount Everest on my back, desperately looking for someone tall to give me directions to the notorious 10A.

I can vividly remember entering St. Nathy's College for the first day of school – convinced I would need every single book packed into my strained bag and terrified that I would get lost among the milling mass of students. I was pleasantly surprised on both counts – it was reassuring to find that only the first years were being brought in on the first day and my back was more then relieved to find my new locker. And now here I was in my final year. No longer was my chequered kilt brushing the floor of our bustling halls, no longer was my timetable permanently clutched in my hand and no longer did I fear getting lost on my way to the baffling room 10A. I was now a mentor, showing the next generation of first years where to go and how to get there. They are only just starting out, just beginning their life as a student of St. Nathy's, and I could only hope that they would have as many great experiences as I have had.

It was a bitterly cold winter, but those assembled inside the Cathedral barely noticed. Every single pew in the church was full and every single face held a smile. A gathered group of students in the St. Nathy's uniform were arranged on the altar, singing Christmas hymns. Each student – from the soaring descant to the sweet soprano, from the low melody of the altos to the rich tenor line – had a grin that mirrored those of the congregation. They were proud to wear the uniform and joyous with the knowledge that they were the cause of such obvious enjoyment. I know because I was one of them.

The St. Nathy's carol service is an annual occurrence that every person in the locality of Ballaghaderreen marks in their calendars – an event that many people claim to be the real beginning of Christmas. During my five years at St. Nathy's College, I participated in four of these services in aid of St. Vincent De Paul. There is no way to describe the feeling of pride that one feels standing on that cramped altar, united with your schoolmates and singing to an enthralled audience. No matter how much the most anti-conforming student may complain about having to wear a uniform, even they could not deny the pride they felt whilst wearing it on that night. For me, one of the most memorable recollections I will ever have of my school days of those carol services.

They say that your school days are the most enjoyable of your life, and I doubt that any past student of St. Nathy's College could ever dispute or deny that fact. Not only is the educational and academic development of the students cared for, but so also is the personal development of each individual. Every student is shown how to care not only for themselves, but also for others. In the school year 2007 to 2008, my fourth year in the College, I remember being part of most fundraising projects in the school along with many other students. We were encouraged to support those less fortunate and do all we could to help them. In that one year alone, we raised €20,000. While we were delighted to have raised such a substantial sum, it was much more satisfying to know that you had played an active part in raising both the money and awareness for each individual project.

Joseph Addison once said: "What sculpture is to a block of marble, education is to the soul." The days spent in school form a huge element of your life and they make up a large part of your memories. These days are incredibly important. They mould you into the person that you are and set the vital foundations for the rest of your life. I firmly believe that the dedication and welcoming atmosphere present in St. Nathy's succeeds in fulfilling and embracing this responsibility. As I look back on my days spent in this school, it makes me wish that I were back at the beginning, starting over once more instead of preparing to leave. From escapades abroad on foreign exchange programmes, to heartily cheering on school teams and to the reassuring, pleasant feeling of simply being able to go into school each day with a smile on your face – this is what made St. Nathy's such an enjoyable place for me during my days as a student.

College days in St. Nathy's, for me, were not only marked by the big events, but also the small ones. The enlightening experience of going abroad in itself was a fantastic memory – but the small aspects, like getting unbelievably lost in translation at a queue for popcorn in a French cinema or wandering around the ballroom in Azay Le Rideau in awe of such renaissance beauty, were the truly unforgettable parts of our journey. The music trips to see Rebecca Storm in Blood Brothers or the production of Mama Mia in The Point were outings that will never be forgotten; not only for the amazing on-stage performances or for the opportunity of being able to sit there and watch them, but for the smaller things like the two hour bus ride up to Dublin, singing catchy songs and telling jokes with friends, driving teachers and students alike absolutely crazy with a seventh rendition of 'Oh Row The Rathlin Bog'.

It was the simple day-to-day experiences that made St. Nathy's so memorable: the good-humoured atmosphere in the classrooms, the friends you met each day and the work you do as a team – be it in sport, music or charity work. St. Nathy's truly is a place of education – never solely in the academic aspect. My college life as a student was one filled with many memories. My five years at St. Nathy's College have been ones filled with fun and education in every sense of the word, and I can only hope that the following years will be as memorable and remunerative.

While I may wish that I were not leaving, I am leaving with the knowledge that St. Nathy's has prepared me for everything ahead.